Past Caring?

PAST CARING?

Women, Work and Emotion

EDITED BY

Barbara Brookes,
Jane McCabe &
Angela Wanhalla

OTAGO

Published by Otago University Press
Level 1, 398 Cumberland Street
Dunedin, New Zealand
university.press@otago.ac.nz
www.otago.ac.nz/press

First published 2019
Copyright © the authors as named
The moral rights of the authors have been asserted

ISBN 978-1-98-853134-2

Editor: Gillian Tewsley
Indexer: Diane Lowther
Design/layout: Fiona Moffat

Cover: Quilt made by Frances Broad, circa 1920, NZ, 138cm x 166cm, GH016392, Museum of New Zealand Te Papa Tongarewa

Printed in China through Asia Pacific Offset

CONTENTS

ACKNOWLEDGEMENTS

The foundations of this collection lie in *Making Women Visible*, a national conference on women's history held at the University of Otago in February 2016. Jane McCabe and Angela Wanhalla co-organised the event with Katie Cooper, Jane Adams and Sarah Christie, ably supported by Radhika Raghav, Violeta Gilabert and Emma Gattey. In an elegant and compelling opening keynote address, Barbara Brookes traced the history and meaning of women's caring work in the past and present, and her address inspired this volume. *Past Caring?* seeks to make care and care work in New Zealand's past visible. It offers different vantage points on women's history and its resonances now, as politicians, commentators and the public debate matters that are important in the lives of New Zealand women, ranging from child poverty to pay equity, both of which have care dimensions.

A year after the conference the editors and invited contributors to *Past Caring?* came together at the Hocken Collections to workshop the book. This was made possible through generous financial support from the Centre for Research on Colonial Culture, a University of Otago Research Centre. We thank the centre's director, Tony Ballantyne, for his support of both events as well as of this volume. In organising the workshop and this volume we have accrued many debts. We would particularly like to acknowledge the assistance and support we received from Sue Lang of the Department of History and Art History, and from staff at the Hocken Collections. Contributors at the workshop benefited from the expertise of invited commentators whose input was essential in shaping the volume:

Vicki Spencer, Annabel Cooper, Jacqui Leckie and, especially, Beatrice Hale who, in her role as keynote commentator, provided a thoughtful and inspiring summary of the papers and the workshop theme, 'Caring Histories'. This volume also benefited from the generous comments of two expert readers whose enthusiastic and insightful response to the collection helped the editors and contributors to think about care in new ways. We want to acknowledge the support of Rachel Scott at Otago University Press for encouraging us in this project. And finally, we thank the contributors for taking up the challenge of thinking and writing about past caring.

INTRODUCTION:
Care matters

Barbara Brookes, Jane McCabe
& Angela Wanhalla

Care comes in many shapes and forms. It can be a state of mind; it can evoke a depth and intensity of feeling; while to describe someone as caring is to conjure images of solicitude, love and devotion. To care is to look after others. It is a relational practice: to provide and receive care is to express a bond between individuals or groups. Care is also a practice that involves physical work associated with ideas about responsibility and duty; it is something undertaken to benefit the health and wellbeing of others. Sometimes care is a physical, emotional and financial burden, but it also encompasses loving attention. It is essential to social warmth and individual wellbeing. It takes thought, attention and time to maintain relationships.

Care is literally stitched into every aspect of our lives. It is woven into our key social institutions, such as the family, and it is embedded in societal expectations around state provision of health and welfare. In fact, care is so vital that it has been taken for granted and has often gone unnoticed in historical and philosophical enquiry – yet it raises profound questions about gender, justice and morality. Is it just, for example, that caregiving falls disproportionately to women? Thinking through these issues – how to integrate women's traditional work of caring into philosophical debates about caring and justice – is at the heart of Heather Devere's discussion of two New Zealand philosophers, Susan Moller Okin and Annette Baier, both of whom brought a feminist eye to questions of morality that acknowledged dependency on others. For Okin, 'a just future is one without gender': in that future, caring would be done by all, and this would lead to a new politics because those in power would have experienced the nurturing of children on a day-to-day basis. In Baier's view, that experience would heighten an individual's 'moral disposition to justice'.

Framed by these urgent questions, this volume is an attempt to instigate a conversation about the history of caring in New Zealand. Our approach is akin to the patchwork quilt that envelops this collection of essays. As a metaphor for 'care' the patchwork quilt evokes the many threads of caring explored by our authors: a beautiful quilt is one that incorporates diversity, colour, textures and a sense of pattern; but as an assemblage it does not communicate a linear story. A quilt also performs a function where the sensory, the social and the emotional meet. Traditionally women's quiltmaking speaks not only to the material expression of care, but to women's predominance as carers in the past. All of these themes – women, work and emotion – are at the heart of this volume.

Understanding care in the past requires attention to personal narratives. In this volume, for example, close attention to a grandmother's story and to a Rarotongan leader's concept of duty situates those narratives in a range of cultural practices and institutional constraints. Women's history, in its early iterations, ignited interest in the recovery of personal narratives of women as an act of retrieval and a way to reinstate women's agency in the historical record. Analysis of caring requires attention not only at the level of personal experience but also at the heart of the political process.

The cost of caring has been in the political spotlight in New Zealand with the success of the Service and Food Workers Union case taken on behalf of Kristine Bartlett, initially in 2012, that led eventually to a $2 billion 'game-changing' equal pay settlement in 2017 that Bartlett hoped would raise care workers out of poverty.[1] But the extent to which this was game-changing has yet to be seen. Paying care workers properly may mean employers expect more work in a shorter timeframe.[2] In August 2017 Diane Moody, who at 75 cares full-time for her profoundly disabled 50-year-old son, lost her case against the Ministry of Health to be recompensed for more than the 21 hours a week at the minimum wage that she was currently paid. Moody estimated she spent 168 hours a week caring for her son, but the government said it would pay only for 'personal care' and 'management', not supervision.[3] The Court of Appeal overturned the original ruling in February 2018.[4] Nonetheless, when it comes to compensating carers, the government's view is that the price tag is likely to be too high.

Expected, indeed demanded, but not to be paid for: this is the paradox of care. To focus on care, therefore, is to pay attention to something we all depend on but often take for granted. One of the reasons for the invisibility of care is that historically it has often been primarily the responsibility of women, in both an unpaid and a paid capacity. Uncovering the historical iterations of care – how it was practised and by whom – is a difficult task when the associated physical and emotional labour was performed at the edges and in the shadows of traditional historical sources, where it was rarely remarked on yet was always present.

As in other realms of academic history, it is the institutional, the problematic, and encounters with the state that have created a documentary record and thus what might be read as an archive of care. A kaleidoscope of scholarship can be drawn around this concept of care. But, as might be expected, state policy, medical and health matters – with their attendant bureaucracy and paperwork – have attracted the most attention from New Zealand historians, as Violeta Gilabert's select bibliography shows.

A particularly rich vein of enquiry in the New Zealand historiography has examined the evolution of social policy, the rise and fall of the welfare state, and public debates about the caring professions (nurses and social workers, for example) as a way to measure the value placed on care by society and the state. Scholars have identified the importance of social, financial and emotional support provided by charitable organisations, which have a long tradition of stepping in to assist when relatives cannot, or when state welfare provision is unavailable.[5] In this volume we build on this scholarship by drawing on personal narratives and recognising the plethora of intermediary and less easily categorised familial–community roles, relationships and scenarios that can be considered care work; and we examine the power relationship between individuals and the state and other organisations. Widening the focus enables a broader depiction of the 'family' in its various forms in the past, generating understandings of how different registers of care overlap and intertwine – as several chapters in this collection show.

These caring relationships do not happen in any kind of set fashion. In seeking new ground on which to make care visible we need to be attentive to diverse cultural perspectives that recognise that care takes place within particular frameworks and that it is performed and valued differently across cultures. In a Māori context the vocabulary of care and its meanings are diverse and therefore difficult to define precisely, but it tends to be characterised as balancing aroha with mana. This can be achieved through the principles of atawhai (kindness) and manaakitanga (generosity), for instance, which highlight the relational elements of caring as a practice that is shared among family and the wider community.

Colonialism disrupted traditional Māori modes of relating to one another. In the extended whānau (family) model of social organisation there were many available caregivers, but this was slowly replaced by the nuclear family model – a shift that was strongly encouraged by the advantages of twentieth-century state welfare support.[6] Alongside Māori and European settlers, New Zealand became home to Pacific, Indian and Chinese peoples whose pathways followed colonial trade and labour routes created out of imperial connections. Just as people moved, so did care practices. Cook Island women, for example, were sought-after as domestic servants in New Zealand families during the 1940s.[7] Through these kinds of migrant journeys, alternative cultural values and principles around care moved across oceans, as a number of chapters in this volume show.

As editors, we are interested in different historical vantage points on care – a subject more readily addressed by policymakers than historians. The Ministry for Social Development's New Zealand Carers' Strategy Action Plan for 2014 to 2018 defines 'carers' as those who 'provide care for someone close to them (family or friend) who needs help with everyday living because of a health condition, disability or injury'.[8] Our focus on care is somewhat wider: we explore the everyday nature of care, not just that demanded by exceptional circumstances. The case studies examined in *Past Caring?* focus on care operating across domestic, institutional and political arenas. They also build on areas of strength in women's history, with its interest in families, motherhood, health, welfare, education and employment. We recognise, however, that this volume only touches on a limited set of perspectives and experiences of caring in the past. We hope that the collection might prompt further explorations of particular caring relationships that exist below the radar of societal norms of care; and of the role of men as carers in the professions as well as their participation in care work within the home.[9]

Past Caring? opens with Barbara Brookes, who sets the wider context for care and its varied histories, detailing the changing landscape of care in New Zealand over the nineteenth and twentieth centuries. Heather Devere's analysis of caring in the context of philosophical debates about justice and ethics demonstrates these are more than abstract issues. In a contrasting personal narrative Melissa Matutina Williams makes explicit the usually unacknowledged texture of care through a close examination of her grandmother's lifetime of care. Patterns of care might also migrate across oceans and across cultures: Jane McCabe explores the elusive and comforting night-time care traditionally provided by an ayah in northeast India, and its transition to New Zealand. Rosemary Anderson considers the public and private duties of care of Takau Rio Love, who was at once bound to serve her people in Rarotonga and her family in New Zealand.

Care might also be enveloped in the material: in the albums carefully curated by women, as Antje Lübcke addresses in her examination of Helen Smaill's photograph album; in the daily tasks of food preparation that are the focus of Katie Cooper's chapter; or in the clothing lovingly made by mothers for their children, the focus of our visual essay 'Stitching the generations together'. In this reflective piece, our contributors share personal stories that reveal the quality of material forms of care. This was often a labour of love: the hours spent making things for children resulted in products that gave women pleasure. For many women of a certain generation, their hands were always busy while listening to the radio or watching television. Sewing and knitting were important economic contributions to the household at a time when bought goods were unaffordable. But sewing and knitting were also creative acts and an aspect of women's work that led to a satisfying finished outcome, unlike the necessary daily round of cleaning and cooking, tasks that were endlessly repeated.

Our contributors highlight the different spaces and locations where care is carried out, from tea plantations and institutions in northern India to missionary homes in the Pacific, and in the rural kitchen. The work of care is often intimate, tactile and labour intensive. Its association with intimacies such as personal hygiene helps explain its invisibility. And, as McCabe's chapter demonstrates, the hidden nature of care can have as much to do with when it takes place as where. Care work might require particular tools and technologies and involve labour-intensive and unpleasant chores, even if they are performed out of love and duty. Cooper's chapter highlights a different set of practices that take place in the kitchen; and the contributions to the visual essay, encompassing knitting needles, the sewing machine and hand stitching, represent material expressions of care.

Two chapters, by Angela Wanhalla and Bronwyn Polaschek, stress the experience of social marginalisation and financial vulnerability of lone mothers, and address how individuals, families, communities and the state respond to them and their children across specific sociohistorical and cultural contexts. Wanhalla's examination of the difficulties faced by the New Zealand mothers of the children of American servicemen in World War II suggests that any ideas of a fatherly obligation to care were undercut by lack of proof of paternity, military rules and distance, leaving women to make do in any way they could. Polaschek's analysis of the 'mother alone' in New Zealand film suggests that the nation has a distinctive tradition of representing mothers caring for their children in a way that resists the isolation of 'man alone' that permeates New Zealand historiography. Both chapters demonstrate through different sources the need to draw on a range of individuals and organisations to create networks of support.

The 'many registers of care' are at the forefront of Margaret Tennant's analysis, in the concluding chapter, of the way informal caring became translated into the 'caring profession' of social work. We now have a variety of 'care work' occupations that distinguish themselves by promoting objectivity towards – as against emotional involvement with – those to whom their services are directed.

By tracing 'registers of care' in specific domains we hope to encourage others to contextualise the urgent issues facing our society. How is it that New Zealand, once thought of as a great place to bring up children, now has high rates of child abuse and child poverty? Why has caring for our children become a problem? Recent studies have produced powerful and deeply moving accounts of state failure when institutions have stepped in as caregivers, exposing stark experiences within a supposedly compassionate society.[10] In order to come to terms with these realities, we urgently require a greater understanding of past notions of familial duty, state welfare and the ways in which caring has become professionalised and commodified. Taking account of past caring may further assist us to identify ways to reshape the future.

Notes

1 Nikki MacDonald, 'National portrait: Kristine Bartlett, equal pay campaigner': www.
stuff.co.nz/national/politics/91759405/National-Portrait-Kristine-Bartlett-equal-
pay-campaigner

2 Annaleese Jochems, 'The cost and value of care': http://pantograph-punch.com/post/
nz-care-workers-experience-pay-settlement

3 Kirsty Johnston, 'Mum to disabled man loses latest family carer court case against
Government': www.nzherald.co.nz/nz/news/article.cfm?c_id=1&objectid=11900968

4 Ana Loren: '"We're absolutely ecstatic": Mum caring for disabled son wins appeal over
pay': www.stuff.co.nz/auckland/101232310/were-absolutely-ecstatic-mum-caring-for-
disabled-son-wins-appeal-over-pay

5 For a comprehensive discussion of this see Margaret Tennant, *The Fabric of Welfare:
Voluntary organisations, government and welfare in New Zealand, 1840–2005*
(Wellington: Bridget Williams Books, 2007).

6 For a discussion of colonialism and its impact on interpersonal relationships and
kin structures see Annie Mikaere, 'Maori women: Caught in the contradictions of a
colonised reality', *Waikato Law Review* 2 (1994), 125–49.

7 Charlotte Macdonald, 'Taking colonialism home: Cook Islands "housegirls" in
New Zealand', in Victoria K. Haskins & Claire Lowrie (eds), *Domestic Service
and Colonisation: Historical and contemporary perspectives* (New York & London:
Routledge, 2015), 273–88.

8 Ministry of Social Development, *Caring for the Carers – He Atawhai i te Hunga
Ngākau Oha o Aotearoa: The New Zealand Carers' Strategy Action Plan for 2014 to
2018* (Wellington: Ministry of Social Development, 2014): www.msd.govt.nz/about-
msd-and-our-work/work-programmes/policy-development/carers-strategy/index.
html#Whoarecarers2

9 There have been some attempts to historicise fathering in New Zealand. See, for
instance, Tim Frank, 'About our father's business: Fatherhood in New Zealand,
1900–1940', PhD thesis, University of Auckland, 2004.

10 See Bronwyn Dalley, *Family Matters: Child welfare in twentieth-century New Zealand*
(Auckland: Auckland University Press, 1998). A confronting set of personal narratives
of abuse in state care has been collated by Elizabeth Stanley in *The Road to Hell: State
violence against children in postwar New Zealand* (Auckland: Auckland University
Press, 2016).

1

CONTEXTUALISING CARING
IN NEW ZEALAND

Barbara Brookes

Richard Cruise, a visitor to New Zealand, remarked in 1824:

> [I]n the manner of rearing children, and in the remarkable tenderness and solicitous care bestowed upon them by the parents, no partiality on account of sex was in any instance observed.... The infant is no sooner weaned than a considerable part of its care devolves upon the father: it is taught to twine its arms round his neck, and in this posture it remains the whole day, asleep or awake.[1]

Cruise's observation transports us to a time when, within Māori society, care of the young might be distributed across whānau, and might change with the development of the child. This was greatly at odds with a new model family promoted to Māori society through British law and by example, after annexation by the Treaty of Waitangi in 1840. An expansive view of care, or manaakitanga (cherishing and respecting others) was more likely, in nineteenth-century European eyes, to be considered the particular domain of women.

Feminist historians have grappled with how to write about the 'hidden lives' of caring; their task is complicated by cultural understandings, and the difficulty of uncoupling caring from gender. From the time of European settlement in New Zealand the economy has relied on the unpaid work of women for social reproduction. Settler society flourished on the expectation that women performed the everyday tasks required to keep families and communities healthy.[2] Women's caring – whether for children, a home or the sick – has involved both physical labour and emotional investment.

We could call much of women's labour in the past 'loving attention' or we could call it 'work'. That naming has implications for how it is viewed by the wider society and how that view has changed over time.[3] Care is not necessarily a glamorous subject, involving as it does attending to bodily needs (think of changing nappies), anticipating dangers (for the blind or deaf, for example), or listening attentively to stories (as we might be required to do) told and retold by the elderly. The Society for Research on Women sensitively documented the difficulties of caring in the mid-1970s.[4] The two images photographer Anne Noble took in the early 1990s of Audrey Thetford and her disabled daughter capture the loving attention and the reciprocal nature of care. Noble's photographs capture the ineffable nature of caring that is so important to us.

The relational notion of reciprocity – that children returned a duty of care that parents had provided for them – governed Pākehā notions of family in the nineteenth century. Unmarried daughters were expected to care for their elderly parents and, by the mid-twentieth century when marriage rates reached their peak, married daughters with children were expected to provide care for elderly parents. State promotion of the idea of the breadwinner wage enabled many women to offer care services to their own families and to take on voluntary roles in the wider community. In the twenty-first century, where the two-income family has become the norm, the general expectation is that care of the elderly will take place in an institution. This chapter considers some of those shifts over time and what they might mean for a re-evaluation of caring.

Ivan Illich named the emotional work of 'enhancing the status and wellbeing of others' 'shadow labour' – 'those unseen efforts, which like housework, do not quite count as labour but are nevertheless crucial' to our daily lives.[5] Some aspects of caring are difficult to put into words. Take, for example, caring as simply being available to family and friends. We do not expect to be paid money for our attention to our friends or family; indeed, to suggest we should be paid risks changing the nature of the relationship. But if our family members require a level of care beyond everyday expectations we might ask for societal recognition through remuneration – and in fact home carers have done just that.

Work or care? One is usually paid for and the other usually not. Much legal time has been spent debating the issue of 'natural support'. The

Anne Noble, *The Thetfords cooking together*, from the exhibition *Hidden Lives: The work of care.*
0.027961/3, Museum of New Zealand Te Papa Tongarewa, Wellington

Anne Noble, *Audrey Thetford assisting Gladys Thetford with washing her hair*, from the exhibition *Hidden Lives: The work of care.*
0.027961/2, Museum of New Zealand Te Papa Tongarewa, Wellington

Ministry of Health in 2012 unsuccessfully opposed paying family members as caregivers on the grounds that this would amount to 'professionalising or commercialising family relationships'. Such relationships, the ministry argued, should be regarded as 'natural supports' – defined as:

> supports that can be accessed by all people who live and work in any community within New Zealand. They are readily available and reasonably easy to access. They describe the personal resource an individual has within them. They describe the support that is available from family members, neighbourhoods and community/social groups, schools, church groups, Scouts, Girl Guides, service groups, sports clubs and so on. They are supports that people access on a very informal basis and in reality are accessed by most New Zealanders.[6]

Despite the carefully gender-neutral language of public policy documents, the fact is that women provide much of that support.

We have seen important transitions in caring. The care of children and the elderly – which, in the past, was expected to be the responsibility of families and to take place in the family home or in some benevolent or church institution – might now take place in a commercial context. My own career has been made possible by that very context: my children were all in daycare from infancy, in after-school care at primary school, and my mother spent her last years in a small rest home near our house. My academic work took priority over caring in a way that would have been unimaginable in my mother's life.

I am not nostalgic for a past where women did the bulk of unpaid caring – if that is indeed in the past – but I want to honour the importance of caring by discussing it in a variety of historically specific contexts. I also want to think about the resources women drew on to make their empathy possible.[7] Those resources included the training in caring from a young age, beginning with dolls and prams, and the care of younger siblings; there were examples of older women engaged in caring work; and there was, what one woman described as 'an inner knowing'. Perhaps most importantly, up until the 1960s there was often a commitment to a church that placed an emphasis on women's selflessness as central to family and community life – and praised such commitment. Women's work might be validated in public weekly in a sacred space, and this empowered them to continue. It was, after all, the religious conviction of the Women's Christian Temperance Union that filled women with confidence that they could 'do anything', including seeking the vote, which they achieved in 1893.

It often seems that we have to move beyond any notion of caring for work to be valued. In order to seek professional respect, childcare had to become 'early childhood education', for example. Somehow this feels like an uncomfortable yardstick of 'progress'. Why is caring not enough? Historian Emily Abel suggests we are seeking 'to create the illusion of independence by disregarding the care on which we depend'.[8] This desire to appear independent is also shaped by gender: traditionally, to be considered a 'good woman' meant putting others first; to be a 'good man' was to put work first.[9]

Arlie Hochschild noted in *The Managed Heart* that there is no real male equivalent for the term 'mothering': 'fathering' is usually used in the biological sense of 'fathering a child', whereas 'mothering' is a much broader concept. How do we think of this unpaid labour of a 'highly interpersonal sort'?[10]

The value of caring to the first people of Ōtākou, a settlement on the Otago Peninsula, was clearly on display in the *Hākui: Women of Kāi Tahu* exhibition at Otago Museum in 2016. Hākui 'are the mothers, grandmothers, aunts and caregivers of whānau (or the wider group)'.[11] The exhibition was a celebration of the caring that Kāi Tahu women have done over the nineteenth and twentieth centuries to ensure the continuity of their culture. Pani Wera, for example, married in the mid 1800s and had several children who accompanied the family on the traditional mahika kai, or food collecting, expeditions. Pani was a gifted weaver – samples of her work were on display in the exhibition – and she passed on her skills to her daughter Hana Te Ururaki.

Nationally, by 1896 the Māori population was less than 40,000 and, of those, only 18,260 were female.[12] By 1900 the Māori proportion of the total population had fallen to 5.5 per cent.[13] One estimate suggests that by the 1890s, 50 per cent of Māori girls died before the age of seven and just 42 per cent reached adulthood.[14] Women such as Hera Te Wahia helped reverse the downward spiral: married in 1883, Hera bore 14 children. For women working for the survival of their communities, the future of their children became paramount. The Kāi Tahu women celebrated in the exhibition focused on that future – they helped build churches and schools; they taught their children to weave and to collect traditional foodstuffs, and to care for their marae. They rebuilt their communities by combining elements of modernity – establishing schools for example – while holding on firmly to traditions.

At the same time as the Māori population was in crisis, the settler population was burgeoning. Pākehā women who married in the 1850s and 1860s bore an average of 7.4 children.[15] Sarah Ann Taylor was an exceptional case: she bore 21 children, only one of whom died at birth. Married at 16 to a Southland banker, she ran a highly ordered household – her eight girls donned a fresh white frilled apron each day, and they and their 12 brothers 'kept splendid health'.[16]

Not all families were blessed with such robustness. The risk of a woman dying in childbirth was high – historian Alison Clarke suggests that, at a conservative estimate, one mother died for every 195 births in the 1870s.[17] Women provided care at either end of life: as midwives and as attendants to the dying. Frequent pregnancies depleted women's physical resources and made them less able to withstand a prolonged labour or septicaemia – both common causes of maternal death.[18]

Frances Porter and Charlotte Macdonald's wonderful collection of writings by nineteenth-century women, *My Hand Will Write What My Heart Dictates*, abounds with instances of care and suggests how women found strength in adversity. Anna Dierks wrote in her diary of her severe illness after the birth of a healthy son in March 1890: 'I fought with every effort and with prayer and sighing … the Lord heard my prayer and permitted me to get better again.' When she gave birth to a premature baby at five months in 1892, Anna faced much suffering, but she noted how glad she was 'that the child was not born dead but would receive emergency Baptism. That is the special comfort of God's grace.' Her baby died 10 minutes after being baptised.[19] The death of a mother required others to step in and care for the rest of the family. 'My Dear Hannah,' Jane Oates wrote of her 19-year-old daughter in 1867, 'was confind on the 16 of July at half past 3 o Clock in the Morning and was Ded at quarter to eleven the same Morning and had left a fine boy and we have got it to nurs and it makes us bisey.'[20]

The health and safety of children was an ongoing preoccupation. Five of Jane Moorhouse's nine children survived, and her 1860s journal records her delight in their progress but also her constant anxiety about them, particularly when her husband was away.[21] Physical ailments such as aches and fevers had to be carefully monitored: five days of a diphtheria epidemic in 1879 took three of Sarah Ricketts' 12 children.[22] Potential accidents had to be anticipated. The home was full of hazards with its open fires, water buckets and dangerous substances; and outdoors, water races, open drains, streams and rivers – all attractive play areas – were equally dangerous. One woman wrote, 'The first place to look [for a lost child] was the well.'[23] For women absorbed in household work it was often impossible to oversee all activities. Older children were expected to look out for the younger ones. Maria Richmond, who was pregnant at the time of her infant niece's accidental drowning in a garden pond, expressed in writing what many mothers no doubt felt: 'Until children are given us, it seems as tho' half the possibilities in human life for bringing joy or sorrow remain unrevealed.'[24]

Women's caring role was part of the family contract and was valued by Christian belief. Sarah Cockburn was a stalwart member of the Queenstown Presbyterian church for more than 70 years.[25] Born in Scotland in 1864, she emigrated to New Zealand with her family and settled in Queenstown. After two years of schooling, from the age of 11 she stayed home to look after her father because her mother was busy and often away from home working as a midwife. At the age of 15 she moved to the Rees Valley near Glenorchy to keep house for her brothers, who were establishing a farm. She used the clear night sky conditions as a chance to forward her interest in astronomy – a passion she shared with her brother George. At 18 she became a governess to three children on a remote sheep station. At 22 she married John Salmond, and went on to have eight children, three of whom became leaders in New Zealand Presbyterianism. Sarah's life involved care of family – her father, brothers, the children of employers, and then her own children.

Historians have argued that colonial New Zealand was distinguished by the expectation of family rather than state support in times of need.[26] Unmarried daughters had an important but often unnoted role to play in that expectation. Obituaries record that the elderly often resided with their 'unmarried daughter'. Sons might contribute to the upkeep of their parents, but it was daughters who provided the daily care. Unmarried daughters who trained in medicine or nursing in the late nineteenth and early twentieth century might be regarded as ideal carers for ailing parents or siblings and be recalled home, expected to give up their profession in the face of family needs.[27] But such training was by no means usual. More common were the youngest daughters who, like Mosgiel Woollen Mills worker Bessie Turnbull, chose not to marry because 'I thought it was my duty to stand by my mother and give her a good ending in life.'[28] One woman, born in 1905, trained to be a teacher but the very day she was appointed to a teaching position she received a telegram from her mother: 'Come home. Grandmother very ill, doctor says long illness.' She recalled:

> I knew at once that, as I was the only daughter, I must be at home with Mother seeing that she had sent for me. I felt it was fair. My mother had helped my father in his work tremendously. Grandmother had helped Mother in the house. Family obligation. I just had to go home, it was an inner knowing.[29]

The expectation that an unmarried family member would care for aging parents continued well into the twentieth century. A Miss H. explained her situation in 1975 to the Society for Research on Women. She had given up her job as a teacher in 1960 in order to serve as a nurse and companion to her father, a duty she accepted since she was the only one of her siblings 'without a family to look after'.[30] Miss H. could no longer work and had left teaching too early to qualify for a pension so the 'future looked grim'. A Mr K. was in the same position, caring for his elderly father; as he said, 'After all, he looked after me while I was young', but he was bitterly aware that he had failed to do many things he had planned as a younger person.[31]

A home could contain multiple generations and a diversity of arrangements. Mary Downie Stewart, for example, acted as hostess and companion to her brother when he became mayor of Dunedin in 1913 and then, when he returned from World War I crippled by arthritis, she supported him throughout his parliamentary career. Her commitment to her brother and her involvement in a number of women's organisations, Yvonne Wilkie has written, 'exemplified her closely held personal belief that a "woman's *real* social value lies in her power of sympathy and service"'.[32]

Single women sometimes found companionship and care in a commitment to each other. A Miss Fergusson, who worked in the Far North as a district nurse, was accompanied by a Miss Kidner who received a small assistant's wage from the Health Department. When Miss Fergusson left the district health service the two women set up a poultry farm together outside Whanganui.[33]

A happy family life and good companionship was of course not guaranteed, and the burdens of caring could sometimes be extreme, when the elderly were cantankerous and ungrateful, or family members were violent or required care beyond the resources of the family. Institutions could play a vital role in relieving those people in intolerable situations. In 1890 a Mrs Fraser found she could no longer nurse her husband, who was driven mad by the pain of his advanced cancer of the rectum: he would not allow himself to be touched or cleaned. Mrs Fraser asked her clergyman to approach Frederic Truby King to have her husband admitted to the Seacliff Asylum. Although he could find 'no evidence of insanity', Truby King admitted the 69-year-old father of nine, who died in the asylum eight months after admission.[34] Violence might be another reason for committal. When Rupert Macdonald (27) attacked his mother sometime in June 1910, she had to run to the neighbours for help.[35] She no longer felt safe caring for him at home and his committal to the asylum relieved her of the fear of her son's uncontrollable rages. These inmates in the asylum were cared for by men – male attendants – a group whose caring role requires more examination.

Margaret Tennant's work has shown that the profile of the aged population in the late nineteenth century was very different to today: there was a predominance of elderly men 'without friends and family' who had no one to care for them. This led to a *sudden* demand for old age welfare services'. In a wonderful piece of writing in the *New Zealand Journal of History*, Tennant discusses how the Wellington Benevolent Institute, which was looking for ways to keep elderly men occupied in 1890, hit on the solution of hiring them out as 'sandwich board men', 'thereby advertising the old men's indigence as well as the products concerned'. When the men used the proceeds from their advertising work on drink rather than warm clothing, they were held to be 'an example of supreme ingratitude'. By 1910, 81 per cent of those in institutions for the elderly were men, and by 1921 they made up 79 per cent.[36] But those in institutions remained a very small minority – under 5 per cent of those aged over 65.

If the elderly had relatives, those relatives were expected to provide their care. When this family contract broke down, those in need might enact proceedings to remind relatives of their duties. In 1916 a 67-year-old mother took proceedings for maintenance against her four sons who failed to support her, because she found the meagre old-age pension inadequate for her needs.

The only son to appear before the magistrate earned £2 a week (equivalent in 2018 to about $263). He had nine children and three of his own sons were serving in the war. The magistrate excused him from contributing but ordered the other three sons to contribute weekly at a rate of 2s 6d to 3s.[37] Some commentators bemoaned the fact that the introduction of the Old Age Pension in 1898 had led to children being less willing to care for their parents; in 1903 the Christchurch *Press* commented that this new trend revealed 'a sad deterioration in the moral tone of the community'.[38]

Children with physical or intellectual disabilities might require a lifetime of care. In March 1919 Elizabeth and William Reylands were charged with depriving their 'mentally defective' son of the necessaries of life. The couple had eight children and farmed in the Paparoa district at the head of the Kaipara harbour. William Reylands had suggested that their son, described as an 'imbecile', 'should be sent to a mental hospital or a home' but had been 'overruled' by his wife. Elizabeth Reylands wanted to keep her son in the family and had done so for 29 years. He was 'of exceedingly dirty habits', tore any clothing that was put on him, and had no control over his appetite; he reportedly ate like an animal. In warm weather he was put in a shed to sleep, and it was the condition of this shed that had enraged a visiting constable, who instituted charges against the Reylands.

Neighbours, however, were quick to spring to the family's defence. The son, they claimed, was treated just like the other children and was always well fed – a view that was confirmed by the medical superintendent of the Avondale Mental Hospital, who could find no signs of ill treatment. In his verdict the judge ruled that the elderly couple had done 'their best' in most difficult circumstances, and he sentenced them to imprisonment only until the court rose that day.[39]

As in the Reylands' case, fathers were much more likely to want to institutionalise an intellectually disabled child than were mothers. In the mid-twentieth-century Pākehā world, a view often prevailed that so-called 'normal' children in the family would suffer if such a disabled child remained at home. The demands of a child unlikely to develop normally were regarded as taking a mother's attention away from her other children, to their detriment, as if families have a closed and limited circle of emotional energy. Some children with Down syndrome, microcephaly and other congenital conditions were sent as infants to a special facility in Nelson. One couple whose eldest daughter, Lorraine, was institutionalised in the 1940s did not discuss her existence although the mother, Mrs D., visited her regularly: they maintained harmony in the family by not speaking about it. When Mrs D. was interviewed in 1966 her two sons, aged 19 and 17, were unaware that they had an older sister.[40]

A large-scale survey carried out in New Zealand in the early 1970s indicated that 'mothers had sole responsibility for considerable numbers of the intellectually handicapped, and for an increasing proportion of those in the older age groups'. Examples ranged from a divorced 22-year-old mother who was working and caring for her son with Down syndrome with the help of her parents-in-law, to a 97-year-old Māori woman living in a rural township who was caring for her 20-year-old great-grandson 'whom she had reared from childhood'.[41] Such caring by kin is powerfully depicted in Vincent Ward's 1980 documentary *In Spring One Plants Alone*, where 82-year-old kuia Puhi lovingly cares for her totally dependent 40-year-old son Niki. The filmmaker's deep concentration on the relationship mirrors the attentiveness Puhi paid to her son.

Māori families, where support of the wider kin group was expected – where it was available – were much less likely to choose institutionalisation for intellectually disabled children. If there was a wider kin network, mothers were released from the primary expectation of care. 'Significantly more' intellectually disabled Māori than Pākehā children were, according to the 1970s study, the responsibility of other relatives, most notably grandparents.[42]

Since the 1980s, technologies and tests such as ultrasound and amniocentesis have raised new societal questions about disability and caring. Rayna Rapp suggests that women are today's 'moral pioneers' as they negotiate the decision-making involved with the choice of abortion in the face of new knowledge about abnormalities derived from new tests.[43] Such tests make it possible to circumvent the burden of caring for the disabled. The group 'Saving Downs' deeply disagrees with this position, which it views as the modern version of eugenics. Instead the group would like to see a society that does not discriminate against those with disabilities.[44]

Individuals may decide to circumvent the burden of caring for disabled infants through prenatal testing, but we cannot escape the needs of the elderly (which we all too soon become) in the same way. Between 1950 and 2000 women's life expectancy increased dramatically – by nearly 10 years. At the start of the new millennium the life expectancy of Pākehā women at birth was nearly 82 years, while for Māori women it was 73 years. Māori women were more likely than other women to keep working over age 65.[45] The late Merimeri Penfold asserted that 'retirement is not in the way of thinking of many Maori elders … We've been taught to survive, how to cope with our responsibilities and a sort of separation between work and retirement isn't our way of viewing the world.'[46] Women are likely to outlive men by five years, meaning that an increasing proportion of women live in homes alone. In 2001, 62 per cent of those over 75 were female and, of those, over 95 per cent were Pākehā.[47] Thirty-one per cent of women aged 85 plus are in residential care.[48] By 2015 the numbers in residential care had increased 8 per cent in just five years.[49]

A 2012 Human Rights Commission report into the aged-care workforce, *Caring Counts*, found that as many as 48,000 workers – the great majority of whom are women – perform the work of care in residential homes for the elderly.[50] Nearly a quarter of those carers are migrants from, among other places, the Philippines, the Pacific Islands and China.[51] Because caring work is done by women, it is underpaid. According to one worker, an 18-year-old working at the fast-food restaurant Burger King was paid more than she was.[52] Maintenance men and gardeners at residential facilities are routinely paid more than the women who do arduous daily tasks assisting residents with showering, dressing, eating and general mobility, as well as providing an essential social contact.[53] As Judy McGregor has written, there are many physically demanding tasks of such caring but at its centre are social relationships: the 'emotional umbilical cord between women working as carers and the older people they care for'.[54] The commission concluded: 'Pay inequality between home and residential based caring and those doing much the same work in public hospitals cannot continue to be condoned when it is publicly funded. Quite simply it is a fundamental breach of human rights.'[55]

Yet decent pay for the workers – which is in line to improve as a consequence of the 2017 decision in the Kristine Bartlett case – is not the end of the story. McGregor noted that the lucky ones in residential care are those who have 'loving partners, friends and families who call in often' and sometimes take the resident for a day out. Those who love their friends and relatives know what matters to them. Beatrice Hale has written movingly of when her beloved great-aunt shifted into residential care. Her Aunt Georgina was proud of her hair, which was always immaculately done up in a bun. When Georgina was admitted to the care facility, however, the first thing they did was to cut her hair because 'it was easier' for them.[56] As Beatrice notes, all the positive associations with the word care – compassion, love, affection – are lacking in this act. A 'care facility' lacked the empathy to respect individual identity. Dignity and fulfilment require care from all directions.

In her book *Hearts of Wisdom: American women caring for kin 1850–1940*, Emily Abel gives a number of explanations for the low status now accorded to caregiving. She suggests that 'the privileged typically depreciate the humanity of subordinate groups and deride the work of caring for them'. Take, for example, the low status of psychiatric or psychopaedic nurses in the past. Abel argues that there has been a decline in the 'cultural value attached to the three major components of caregiving – instrumental, spiritual, and emotional – between 1850 and 1940'. By 'instrumental' she is referring to the medical care that was once women's realm – the poultices and plasters found in recipe books, for example – that were undermined by the professionalisation of medical care, both in medicine and nursing. By the 'spiritual' she is referring to the way in which 'sickness and death were regarded as religious as well as medical events' when, in European society, Bible reading and prayer were part of the ritual of attending to others. And in her discussion of the 'emotional' dimension of care, she suggests that literature once celebrated women's emotional involvement. In the past women were encouraged 'to find meaning in their closeness to the sufferings of others', but as nursing became professionalised, too much intimacy was discouraged. Emotional attachment became seen as an indulgence, and likely to distort patients' needs.[57]

We can add secularisation more broadly to Abel's explanation for the low status of caregiving. Callum Brown's work on secularisation in Britain demonstrates that women remained the heart of organised religion in the 1950s. In the 1960s, with a growing emphasis on self-fulfilment, church involvement declined markedly. Brown traces the way in which cultural narratives of feminine fulfilment through home and family fell away. Instead, the burdens of family and marriage as a trap became the focus of feminist critique. It was this climate that empowered Susan Moller Okin to question theories of justice that ignored gender and to highlight how the gendered division of labour within families constrained women. Increasingly women's magazines paid less attention to how to achieve contentment in the domestic sphere and gave more emphasis to careers and women's rights.[58] According to Brown, the 1960s saw 'the dissolution of Christianity from the everyday culture, family life and meaningful identity of most people'.[59] The churches' validation of women's caring role became discounted just as the feminist movement arose to assert women's independence and rights.

Yet feminism itself aimed to care for those in the 'sisterhood': to promote the interests of women against male power. Whereas a Christian commitment to temperance inspired the first wave of feminists seeking the vote, second-wave feminists were inspired by a raft of ideas, and particularly by the slogan 'the personal is political'. The Society for Research on Women, founded in 1966, set out to remedy the lack of information about women's status in New Zealand society: it carried out studies of all kinds of issues, including caring. The difficulty of uncovering answers to questions about care was apparent in the Department of Statistics refusal of the society's request to include questions about caregivers in the 1976 Census.[60]

Women's subordination in a number of domains became clearly delineated and subject to critique: why did women do the flowers in church while men preached? Why was a woman's labour worth less than a man's? Why were women's sexual histories on trial when men were charged with rape? In order to change society, feminists created new institutions that provided care unshackled from the family, such as childcare centres, women's refuges, rape crisis and women's health centres. They also began to study what women had been doing and what they wanted to do.

In the last decades of the twentieth century, women's participation in the labour force increased at double the rate of men's. Caring for children, for parents and others in need increasingly has to be squeezed in around work commitments. As long ago as 1945, Swedish feminist and driving force in the creation of the Swedish welfare state, Alva Myrdal, wrote that 'unproductive age groups have no assured place in the new economic order of individualistic money-making in nation-wide competitive markets'.[61] Building on Myrdal's observation, economist Nancy Folbre remarked that the same may be said for those who take care of those 'unproductive groups'. She suggested that 'It has proved much easier for women to win new rights for themselves than to impose new obligations of caring on men.'[62]

Modern work, as Marilyn Waring powerfully reminded us in *Counting for Nothing*, has globally been counted as men's work.[63] In a more recent study, Waring and Christa Fouché have highlighted the difficulties in determining work–life balance and gaining justice for those who are in unpaid labour.[64] Feminist economist Prue Hyman in *Hopes Dashed? The economics of gender inequality* (2017) analyses the ways in which discrimination against women continues to limit equal opportunities in the workforce.[65] This is the kind of injustice, Okin argues, that was hidden from view in the traditional family.[66] Is there a way to re-evaluate work – uncoupling work and caring from gender – so that there is time in our lives for the 'shadow labour' on which we all depend?

New exhortations about self-fulfilment (and the needs of global capital) propelled women out of the church and voluntary work into the paid workforce. But that workforce was still organised on traditional models of the male working week. We need new ways to think about the organisation of work to take account of caring, and a language to validate it. Political philosopher Nancy Fraser argues for the concept of a 'universal caregiver' where gender is uncoupled from caregiving – where men take equal responsibility and where 'citizens' lives integrate wage-earning and caregiving'.[67]

What would happen if caregivers withdrew their labour? How many children would be wandering the streets? How many disabled people would be stranded in their beds? How many elderly would starve? Imagining this reminds us of the centrality of caregiving today. Such 'social reproduction', Fraser argues, 'is indispensable to society'; without it there would be 'no culture, no economy, no political organisation'.[68] Once we make it visible, we see care everywhere in the current world and in the historical record. Yet feminists who saw their mothers' lives as trapped within the needs of family and community perhaps overestimated the value of monetary reward as a personal goal. The current movement for work–life balance suggests that many in paid work would prefer to have more time for family.

It has, perhaps, been easier for Māori to openly acknowledge the value of caring, because of the very precariousness of their communities and because of an appreciation of elders – as volumes such as *Kaumātua: Anō to Ātaahua:*

Honouring the gifts of our elders suggest.[69] Ruku Te Kauki Taiaroa Arahanga says in *Kaumātua*:

> I have had a good life. We were taught at a very early age how to care for one another. We had a dairy farm at Raetihi. My parents brought all their children up in a Christian atmosphere. This upbringing has stood me in good stead all these years.[70]

Equating a good life with caring is an unusual association in a market-driven world. By making caring visible in a variety of contexts we can see the complexity of social change.

Women gained financial independence by entering the paid workforce and abandoned the dependency involved in the 'breadwinner wage'. That very dependency, which allowed women time for a family and a community life and tied men closely to their paid employment, has been replaced by a model where there are two adults with full-time jobs. Some may have envisaged that a male 'househusband' might make family life possible but this turned out to be a mirage. Caring can be bought in the marketplace if you have sufficient income, but the irony is that for those who work in caring roles, their income denies them that resource. And women remain tightly tied to caring work whether inside or outside the paid sector. The context of caring has shifted but the gender of carers remains essentially the same.

The dilemmas raised by the question of 'who cares?' are not easily resolved, but they are questions that are crucial to contemporary New Zealand society, where a quarter of children are raised in poverty and where, in 2012, a child was admitted to hospital every second day 'with injuries arising from either assault, neglect or maltreatment'.[71] If the good treatment of the most vulnerable is the hallmark of a decent society, New Zealand is failing. Understanding our history may make us aware of how we have come to this pass and better equip us to seek solutions.

Notes

1 Richard A. Cruise, *Journal of a Ten Months' Residence in New Zealand [1820]*, edited by A.G. Bagnall (Christchurch: Pegasus Press, 1957), 188–89.

2 Nancy Fraser, 'Contradictions of capital and care', *New Left Review* 100 (2016), 104. Fraser writes of 'three-regimes of social reproduction-cum-economic production' in capitalism's history. First, 'the nineteenth century regime of liberal competitive capitalism', which cast 'social reproduction as the province of women within the private family'. Second, the state-managed capitalism of the twentieth-century

promoted the idea of the 'family wage'. Third is the 'globalized, financialized capitalism of the present era', posited on the ideal of the 'two-earner family'. The latter has led to 'a dualized organisation of social reproduction, commodified for those who can pay for it, privatized for those who cannot'.

3   Marilyn Waring asks 'If it's not work, what is it?' in her chapter 'Do unpaid workers have rights?' in Marilyn Waring & Christa Fouché, *Managing Mayhem: Work–life balance in New Zealand* (Wellington: Dunmore Publishing, 2007), 59–61.

4   Society for Research on Women in New Zealand Inc. (SROW), Wellington Branch, *Those Who Care* (Wellington: Society for Research on Women, 1976); SROW, Auckland Branch, *Those Who Care in Auckland* (Auckland: Society for Research on Women, 1979).

5   Arlie R. Hochschild, *The Managed Heart* (Berkeley, CA: University of California Press, 2003), 167.

6   Ministry of Health v Atkinson [2012] NZCA 184: www.nzlii.org/cgi-bin/sinodisp/nz/cases/NZCA/2012/184.html?query=title(atkinson%20near%20ministry%20of%20health. See: Attorney General v Spencer [2015] NZCA 143: www.hrc.co.nz/files/9214/3079/3116/Attorney-General_v_Spencer_2015_NZCA_143.pdf

7   Ailsa McKay, 'Rethinking work and income maintenance policy: Promoting gender equality through a citizens' basic income', *Feminist Economics* 7, no. 19 (2001), 97–118.

8   Emily K. Abel, *Hearts of Wisdom: American women caring for kin 1850–1940* (Cambridge, Mass: Harvard University Press, 2000), 262.

9   Julia T. Wood, *Who Cares? Women, Care and Culture* (Carbondale: Southern Illinois University Press, 1994), 9.

10 Hochschild, 170.

11 *Hākui: Women of Kāi Tahu*, exhibition catalogue, Otago Museum, 2015.

12 'Census of the Maori Population', *Appendices to the Journals of the House of Representatives* (AJHR), 1896, H-13b, 12.

13 Bronwyn Elsmore, *Mana from Heaven: A Century of Maori prophets in New Zealand* (Auckland: Reed, 1999), 141.

14 Ian Pool & Rosemary du Plessis, 'Families: A history – Late 19th and early 20th century families', Te Ara – The Encyclopedia of New Zealand: www.teara.govt.nz/en/families-a-history/page-3

15 David Thomson, 'Marriage and the family on the colonial frontier', in Tony Ballantyne & Brian Moloughney (eds), *Disputed Histories: Imagining New Zealand's pasts* (Dunedin: Otago University Press, 2006), 131.

16 'Sarah Ann Taylor, 1856–1924', in Tauranga Women's Centre (ed.), *New Zealand Herstory* (Dunedin: John McIndoe, 1982), 27. The *Herstory* diaries were an initiative begun by the Dunedin Collective for Women in 1977. Other women's collectives throughout the country helped produce subsequent editions and the diaries served to draw attention to the history of New Zealand women.

17 Alison Clarke, *Born to a Changing World: Childbirth in nineteenth-century New Zealand* (Wellington: Bridget Williams Books, 2012), 174.

18 J. Graham, 'The pioneers: 1840–1870', in Keith Sinclair (ed.), *The Oxford Illustrated History of New Zealand* (Auckland: Oxford University Press, 1990), 72.

19 Frances Porter & Charlotte Macdonald (eds), *'My Hand Will Write What My Heart Dictates': The unsettled lives of women in nineteenth-century New Zealand as revealed to sisters, family and friends* (Auckland: Auckland University Press/Bridget Williams Books, 1996), 371.

20 Jane Oates, *Dear Sister: Letters between a pioneer Wairarapa family and relatives in rural England, 1856–1883*, edited by M. Morten, R. Holes & A. Farley (Masterton: Wairarapa Archive, 2006), 126.

21 Jane Ann Moorhouse, Journal and Household Account Book, 1867–1869, MS Moo, Alexander Turnbull Library.

22 Charlotte Macdonald, *A Woman of Good Character* (Wellington: Allen & Unwin/ Historical Branch, 1990), 168.

23 Charlotte E. Warburton, *Changing Days and Changing Ways* (Palmerston North: C.E. Warburton, 1954), 77.

24 Frances Porter, *Born to New Zealand: A biography of Jane Maria Atkinson* (Wellington: Allen & Unwin/Port Nicholson Press, 1989), 156.

25 All details about Sarah's life drawn from John A. Salmond, 'Salmond, Sarah', from the Dictionary of New Zealand Biography: www.TeAra.govt.nz/en/biographies/2s2/ salmond-sarah

26 David Thompson, *A World Without Welfare: New Zealand's colonial experiment* (Auckland: Auckland University Press, 1998).

27 Barbara Brookes, 'A corresponding community: Dr Agnes Bennett and her friends from the Edinburgh Medical College for Women of the 1890s', *Medical History* 52, no. 2 (2008), 237–56.

28 Helen Frizzell, recorder, 'Bessie Turnbull', in Charlotte Macdonald, Merimeri Penfold & Bridget Williams (eds), *The Book of New Zealand Women: Ko Kui Ma Te Kaupapa* (Wellington: Bridget Williams Books, 1991), 700.

29 Society for Research on Women in New Zealand (SROW), Wellington Branch, *In Those Days: A study of older women in Wellington* (Wellington: Society for Research on Women, 1982), 55.

30 SROW (Wellington), *Those Who Care*, 40.

31 Ibid.

32 Yvonne M. Wilkie, 'Stewart, Mary Downie', from the Dictionary of New Zealand Biography: www.TeAra.govt.nz/en/biographies/3s34/stewart-mary-downie

33 *Kai Tiaki*, 12 January 1929, 44.

34 1890 Case no. 2396, Seacliff Archives, Archives New Zealand, Dunedin, cited in Barbara Brookes, 'Women and madness: A case-study of the Seacliff Asylum, 1890–1920', in Barbara Brookes, Charlotte Macdonald & Margaret Tennant (eds), *Women in History 2* (Wellington: Bridget Williams Books, 1992), 129.

35 1910, case no. 4709, cited in Brookes, 'Women and madness', 133.

36 Margaret Tennant, 'Elderly indigents and old men's homes, 1880–1920', *New Zealand Journal of History* 17, no. 1 (1983), 4 (emphasis on 'sudden' in the original).

37 *Star*, 13 June 1916, 5.

38 *Press,* 28 January 1903, 6.

39 *Taranaki Daily News*, 7 May 1919, 5.

40 S.B.C., 'The families, the doctors, the community and 14 intellectually handicapped children', preventive medicine dissertation, University of Otago School of Medicine, 1966, 13.

41 A.A. Morrison, D.M.G. Beasley & K.I. Williamson, *The Intellectually Handicapped and their Families* (Wellington: Research Foundation of the New Zealand Society for the Intellectually Handicapped, 1976), 100.

42 Ibid., 103.

43 Leslie J. Reagan, *Dangerous Pregnancies: Mothers, disabilities, and abortion in modern America* (Berkeley, CA: University of California Press, 2010), 103; Rayna Rapp, *Testing Women, Testing the Fetus* (New York: Routledge, 1999), 306–11.

44 www.savingdownsyndrome.org/

45 Statistics New Zealand, *Focusing on Women 2005* (Wellington: Statistics New Zealand, 2005), 63.

46 New Zealand Human Rights Commission, *Caring Counts* (Wellington: New Zealand Human Rights Commission, 2012), 136.

47 Statistics New Zealand, *Focusing on Women*, 109.

48 Judith A. Davey, *Two Decades of Change in New Zealand: From birth to death* (Wellington: Institute of Policy Studies, 2003), 161.

49 *InSite Magazine: Aged Care and Retirement*, December 2015: www.insitemagazine. co.nz/assets/Issues/December-2015/INsite-Dec2015-E-Edition.pdf, 2.

50 New Zealand Human Rights Commission, *Caring Counts*, 1.

51 Ibid., 10.

52 Ibid., 53.

53 Ibid., 52.

54 Ibid., 132.

55 Ibid., 60.

56 Beatrice Hale, 'Care?', http://corpus.nz/care/

57 Abel, *Hearts of Wisdom*, 264.

58 Callum Brown, *The Death of Christian Britain: Understanding secularisation 1800–2000*, 2nd edn (London: Routledge, 2009).

59 Callum Brown, *Religion and the Demographic Revolution: Women and secularisation in Canada, Ireland, United Kingdom and USA since the 1960s* (Cambridge: Cambridge University Press, 2013), 2.

60 SROW (Wellington), *Those Who Care*, 8–9.

61 Alva Myrdal, *Nation and Family: The Swedish experiment in democratic family and population policy* (Kegan Paul, Trench, Trubner & Co., 1945), 5.

62 Nancy Folbre, 'Family unfriendly', *American Prospect,* 9 November 2001: http://prospect.org/article/family-unfriendly. For her extended discussion see Nancy Folbre, *Who Pays for the Kids? Gender and the structures of constraint* (London: Routledge, 1994).

63 Marilyn Waring, *Counting for Nothing: What men value and what women are worth* (Wellington: Allen & Unwin/Port Nicholson Press, 1988).

64 Waring & Fouché, *Managing Mayhem*.

65 Prue Hyman, *Hopes Dashed? The economics of gender inequality* (Wellington: Bridget Williams Books, 2017).

66 Susan Moller Okin, *Justice, Gender and the Family* (New York: Basic Books, 1989).

67 Nancy Fraser, *Fortunes of Feminism: From state-managed capitalism to neo-liberal crisis* (New York: Verso Books, 2013), 135.

68 Fraser, 'Contradictions of capital and care', 99.

69 Elizabeth Kerekere (ed.) & Nicolas Twist (photos), *Kaumātua: Anō to Ātaahua: Honouring the gifts of our elders* (Auckland: David Bateman, 2001).

70 Ibid., 24.

71 Blair Ensor, 'New Zealand's shocking child abuse statistics': www.stuff.co.nz/national/crime/68936884/new-zealands-shocking-child-abuse-statistics

2

ANNETTE BAIER AND SUSAN MOLLER OKIN:
Debating the ethic of care and the ethic of justice

Heather Devere

Two New Zealand women have been at the forefront of late twentieth-century debate on the ethic of care and the ethic of justice, issues that are still urgent and pertinent in the twenty-first century. Annette Baier is regarded as one of the key ethic of care theorists. She has also won distinction more broadly as a moral philosopher, especially for her work on the emotions, and she has been an active contributor to philosophical debate about the most ethical way politics and society should operate. Susan Moller Okin introduced a feminist perspective into the ethic of justice side of the debate that is considered to be 'of central importance'.[1] Both women graduated from New Zealand universities – Baier from the University of Otago in Dunedin, and Okin from the University of Auckland – and both went on to become pre-eminent philosophers internationally. They have opened up questions about care at a philosophical level in the same way as feminist historians have begun highlighting the importance of care in the past.

Baier and Okin, starting from different sides of the justice/care debate, play an important role in the integration of these concepts and advocate a politics that takes account of both. Both writers believe that a woman's perspective needs to be incorporated into traditional philosophical and political theories, and both are critical about the continued omission of female 'voices' from the mainstream debate.

This chapter first outlines the ethic of justice. It looks in particular at the work of John Rawls, who was one of Okin's teachers, and at some of the critiques of Rawls' theory of justice from different sides of the political spectrum. It then looks in detail at the critique from the theorists who advocate an ethic of care, in particular the work of moral development psychologist Carol Gilligan. The chapter then examines the contributions of Baier and Okin to this debate. Finally, it brings their work together and proposes how we might start to integrate the ethic of justice and the ethic of care.

The ethic of justice debate

The ethic of justice debate centres on how to create a society where there is a fair distribution of wealth and benefits. Proponents of the ethic of justice approach claim that the most ethical form of decision-making is to develop universal and objective principles and rules to ensure that people are treated fairly and equitably. Liberal philosopher John Rawls uses contract theory to argue for a society based on distributive justice that considers equality and fairness as of paramount importance. In *A Theory of Justice* (1971) he uses the device of a 'veil of ignorance' to examine how a just theory of distribution might be developed.[2] Rawls advocated that when considering a fair society, we should try to imagine that we are making decisions from behind a 'veil' where we are unaware of what our own position might be within that society. From a perspective of 'ignorance' about our status, talents, gender, ethnicity and so on, we should be able to perceive the conditions that would create a just society. The Rawlsian thought experiment follows the tradition of imagined political contracts described by Western political philosophers such as Hobbes, Locke and Rousseau to justify certain distribution patterns of power and resources. Rawls' liberal theory emphasises the need to satisfy the value of fairness as the basis for political organisation.

Rawls' theory of justice has, however, been challenged from various directions. From the right comes the critique epitomised in Robert Nozick's libertarian theory of distribution proposed in *Anarchy, State and Utopia* (1974), which advocates for property rights based on legal acquisition and legal exchange.[3] From a feminist perspective, Carol Pateman's *Sexual Contract* (1988) highlights the way in which contract theory has been based, in the main, on men being the decision-makers and women being subordinate.[4] From a critical race perspective, Charles Mills builds on

Pateman's criticism in *The Racial Contract* (1997) and asks whether Rawls' imagined contract would involve free and equal people agreeing to 'be positioned as non-white in a racist society'.[5]

Increasingly, the unemotional, impersonal, objective values of modern politics and philosophy have been criticised as unrealistic, impractical and harmful to the development of a just and caring society. Communitarians such as Alasdair MacIntyre, who are concerned with how society has become more divided and divisive, advocate a return to Aristotelian ethics that identify values that are important for society, and where individuals strive to become better members of the community. Others are engaged in incorporating emotions or the passions into the study of ethics and politics, as a counter to the privileging of reason and rationality in traditional ethical theories such as Kantianism and utilitarianism. Late twentieth-century feminism, with its slogan of 'the personal is political', argued that female values and contributions were being ignored in the political process, and that it needs to take more account of interpersonal relationships. And in the discipline of psychology an awareness of the importance of interpersonal relationships for both psychological and physical health has developed.

The ethic of care debate

The ethic of care, sometimes known as feminist ethics, is a theory that emerged in the late twentieth century as a challenge to traditional justifications for moral decision-making. Rather than emphasising objective, detached decision-making that should be applied universally, ethic of care advocates argue that decisions should include the context and the specific needs of people to ensure harmonious caring relationships. The ethic of care theory now spans about 40 years. It has been influenced by a variety of historical philosophical perspectives and can be divided roughly into four progressive stages of development: 'breakthrough' (mid 1970s to early 1980s), 'analytical' (late 1980s), 'practical political' (1990s) and 'revisionary reconstructive' (2000s).[6] From the foundational works of Carol Gilligan in 1982 and Nel Noddings in 1984, to Virginia Held's 2006 contribution and Michael A. Slote's in 2007, the ethic of care debate has influenced analysis across a wide range of disciplines from nursing, medical and teaching practices to moral and political philosophy.[7] Increasingly, the 'universal appeal and utility' of this feminist-inspired ethic has been explored by many theorists and philosophers who are keen to expose any misconceptions that 'caring' is limited to the personal.[8]

The initial impetus for an ethic of care came from the work of developmental psychologist Carol Gilligan; her influential book *In a Different Voice: Psychological theory and women's development* (1982) is cited in almost all subsequent works on the subject. Gilligan identifies a distinct moral voice that reflects a relational 'ethic of care' that differs from the standard ethic of justice identified by traditional 'masculine' theories of moral development. She critiques the empirical research that underlies models of moral development, which found that the highest level of ethical decision-making was based on the impartial application of universal principles. Both Lawrence Kohlberg (1981) and Erik Erikson (1968) associated moral maturity with detachment and independence, subordinating relationships to rules.[9] When women were measured against a hierarchy of ethical progress – with six levels of moral development from infancy to adulthood – they reached only level three. This stage was at the level of adolescents and early adults according to Kohlberg's moral development theory, and was related to the development of good interpersonal relationships. The conclusions were that women were either deviant or deficient in their development, which was often attributed to their being overly emotional. The later stages – identified as relating to maintenance of social order; social contract and rights; and decision-making based on universal principles – were seen as being beyond their grasp.

These developmental levels had been created based on research using male subjects only. Gilligan pointed out that the findings of developmental inferiority in women may have more to do with the standard by which development has been measured rather than the quality of women's thinking. Based on empirical data collected from three studies where women as well as men were interviewed on their experiences of and attitudes towards a variety of moral dilemmas and life choices more generally, Gilligan constructed a model of moral development that considers appropriate caring as a moral strength and recognises the primary interdependence of self and other. Her three-level development sequence traces how women's moral judgements proceed from an initial focus on the self, to a second level where the good is equated with caring for others, to a third level where the self integrates caring for both oneself and others under the moral principle of nonviolence. When she applied this moral development hierarchy, Gilligan found that women tended to have a heightened sense of responsibility for other people.

It is Gilligan's claim about women's 'different voice', as well as her critique of traditional theories of moral development, that link her into the feminist philosophical debate. According to Samantha Brennan:

> Feminist ethics as an academic pursuit begins with the claim that traditional or mainstream ethics, as practiced largely by white middle- and upper-class men, has constructed ethical theories which reflect the experiences of this group and leave out, or make it impossible to make sense of, the experiences of women and others.[10]

There has been a wide-ranging dispute between feminists as to whether the ethic of care is 'feminine' rather than 'feminist'; whether an emphasis on a woman-specific approach to morality reinforces stereotypes of women as more caring than men and, therefore, more suitable to be the carers for society. This seemed to work against the feminist project, as it confirms women 'in their "otherness"', and thus prevents them claiming access to the moral and political order on equal terms, as full-fledged, independent individuals'.[11] Charges of 'essentialism' and 'false universalism' have been laid against the ethic of care, and this debate intersects with feminist debates about the importance of recognising differences between women in terms of race, class and culture.[12]

Debate has moved away from emphasising the gendered division of care as feminine and justice as masculine, towards an attempt to integrate the ethic of care and justice. The feminist commitment to make the personal political and to ensure that inequalities that were previously regarded as part of the private realm should be of public concern, also focuses on the epistemology of care as an applied and broad-ranging ethic that is aimed at making the 'real' world (as opposed to the one we rationalise and idealise) a better and more inclusive place for all to live in.

The debate has ranged from the claim that these are two distinct and incompatible approaches to morality, to the assertion that there is no true morality if care and justice are not able to be reconciled. For example, Fiona Robinson (1999) offers a 'thorough-going critique of the justice tradition' in her book *Globalising Care* and is 'skeptical of attempts to combine the universalist tendencies of the justice tradition with the situated approach advocated by proponents of the ethic of care'.[13] Selma Sevenhuijsen, on the other hand, writing on citizenship and the ethic of care, argues for a 'caring justice' and suggests 'starting with the vocabulary of care and reformulating the central concepts of a justice orientation in light of this'.[14] Grace Clement argues that the two approaches 'are more fundamental than other possible ethics because they thematise two basic dimensions of human relationships, dimensions that might be called vertical and horizontal' – with justice focused on equality and inequality, and care focused on attachment and detachment.[15] She believes that the 'gender-coding' of the two approaches has to some extent concealed the great importance for morality in general of an understanding of the relationship between care and justice, and that both inequality and detachment are problems for morality.[16] Sybil A. Schwarzenbach proposes 'civic friendship' as a model that 'includes women in the state' by recognising the traditional caring labour and activities performed by women that she regards as essential for a just society.[17]

Annette Baier (1929–2012)

Annette Baier was born in Queenstown and graduated from the University of New Zealand in 1952. She earned a BPhil from Oxford with a thesis supervised by J.L. Austin, and taught in Australia, Scotland and America. She spent the last 22 years of her academic career at the University of Pittsburgh. In 1995 she returned to Dunedin, where she continued to contribute to the debate on moral philosophy at the University of Otago until her death in 2012. Baier is much published and, in 1990, was elected president of the Eastern Division of the American Philosophical Association, 'one of only a few women to be so honored in the first hundred years of the association's history'.[18] In October 2007 she was included in the list compiled by the *Daily Telegraph* of 100 living geniuses, the only New Zealander on the list.[19]

Baier is honoured for her work on Descartes, Hume and Kant in a collection of essays by contributors who acknowledge her as 'trusted teacher, mentor, confidante, and friend'.[20] She advocated an approach of 'fidelity to complex facts' that avoids simplification and dualism and attends to real complexities in the writings of the philosophical canon.[21] As her student Amy Schmitter claims, Baier avoids the 'document and deplore' strategy of some feminist historians of philosophy, and shows us 'firsthand that a philosopher need not compromise her feminist commitments by falling in love with the works of a long-dead, quite white and almost certainly male philosopher'.[22]

Rather than discarding traditional philosophers as anti-feminist, Baier and her followers have sought aspects within their work that are important to feminism. Baier took inspiration from the ideas of Descartes, Spinoza, Hume and Darwin in an approach that 'recognises both the complex psychophysical and the sociocultural nature of the emotions'.[23] Schmitter, drawing on Baier's example, applauds Descartes' 'explicit and published insistence on respecting the intellect of women' and, at the same time, acknowledges that the Cartesian tradition has supported 'a suspiciously gendered view of reason'.[24]

Baier is well known for her work on the emotions and the passions in Western philosophy. Donald Ainslie claims that her 1991 book *A Progress of Sentiment: Reflections on Hume's Treatise* 'changed the way we read Hume', and that she finds in his *Treatise* a study of human nature that is 'a careful, naturalistic investigation of the "social and passionate"'.[25] According to Ainslie, Baier offers us an account of humans 'as animals who relate to one another (and to our environments) both emotionally and cognitively and who can reflectively correct these ways of relating to one another at an individual and social level'.[26] For Baier, 'Persons are essentially successors, heirs to other persons who formed and cared for them.'[27]

Baier does not believe it is 'possible for a person to think and to act in complete isolation from the nurturing activities of fellow thinkers and agents'.[28] While she acknowledges that some people are autonomous and either choose or are forced not to trust others, she believes that 'we are never in a position ... that is not dependent on the concurring judgment or the enabling cooperation of our fellows'.[29] Moral philosophers, therefore, need to consider the circumstances in which we ought to trust or distrust another person. Our dependence makes us vulnerable – in particular, our emotional attachment to certain people. It is this vulnerability and attachment that Kantians and contractarians fear because it prevents us from acting in a dispassionate and detached manner. Baier argues that emotions have a positive influence on our judgements, involving the need to trust, which is important for our continued interrelationships.

Baier has 'opened up a path' for others to follow.[30] She agrees with Gilligan's claim that concerns expressed by women overall reveal a 'different voice from the standard moral philosophers' voice'. She argues that the standard voice has limited application in addressing concrete moral dilemmas such as those that tend to concern women in their relationships with children, family, friends and lovers, and the ill. She claims that women's insights and concerns about these relationships reflect the 'ethics of love', whereas the standard approach of male theorists reflects the ethics of obligation, which, in turn, justifies coercion. She considers Hume to be 'the best' of the traditional moral philosophers and draws on his work to develop the notion of a 'climate of trust' to be progressively enlarged and to expand morality beyond 'a system of threats and bribes'.[31]

According to Elizabeth Porter, Baier defines trust as 'reliance on others', a 'competence and willingness to look after, rather than harm, things one cares about which are entrusted to their care'.[32] Baier 'is convinced that a morality of love is part of all its variants, like parental love, children's love for their parents, love of other family members, friends, lovers, co-workers, figureheads because "love and loyalty demand maximal trust of one sort, and maximal trust worthiness"'.[33] But Baier is also wary of advocating that anyone should be trusted because of situations where trust has been betrayed.[34] Trust is allowing ourselves to be vulnerable and depends on the goodwill of other people. Therefore we need to be aware of appropriate trust and distrust. Not all trust relationships are good and if there is no goodwill between people, 'judicious untrustworthiness, selective refusal to trust, discriminating discouragement of trust' are also necessary.[35] Trust is integral to caring, and is an important concept to be considered by ethic of care theorists.

Baier, like Gilligan, hears from women 'a different voice from the standard moral philosophers' voice'. She also hears a 'different tone and approach' from women such as Elizabeth Anscombe, Iris Murdoch, Claudia Card, Virginia Held, Alison Jagger and Marilyn Frye, who have followed in the footsteps of the great male moral and political philosophers.[36] Baier thinks, for example, that it is 'significant that women have not rushed into the field of game-theoretic moral philosophy, and that those who have dared enter that male locker room have said distinctive things there'.[37] She is critical of liberal theorists for omitting from their 'justified list of obligations' the obligation to properly care, in particular for the young, thus 'doing nothing to ensure the stability of the morality in question over several generations'.[38] Although she regards Rawls' theory of justice as 'the best of men's recent theories' because it attends more than most to 'the question of the stability of his just society, given what we know about child development', she argues that we cannot just take for granted the existence of loving parents who are able to instil a sense of justice in their children. Instead, she says, 'the virtue of being a *loving* parent must supplement the natural duties and the obligations of justice, if the just society is to last beyond the first generation'.[39]

While she acknowledges gender differences in the way men and women develop their moral thinking, she is optimistic about women and men being able to morally reason together. She talks in terms of 'the insights that men have more easily than women, and those that women have more easily than men', rather than there being innate and incompatible differences. Baier's advice to women and to feminist philosophers is to take advantage of being latecomers and to 'stand on the shoulders of men moral theorists ... and connect their ethics of love with what has been the men theorists' preoccupation, namely obligation'.[40] She argues that putting trust at the centre of the problem 'could do better justice to men's and women's moral institutions than do the going men's theories'.[41]

Susan Moller Okin (1946–2004)

After graduating in history from the University of Auckland, Susan Moller Okin gained a master of philosophy degree in politics from Oxford University in 1970 and a doctorate in government from Harvard University in 1975. She died unexpectedly in March 2004, aged 57. She had been teaching at Stanford University and at the time of her death was at the Radcliffe Institute for Advanced Study at Harvard.[42] She wrote three books: *Women in Western Political Thought* (1979), *Justice Gender and the Family* (1989) and *Is Multiculturalism Bad for Women?* (1999).[43] She has been described by Amy Baehr as 'John Rawls's foremost feminist critic and advocate'.[44]

Like Baier, Okin had ideas about amending some of the contractarian theories to more closely address women's concerns. And like Baier, she saw merit in Rawls' theory of justice and had suggestions about revisions to that theory to make it more appropriate for women. She was critical of Rawls' assumption that the family was a just institution of society that ignored the role of sex and gender.[45] Okin proposed that Rawls' device of considering a just society from behind the 'veil of ignorance' might be useful in addressing the inequalities between the sexes and the division of work within the family.[46]

Okin, a much more overt feminist than Baier, was considered to be 'a leading feminist political theorist'.[47] In a collection of papers in her honour there is both praise and criticism of her political philosophy.[48] Baehr proposes that there might be 'two Okins' – one who argues for cultural transformation as 'comprehensive genderlessness'; the other as merely 'political genderlessness'.[49]

Okin's 1989 seminal work entitled *Justice, Gender and the Family* highlighted the fact that theories of justice, 'ostensibly about people in general, neglect women, gender, and all the inequalities between the sexes'. According to her, one of the reasons for this is that these theories 'assume' rather than 'discuss' the traditional gender-structured family.[50] She pointed out that 'typical current practices of family life, structured to a large extent by gender, are not just',[51] and she argued that it is difficult to imagine how families that do not live according to principles of fairness can play a positive role in the moral education of citizens in a just society. The strict gendered division of labour, she argued, means that 'women's self-conceptions, life opportunities, and access to political power' are considerably more constrained than those of men; and when girls are 'raised in fundamentalist, orthodox or religious households or highly traditionalist families' these constraints are even more extreme.[52] Okin believed that an ethic of justice should accommodate the ethic of care, and that 'the best theorizing about justice has integral to it the notions of care and empathy'.[53] However, she also had concerns that the ethic of care could reinforce negative stereotypes of women that could be used to perpetuate women's exclusion from the public sphere.[54] While Okin is remembered primarily as a feminist theorist of justice, her contribution to the debate about the nature and role of women in society is often cited in the literature on the ethic of care, and her extension of Rawls' theory to include the family more explicitly has opened up a debate between feminists about reconciling justice and care.

While Baier argues that an ethic of love is needed within the family and in society more generally to ensure that just principles are practised and passed on, Okin believed there is something much more fundamentally unjust about the structure of the family. In particular, Okin criticised the institution of marriage which, she claimed, has 'an earlier and far greater impact on the lives and life choices of women than on those of men'.[55] She believed that women are made vulnerable by marriage – vulnerable by anticipation of marriage, vulnerable within marriage, and vulnerable by separation or divorce.

Okin focuses more on political theory than does Baier. Brooke Ackerly claims that scholars have underutilised 'her argument that justice requires *political* antidotes to the range of social and economic institutions that perpetuate gender-based vulnerability'.[56] Okin is recognised as having helped to extend the justice debate by arguing that an ethic of justice should not be 'relegated to public relations and banned from private relations'.[57] This has enabled ethic of care theorists to move beyond relegating care to personal relations, and to bring it into the political realm. The issue of inequalities of the family has been taken up by those who advocate an ethic of care, although the concerns of some of these theorists are different from Okin's own focus. For example, Deborah Stone calls for a 'care movement' out of concern about the collapse of the family and the 'erosion of the traditional gendered division of labor'; and Julie White argues that 'the transformation of the family provides an opportunity to critically reflect on the organisation of care within society more generally'.[58]

Where Baier and Okin stand in the justice/care debate

Both Baier and Okin advocate that women's perspective needs to be incorporated into traditional philosophical and political theories, and both are critical of the omission of female 'voices' from the mainstream debate. They believe it is essential that women are more visible and audible, in order not only to ensure equality for women, but to improve society's morality. However, they differ in their attitudes towards the ethic of care, and the benefits or harms incurred for the feminist cause.

In terms of the feminist debate, Baier takes a 'softer' approach to gender: she proposes that the characteristics and values of women need to be 'added in' to the philosophical mix, for the benefit of all. She identifies women as 'latecomers' and believes that they are advantaged by being able to observe from the outside and to critique from their own experience, with their 'different voice', the models provided by male theorists. For Baier, the ethic of care enables women to work within their comfort zone, to have their perspectives acknowledged and valued and, at the same time, to produce a more inclusive and caring society by prioritising relationships.

It is this aspect of the ethic of care that Okin is suspicious about. Although Baier is careful to acknowledge women's vulnerability, Okin questions the wisdom of advocating an ethical approach that seems to reinforce women's responsibility for caring, and to allow the institution of the family to go unchallenged. Okin takes a more radical feminist stance, and analyses the discussion from more of a political perspective. As we have seen, she does concede that care and justice are both needed, but she cannot sanction an ethical theory that could lead to inequality, particularly if it is women who continue to be the disadvantaged. For her, 'a just future is one without gender'. There would be no assumptions about different gender roles: men and women would be equally responsible for child rearing and for contributing and participating in the workforce and in politics.[59] The policies that would come from such a society, Okin suggests, would probably differ markedly because they would be made by people who had experienced nurturing children on a day-to-day basis.[60] She claims that this would lead to better policies that are more 'humanist' but not necessarily more caring or nurturing.[61] This is a logical rational change that is not based on the emotions, but is part of a rights-based discourse.

Baier and Okin locate themselves in different places on the justice–care continuum. Both are familiar with the work of traditional male philosophers and have a sympathy and respect for the justice tradition. Okin comes down on the justice end of the continuum, and Baier is further to the care end. Okin is, of course, very critical of the justice theorists who, she claims, 'have displayed little interest in or knowledge of the findings of feminism'.[62] She names, for example, Ackerman, Dworkin, Galston, MacIntyre, Nozick and Unger as contemporary theorists of justice who 'pay even less attention to issues of family justice than Rawls'. But she also believes that the emphasis on the morality of care and claims that justice and rights are masculinist ways of thinking about morality are 'misplaced'.[63] It is not that the concept of justice is flawed; rather, it has not been applied correctly. Not including women's perspectives as fully as men's, but implying that these theories are applicable to everyone, produces anomalies. Assuming that institutions such as families are 'just', when they are not, means that the theories of moral development such as Rawls' 'seem to be built on uncertain grounds'.[64]

Okin believes that in order to achieve a just society, the family – that institution that is primarily responsible for passing on values – must also be based on justice. Baier and Okin agree that justice theorists and others have failed to include family relationships in their analysis and that their theories are therefore inadequate. Both women consider that the family plays an essential role in socialisation and that it is therefore an omission to ignore this role. Yet Baier finds positive values in the family in contemporary society: she sees it as a source of love and care that can be extended into society. Her work on the emotions and her emphasis on the psychological elements of theories of justice link her more closely with the ethic of care. Significantly, both Baier and Okin believe not only that justice and care are compatible but that society requires both these values.

Integrating justice and care

The thinking work of Baier and Okin on integrating justice and care is part of a larger debate about how the contribution of women might make for a different sort of politics. While justice is a value intrinsically associated with politics, care is still seldom regarded as 'political' in mainstream debate.

The justice/care debate makes explicit reference to the role of care for citizenship and civic participation. White has identified care as 'defacto if not de jure a citizenship value'.[65] Deborah Stone claims that 'caring for each other is the most basic form of civic participation'.[66] Eva Kittay proposes that Rawls' principles of justice should have added to them 'the principle of the social responsibility to care'.[67] Schwarzenbach's civic friendship incorporates justice and care in 'ethical reproductive praxis', which is the traditional form of caring labour and activity usually performed by women.

Baier's work challenged those who proposed traditional theory to look more carefully at their models and consider the realities of how their politics might work. Her insight into Hobbes' state-of-nature hypothesis, for example, is that 'it ignores the fact that for any human interaction to take place, including even "a war of each against each," there must first be family and nurturance. Otherwise the helpless infant will not survive its first nights.'[68] She demonstrates that without care and attachment to those one loves and a wider community, 'the moral disposition to justice – as opposed to the purely prudential disposition to justice – has no place to take root'.[69]

Okin has also challenged the justice tradition of politics, along with those who are concerned that 'moral theorists fail to take seriously the actual desires of women'.[70] Okin wanted women to be taken seriously as individuals and citizens. Her work on justice highlighted the way in which a focus on justice between households made injustice within households invisible. She also suggested that the Rawls' veil of ignorance had potential for feminists. By bringing into the justice debate the reality of family considerations and of women being primarily the carers within the family, Okin helps to make the link with the role of care in politics.

Links to historical case studies

In the historical case studies in this volume, the authors explore different aspects of care, from the personal to the political – conscious that doing justice to the concept requires the type of hard reasoning that Baier and Okin brought to the subject. Following Baier, many of these chapters detail the importance for care of the context and needs of specific people, both those receiving and those providing the care. Emotional attachment, the development of trust and the focus on family and children as objects of love and care are vital aspects of these accounts. Melissa Matutina Williams, in a personal narrative, explores the caring undertaken by her maternal grandmother Tina Murphy. Trust is especially poignant in Jane McCabe's chapter on the night-time care of children. Others explore the materiality of care: Antje Lübcke in an examination of a missionary woman's photograph album, and Katie Cooper through the provision of food in the rural kitchen. Some of the dilemmas that women face in their loving and caring are explored in Angela Wanhalla's chapter on the interrupted relationships between New Zealand women and American servicemen, and in Bronwyn Polaschek's examination of the screen portrayal of single mothers.

Whereas Baier emphasises the need for women's insights into care, Okin is concerned that women's care work is often not justly rewarded and that women can be disadvantaged by marriage and the responsibility for the care of the family. The more political aspects of justice and caring that Okin examined are evident throughout this volume. In Chapter 1 Barbara Brookes alerted us to the historically shifting concepts of care in New Zealand over the nineteenth and twentieth centuries. Margaret Tennant notes the shifting 'registers of caring' in care work undertaken as 'social work' – an occupation that becomes more defined over the twentieth century. Rosemary Anderson looks at the constraints on High-Elect Chief, Takau Rio Love in serving both her New Zealand family and her Rarotongan nation; and Angela Wanhalla speaks about how different aspects of marriage make women vulnerable.

This volume has focused on historical case studies, but the debate about care and justice continues in Aotearoa New Zealand. For example, recent debates about the adequate payment of care workers have combined questions of care and justice and are integral to concepts of gender pay equity. Legislation that extends parental leave entitlements and ensures that both men and women take those entitlements is addressing some of the inequities in expectations about women's role in caring.

At the time of writing, the issue of care and justice played out in New Zealand's highest political forum. Prime Minister Jacinda Ardern gave birth while in office. To critics this seemed a very undesirable situation: how could the leader of the country do her job while also caring for a baby? To many feminists, however, the news brought celebration: this was another opportunity for politics to have to recognise the relevance of caring.

Notes

1   Amy R. Baehr, 'Toward a new feminist liberalism: Okin, Rawls, and Habermas', *Hypatia* 11, no. 1 (1996), 49.
2   John Rawls, *Theory of Justice* (Cambridge, MA: The Belknap Press of Harvard University Press, 1971).
3   Robert Nozick, *Anarchy, State and Utopia* (Oxford: Blackwell, 1974).
4   Carole Pateman, *Sexual Contract* (Cambridge: Polity Press, 1988).
5   Charles Mills, *The Racial Contract* (Ithaca: Cornell University Press, 1997), cited in Janice Richardson, 'Feminism, property in the person and concepts of self', *British Journal of Politics and International Relations* 12 (2010), 56–71.
6   I would like to acknowledge Sally Simmonds for her unpublished work and her insightful analysis.
7   Carol Gilligan, *In a Different Voice: Psychological theory and women's development* (Cambridge, MA: Harvard University Press, 1982); Nel Noddings, *Caring: A feminine approach to ethics and moral education* (Berkeley, CA: University of California Press, 1984); Virginia Held, *The Ethics of Care: Personal, political and global* (Oxford: Oxford University Press, 2006); Michael A. Slote, *The Ethics of Care and Empathy* (London: Routledge, 2007).

8   Held, *The Ethics of Care.*

9   Lawrence Kohlberg, *Essays on Moral Development, vol. 1: The Philosophy of Moral Development* (San Francisco, CA: Harper & Row, 1981); Erik H. Erikson, *Identity: Youth and crisis* (New York: Norton, 1968).

10 Samantha Brennan, 'Recent work in feminist ethics', *Ethics* 104, no. 4 (1999), 860–61.

11 Selma Sevenhuijsen, *Citizenship and the Ethics of Care* (London: Routledge, 1998), 38.

12 Grace Clement, *Care, Autonomy, and Justice: Feminism and the ethic of care* (Boulder, CO & Oxford: Westview Press, 1996), 3. In fact, some feminist writers, such as Patricia Hill Collins, refer to care as an Afrocentric value (see Clement, *Care*, 9, n. 1).

13 Fiona Robinson, *Globalizing Care: Ethics, feminist theory, and international relations* (Boulder CO: Westview Press, 1999), cited in Julie Anne White, 'Citizenship and the labor of care', *Polity* 33, no. 3 (Spring 2001), 492.

14 Sevenhuijsen, cited in White, 'Citizenship and the labor of care', 494.

15 Clement, *Care*, 1.

16 Ibid., 2.

17 Sybil A. Schwarzenbach, *On Civic Friendship: Including women in the state* (New York: Columbia University Press, 2009).

18 Christopher Williams, 'Persons and passions: An introduction', in Joyce Jenkins, Jennifer Whiting & Christopher Williams (eds), *Persons and Passions: Essays in honor of Annette Baier* (Notre Dame: University of Notre Dame, 2005), 2.

19 'Top 100 living geniuses', *Daily Telegraph*, 28 October 2007: www.telegraph.co.uk/news/uknews/1567544/Top-100-living-geniuses.html

20 Williams, 'Persons and passions', 18.

21 Ibid., 2.

22 Amy Morgan Schmitter, 'The passionate intellect: Reading the (non-) opposition of reason and emotion in Descartes', in *Persons and Passions*, 45.

23 Lilli Alanen, 'Reflection and ideas in Hume's Account of the Passions', in *Persons and Passions*, 122.

24 Schmitter, 'The passionate intellect', 70.

25 Donald Ainslie, 'Sympathy and the unity of Hume's idea of self', in *Persons and Passions*, 143.

26 Ibid., 143–44.

27 Annette C. Baier, 'What do women want in a moral theory?', *Nous* 19 (1985), 85, reprinted in Mary Jeanne Larrabee (ed.), *An Ethic of Care: Feminist and interdisciplinary perspectives* (New York & London: Routledge, 1993), 19–32.

28 Williams, 'Persons and passions: An introduction', 4.

29 Ibid., 5.

30 Larrabee (ed.), *An Ethic of Care*, 12.

31 Baier, 'What do women want in a moral theory?'

32 Elizabeth Porter, *Feminist Perspectives on Ethics* (Harlow, Essex: Pearson Education, 1999), 44.

33 Ibid., 45.

34 Baier, 'What do women want in a moral theory?', 28.

35 Ibid., 31.
36 Ibid., 19.
37 Ibid., 20.
38 Ibid., 23.
39 Ibid., 22.
40 Ibid.
41 Ibid., 32.
42 Brendan McCarthy, 'Susan Moller Okin, author, professor, feminist theorist', *Boston Globe,* 11 March 2004, C20.
43 Susan Moller Okin, *Justice, Gender and the Family* (New York: Basic Books, 1989); Susan Moller Okin, *Is Multiculturalism Bad for Women?* (Princeton, NJ: Princeton University Press, 1999); Susan Moller Okin, *Women in Western Political Thought* (Princeton, NJ: Princeton University Press, 1979).
44 Baehr, 'Toward a new feminist liberalism', 49.
45 Okin, *Justice, Gender and the Family*; Brennan, 'Recent work in feminist ethics'; Susan Moller Okin, 'Political liberalism, justice and gender', *Ethics* 105, no. 1 (October 1994), 23-43; and thanks to Vicki Spencer for her advice on Rawls and Okin.
46 Brennan, 'Recent work in feminist ethics', 876.
47 McCarthy, 'Susan Moller Okin', C20.
48 Debra Satz & Rob Reich (eds), *Toward a Humanist Justice: The political philosophy of Susan Moller Okin* (New York: Oxford University Press, 2009).
49 Amy R. Baehr, 'Book review of Debra Satz and Rob Reich (eds), *Toward a Humanist Justice: The political philosophy of Susan Moller Okin,* Oxford University Press, 2009', *Social Theory and Practice* 36, no. 3 (2010), 533.
50 Okin, *Justice, Gender and the Family*, 8.
51 Ibid., 4.
52 Porter, *Feminist Perspectives on Ethics*, 43.
53 Okin, *Justice, Gender and the Family*, 15.
54 Julie Anne White, 'Citizenship and the labor of care', *Polity* 33, no. 3 (Spring 2001), 489, n 3.
55 Okin, *Justice, Gender and the Family*, 142.
56 Brooke Ackerly, 'Susan Moller Okin (1946–2004)', *Political Theory* 32, no. 4 (2004), 447.
57 See, for example, Clements, *Care, Autonomy, and Justice*, 69.
58 Deborah Stone, 'Why we need a Care Movement', *Nation,* 13 March, 13–15, cited in White, 'Citizenship and the labor of care', 487. Second quote is from White, 'Citizenship and the labor of care', 487.
59 Okin, *Justice, Gender and the Family*, 171.
60 Ibid., 179.
61 Ibid., 184.
62 Ibid., 8.
63 Ibid., 9, 15.
64 Ibid., 22.

65 White, 'Citizenship and the labor of care', 488.

66 Cited in White, 'Citizenship and the labor of care', 487.

67 Eva Feder Kittay, 'A feminist public ethic of care meets the new communitarian family policy', *Ethics* 111, no. 3 (2001), 523.

68 Owen Flanagan & Kathryn Jackson, 'Justice, care and gender: The Kohlberg–Gilligan debate revisited', in Larrabee (ed.), *An Ethic of Care*, 77.

69 Ibid., 78.

70 Brennan, 'Recent work in feminist ethics'.

3

TINA:
Whānau, whenua and care

Melissa Matutina Williams

was playing in the lounge at my grandmother's house the day I heard she was once a servant. My mum and Aunty Therese were talking about her occupation and I remember the description confused me. It was the 1970s, I was a child, and I was not supposed to be listening. The wider context of their conversation is forgotten and over the years I have questioned the accuracy of that memory. But while researching for this chapter I discovered that I probably remembered rightly. My grandmother's occupation is recorded in my mother's handwriting as 'servant' in our family history book.[1] I know my mum and aunty loved and respected their mother, and I like to think that their view of her life work, and their attempt to define it, came from a place of aroha, understanding and pride. But it may have also come from a place tinged with resentment about how others had taken so much of their mother's time and care. Forty-odd years later, I too reflect on the life history of the woman I always knew as 'Nan', to explore the crucial role she played in our whānau as a caregiver to her father, husband, children, mokopuna (grandchildren) and tamariki atawhai (children she raised).[2]

This chapter is about my maternal grandmother, Tina Murphy, but it is also about my wider whānau and how our understandings about caring for people have been integral to our relationships over time and across place. Nan cared for many throughout her life. Sometimes she had little choice, and those she cared for may not have always expressed gratitude. Yet she was never a submissive attendant to the needs of whānau members – as the term 'servant' implies. Nan *gave* her time and care, it was not taken. Also, her care of whānau was seldom one-directional; it entailed a reciprocity of care that extended beyond the physical to cultural, emotional, financial and spiritual support. My Nan's story illustrates an 'ethic of Māori care' that will resonate with whānau throughout te ao Māori and many other families beyond it. Indeed, Annette Baier's theory on the ethic of care highlights how trust and dependency are integral to the reciprocity of care and, moreover, that we 'are essentially successors, heirs to other persons who formed and cared for them'.[3] The importance and value of caring has been passed down and has changed little in our whānau, but ways of showing and giving care did change over Nan's lifetime. Intergenerational factors and migration to and from Auckland city from North Hokianga drove much of this change, as the pressures and priorities of city living and working, underscored by persistent assimilationist policies, altered how care could be shown and provided. This chapter highlights how Nan's care of others (and, in turn, our care for her) shaped our relationships to each other as a whānau, and our connection to our papakāinga (our whānau home and whenua/land) in the small North Hokianga community of Whakarapa (Panguru).

Born into a Māori world

Tina was born in Whakarapa in 1910, the eighth of 11 children to Pipiana Morunga and Tamati Peita.[4] In addition to her large family, she was surrounded by many elders, uncles, aunties and cousins, all members of the Te Waiariki and Kaitutae hapū (local tribal groups). Her father was one of 13 children, many of whom had large families of their own – such was life at the turn of the century in this remote Catholic Māori community. At nine days old she was baptised Matutina Tamati Peita, a Latin name derived from a biblical reference to Stella Matutina, the Morning Star.[5] The name Matutina reflected her father's deep commitment to te Hāhi Katorika (the Catholic Church). Indeed, Tamati's gravestone reminds everyone that he was 'he pou note hahi' (a pillar of the church). Tamati was also a farmer, kaikōrero (speaker) on the paepae (orators' bench) of Waipuna marae, community katekita (lay preacher), midwife, and a philosopher who recorded how the community's faith influenced interpretations of, and responses to, significant natural events in Whakarapa.[6] Although Christianity, a capitalist economy and other Western ideas and practices were adopted in the area by the early

Tamati Peita at
Whakarapa, c.1950s.
Author's collection

twentieth century, customary ways continued. Tamati frequently attended
births in the community, an example of customary midwifery practices that
persisted in many Māori communities despite (and sometimes supported by)
district nurses who were dispatched to those communities by the Department
of Public Health in the early twentieth century.[7]

During Tina's childhood, contagious diseases were ravaging Māori
communities. In 1906 a typhoid epidemic hit Whakarapa, and influenza
swept through whānau homes in October 1918.[8] Tuberculosis claimed lives
well into the mid-twentieth century. Economically times were grim, too. By
the 1920s and 1930s, as the Great Depression hit New Zealand, the timber
milling industry that had brought some prosperity to the Panguru region in
the late nineteenth century had begun to decline, and people were travelling
out of the area in search of labouring work. Whina Cooper, who emerged as
a community leader at the time, claimed that the land development schemes
introduced by Māori MP and leader Āpirana Ngata in the early 1930s saved
some from starvation.[9]

Whānau engaged in labour-intensive activities in order to remain self-
sufficient. The Hokianga Harbour and Warawara forest provided a wide
range of foods and traditional medicines. Large land blocks surrounding

Tamati and Pipiana's home were used for maara kai (community gardens). Tamati and Pipiana built their home before Tina was born, at the foot of the mountains Panguru and Papata, at a place called Taiamai. Although it was humble, their home was comfortable, with a kāuta (cooking shelter) attached for kai preparation and meals and a veranda facing the marae and the urupā (cemetery) beyond the creek by their home.

Isolated by poor roads, Whakarapa was a bustling community during Tina's childhood. In addition to the marae and church, the community had a general store and a convent school, and it engaged in sports tournaments across the wider Hokianga region.[10] Between 1918 and 1925 Tina walked to St Joseph's Convent, where she acquired a basic education in reading, writing and arithmetic.[11] At home she helped with cooking, cleaning and other chores, but her lifetime role as a caregiver began in earnest in the mid-1920s when her mother died. Tina's younger sister Hoana was still at home, possibly with a few other siblings, but most of her older brothers and sisters were by then getting married and moving around the region in search of paid work.[12] Tina's whānau and whenua, her tūrangawaewae (place to stand), were tightly interwoven aspects of her life and identity. She did not leave home for an extended length of time for another 40 years, until 1967, during which time she looked after the papakāinga and took care of her husband and children, her nieces and nephews and their children. It was her father who anchored her at home – a number of factors motivated her to stay and care for him, and her decision to do this still impacts on our whānau today.

He aha te mea nei: care?
What is this thing: care?

My whānau never talked about what 'care' meant. We sometimes discussed who and how people needed to be looked after, but usually what we meant by care, in both the broadest cultural and narrowest whānau context, was simply understood as manaakitanga (extending care and hospitality to others), providing awhi to those in need of help, showing aroha or compassion, or just being there to tautoko or support friends and whānau. This list is not exhaustive but it shows that we cared in different ways and according to values and customs learned over time within our whānau. Mason Durie describes manaakitia as 'the capacity to care', which entails being responsive and responsible to those less abled by exhibiting the qualities of love, compassion and protection, especially to the elderly, children and the sick.[13] Manaakitia is what strengthens whānau ties and responsibilities, and is 'based on the principle of [everyone, regardless of gender or generation] supporting and working alongside each other'.[14] Other scholars highlight how whakapapa and principles such as mana, utu and aroha underpin the various ways we give and receive care, and how caregiving essentially entails upholding reciprocal obligations and maintaining a balance of respectfulness in social and whānau relationships.[15] Although such duties and obligations are theoretically neat and tidy, in reality they are continually mediated according to changing personal and whānau circumstances.

Concerns about the capacity of Māori to care for themselves and, in particular, their children, have complex historical and political roots extending back to the outset of colonisation when Western values and standards of care and ideas about 'race' were used to judge how Māori practised caregiving. The unwillingness of Māori to physically or otherwise discipline their young was romanticised as characteristic of a tender native disposition, but it was also criticised as negligent when European children were being raised according to the adage, 'spare the rod, spoil the child'. Emerging concerns about 'racial purity, racial improvement, and racial destiny' at the turn of the twentieth century, along with fixed ideas about the gendering of care, further fuelled critical accounts of Māori communal ways of living and caring.[16] A recent summary of early accounts highlights how communities traditionally shared care of children and how, depending on the age of the child, both men and women oversaw their wellbeing. Children were seen as taonga, or gifts, the mana of which needed to be nurtured into adulthood. Elders often took care of their mokopuna, and they were viewed as valuable members of the wider whānau group.[17] This collective form of caregiving continued with the arrival of Europeans, but the introduction of laws and regulations designed to assimilate Māori into European ways of caregiving for individuals created challenges for the ongoing practice of Māori customs into the twentieth century. Indeed, 'care' in our whānau context was sometimes a challenge and imperfectly practised, but ultimately it is what stitched and continues to stitch our whānau and whenua together.

A caring daughter

Tina was 16 and living at home when her mother died in 1926. Her presence in the home placed her in the position to take on the role of her mother, caring for younger siblings until they left home, maintaining the house and looking after her father. Daily caregiving was labour intensive, with no electricity in the home until the 1950s. It involved collecting water from the creek, boiling clothes in the copper, chopping wood for the stove and cultivating and harvesting the orchard and vegetable garden of the papakāinga. From the 1930s Tamati also ran a small dairy farm and the cows had to be milked. Tina would have been well used to this mahi, but she also had to contend with her father's disposition, ways and expectations of her. He was a frugal man, strict, always thinking and planning, and was viewed by some in the community as someone who preferred to stick to himself. He also had a vulnerable and soft side – as was evident when he cried the entire walk home from church after hearing his son Fred had been killed in the war.[18] We do not know the nature of the relationship between father and daughter, but there must have been a degree of mutual respect and support. Tamati stood by Tina when she fell hapū with her first child in January 1933. Her pregnancy was probably controversial given Tamati's position in the church, but she stayed at the papakāinga to look after him and, after the birth of her son Rapata in 1933, she raised him with the support of her father.

Tina's story as a caregiver clearly transitions here into one of mutual whānau care on many levels besides physical care. The relationship between father, daughter and mokopuna entailed each of them giving and receiving some form of care or support. Tamati supported his daughter and mokopuna both morally and financially; Tina was committed to looking after her father and the farm; and Rapata, whose presence comforted Tamati, eventually helped take care of his grandfather too. Rapata's recollections of 'the old man' illustrate that Tamati felt it was his role to pass on life lessons to his eldest mokopuna, to teach him the value of hard work and discipline:

> The old man used to tell me how to grow things. [Our garden] had potatoes, cabbages, everything. Yeah, lots of things I learned. We had beautiful fruit trees. Beautiful bloody pears, peaches. We had every bloody thing, plums! And all underneath, they had grass. And every morning 'Hey, hey, hey, haere tiki ngā pears, and go and get the peaches, all that type of thing.' And I said to him, why don't we get the cows in [to eat the grass]?

'Oh,' he said, 'sit down.' He said, 'You know why I don't cut the grass? Well, listen.' [He said it like that] to make it so he could really explain it to you. And he said, 'The pear drops on the grass, and it doesn't split. The grass cushions it, you see.' When you look at it, aye, all those things – right. And the smell of the house was beautiful – right through [to] the smell of ripe fruit.[19]

Another mokopuna, Karora Thomas, who stayed with Tamati and Tina in the 1930s, recalls his stay at the papakāinga until he was about eight years old:

I was with my grandfather... because my father is the first son of Tamati Peita, they [the elders] normally ... take the first son. Well, that's what happened to me. But I ended up with my grandfather at about the age of two, I suppose. My grandfather had a farm ... Tamati, Tina and Jock [Hoana] used to milk. Well, by the time I was five, I was milking cows. I had to feed the pigs, the calves...wash the separator. It wasn't easy.[20]

Mokopuna came and went but Rapata remained at the papakāinga until adulthood. Mutual care within the whānau did provide him with many life lessons, but it was far from a warm and fuzzy learning experience. Tamati disciplined Rapata and taught him the consequences of failing to look after belongings and keep things clean and tidy:

One day he said to me 'Where is my hammer? Kei hea? Where?' And he said, 'Go and find it.' So I went and looked for it for hours. And I found it and I took it to him, 'Kitea', here it is. And he took my hand and he took my ear and he said to me, 'How am I supposed to find it if you can't find it yourself? Put the thing back.' He was lecturing me, twisting my ear. I went up [motioning head going upwards] like this, until I had no toes left on the ground. And the last twist is the reminder, you're going away saying 'ok' and squealing, you see. That's why, in my shed now, I know where everything is. He means it when he says something to you. Very strict. He means it.[21]

It would have been challenging looking after a strict man like Tamati. He was a stickler when it came to keeping things in order, super-organised, and willed his mokopuna to be the same. Rapata recalled, 'They used to say, oh he's a mean old bastard and all sorts. But when he died everything was organised. We paid for the bloody thing (the tangi). But, he had everything worked out, that's him.'[22] Tamati was also a pragmatist and to some degree a nonconformist, indifferent to the expectations of the wider community, especially when reconciling his faith with the realities of his whānau life.

Tina and George

Something that Tamati also had to navigate was Tina's marriage to George (Hori) Murphy, who Rapata described as a 'small fulla' with a 'voice like Jim Reeves'.[23] When they married on 17 December 1946, Tina was 36 and George was 54. Tina's marriage can also be couched within the context of her role as a caregiver. George was Tina's uncle by marriage, the widower of Tamati's younger sister Rawinia (Rawi). Kōrero passed down in Tina's whānau has it that when Rawi fell terminally ill she asked Tina to look after George when she died. Arrangements like this were not uncommon within Māori families and led to complex whakapapa connections, as explained in the instance of the mother of Maggie Papakura, a Rotorua entertainer and scholar, who married her deceased sister's husband:

> In those days if a husband was widowed, you'd match them off to the deceased person's surviving sibling ... To take it the Māori way, from his first wife he [William Thom] had Bella. But his second wife was a sister to the first wife and she had Maggie Papakura. So Bella and Maggie were not only first cousins, but half-sisters too.[24]

Regardless of whether or not Rawi made a formal arrangement with Tina, it is clear that Tina was determined to live her own life and she married George. It was not a loveless marriage bound by duty. In old age, Tina fondly recalled her wedding day as something she enjoyed and helped organise. She remembered that she wore a 'blue polyester frock' that she purchased by mail order from a store in Auckland, and a hat and 'nice shoes'. George wore a blue-striped shirt, pants and a 'nice pair of shoes'. Preparations for the wedding took place the night before at her aunty's home at Otengi Road, not far from the papakāinga, where she prepared kai for the wedding reception and put the finishing touches to the wedding fruitcake with Meri-Meri Te Tai and other women in the community. They were married at the private chapel of the convent at Panguru.[25] Not many attended the wedding, but some of her whanaunga gathered at Otengi for the reception afterwards. Tina and George then rode by horse over the hills to Motutī where they spent the night on a mattress on the floor of a nīkau house.[26]

The marriage marked the beginning of a pause in Tina's care of her father and the beginning of Rapata's turn to singlehandedly look after his grandfather and the papakāinga. He was a teenager and he resented the way

George had diverted Tina's care and attention from him. He reflected on this years later:

[George] might be a good man, but how would I put it – say your mum went with another man and all this. You never have the same [view of that man] ... might be months, years after before you're starting to talk to him, you know what I mean. I was like that with George. But he was harmless, his wife was dead. And the old lady used to say [to me], 'kaua e pena', you know, don't do that.[27]

George and Tina had their first two children while living at Tautehihi, close to George's labouring job on the roads around Kohukohu. His income barely supported them and Rapata recalls visiting often, catching fish for them to eat and putting the babies to sleep. Tragedy struck when the second baby, Dominic, died. Tina, who was pregnant with her third child, went home to Tamati while George carried on working and came back to the papakāinga on weekends. There are many reasons why Tina may have returned to the papakāinga: she would have been grieving over the death of her child; Tamati may have asked her to return; and Rapata was planning to leave for Auckland. The relationship between Rapata and George seems to have eased by this stage, and we can see from Rapata's description that Tina was a no-nonsense woman. She was not a submissive handmaiden to George. She had expectations of him and was not reticent about expressing her frustration when he failed to meet them. Rapata felt sorry for George: 'That fulla, never swear. You know Mum, eh, he used to come back from Kohukohu right back to Panguru on a pushbike, on the weekends, And Mum, all of a sudden, "You bloody –", start swearing at him. But George never said a thing, never. What a man, eh.'[28]

Tina's marriage to George was short – barely five years. He died of tuberculosis under a lemon tree near the papakāinga in December 1950. Nevertheless, it was a productive marriage, with four children born in quick succession. Their youngest daughter, Hoana, was born in 1951 after George died. Tina, now a widow and single mother of four young children, was financially independent for the first time in her life – after George's death she received a widow's pension and continued to care for Tamati, who by now was 73 years old.[29]

Tamati sitting on the veranda of the papakāinga with Tina's daughters. Terehia sits next to Tamati, obscured by Hoana on her lap. On the right is Elizabeth, c.1954. Author's collection.

Tina's daughters attended the local convent and then Panguru High School, which opened in 1961. For the first time, all children in the area had access to secondary education locally. Rapata, meanwhile, had moved to Auckland in about 1954–55, where he soon met a young woman named Delia, who recalls:

> He took me back home ... Mum was there, the old man was there ... And then Bob [Rapata] says to him, this is my girlfriend, we want to get married. We want to have your blessing. And in the meantime [an aunty] had found out that I'd had a child before I met Bob, and she was saying that it's not right, he shouldn't marry me. And then the old man says, she's single, she's not a married woman, and so what if she's had a child, she's not the first and she won't be the last. So that sort of quietened her. So anyway ... the old man wanted us to go home and get married. I said to Bob, no way.[30]

Bob and Delia married in Auckland in 1956. They returned home to visit when Delia was pregnant with their first child, Heather.

> When I was expecting Heather, he [Tamati] says to Bob to leave me behind, have the baby up there. Because being Bob's first child – he brought Bob up as his son, and he wanted to be there when the baby arrived. And I says to Bob – no way ... the nearest hospital is at Rawene! And Bob said, no, [Tamati] was going to do it [deliver our baby at the papakāinga]. No thank you! And I says to Bob, no, I'm going back to Auckland. And Papa

was quite hurt. Well, we came back, I had Heather, and she was just a few weeks old and I said to Bob, we should go home to see the old man. And then somebody said to me she's too young to travel. Anyway we didn't go and we heard not long after that Papa had passed away. But we were both disappointed that we never took Heather back to see him, because he would have loved to have seen her.[31]

Tamariki atawhai

Many tamariki came to the papakāinga to live, work and learn alongside Tamati, and Tina looked after them. Even after her father and her husband had died she continued to take care of tamariki, almost all of them nieces and nephews, or their children. Some stayed for years, others for short periods, as arranged within the whānau. The children in her care knew Tina was their aunty, though some called her mum. The customary practice of atawhai (also referred to as whāngai) still occurred everywhere in te ao Māori, despite state attempts to stop it.

Drawing on Suzanne Pitama's research, Karyn Okeroa McRae and Linda Waimarie Nikora illustrate how the practice of taking tamariki into the home was viewed negatively by state authorities and was undermined by a series of laws through the twentieth century.[32] In 1901 the Native Land Claims Adjustment and Laws Amendment Act made it necessary to formally 'register whangai placements in the Native Land Court to qualify the child to succeed to lands of their whangai parents'.[33] The Act legalised the adoption of children outside of the kin-based network.[34] Further changes were made when the Native Land Act 1909 prohibited customary whāngai practices: instead, formal adoptions had to be legally registered through the Native Land Court. As McRae and Nikora note, Māori continued to whāngai children, but at 'the risk of whangai not being able to legally succeed to land'.[35] By 1915 the concept of 'secrecy' dominated adoption laws, but allowances were made for Māori values, and Maori Land Court adoption hearings remained open and were published in *Te Kahiti Tuturu mo Aotearoa* (the Maori Gazette) and the *New Zealand Gazette*.[36] The 1955 Adoption Act and the 1962 amendment to that Act further tightened the principle of secrecy via 'closed adoption' – legislation that inferred that the transparency inherent to 'whangai practices [was] somehow detrimental to the child and their whangai parents'.[37] The whāngai practice was about leaving the doors open between tamariki and their whanaunga; and from a Māori perspective, closed adoption effectively closed the door to one's whakapapa, identity and whenua.[38]

Severing connections between tamariki and their whānau was further facilitated in the 1960s and 1970s when Māori children who were deemed to be living with 'unfit' parents were placed with Pākehā families or institutionalised. This form of child 'care' was consistent with assimilative policies that promoted the Pākehā nuclear family over whānau.[39] The *Puao-Te-Ata-Tu* report of 1986 'set out a Maori perspective for the Department of Social Welfare' in an attempt to 'incorporate tikanga Maori' into New Zealand's welfare system and 'to correct those deficiencies in law and practice which undermined the connection between Maori children and young people and their whanau, hapu and iwi'.[40] The *Puao-Te-Ata-Tu* report became official policy in 1987. But the attempt in 2017 by Oranga Tamariki Ministry for Children to undo that policy by deprioritising the placement of Māori children with their own whānau and iwi merely confirms persisting cultural tensions between Māori and state ideas about what 'care' really means to Māori.[41] A welfare system that is devoid of Māori values and cultural protocols will continue to fail Māori tamariki and whānau. This is evident in the outcomes of past policies that are now surfacing as people, mainly Māori, who were lost and abused in the welfare system seek acknowledgement of the abuse and trauma they experienced in state care.[42] Meanwhile, media commentary and public debate remain focused on instances of Māori child abuse and its causes, and proactive Māori organisations such as Mana Ririki look to tikanga and positive parenting as a means of supporting communities.[43]

Given the culturally alienating bureaucracy of New Zealand's social welfare system, and the risk of losing children to it, it is unsurprising that the practice of atawhai carried on under the official radar in Māori communities. It is unlikely that Tina considered legally adopting any of the children in her care. For her, the practice of atawhai was never about taking ownership of a child. As McRae and Nikora explain, it was about looking after a child while also 'establishing, nurturing and strengthening relationships between whanau members' and broader relational networks.[44] Also, quite simply, Rapata believed that Tina cared for the children because 'she just loved them. She loved kids.'[45]

Reciprocal care in the city

In 1957, the year Tamati died aged 80, the Māori world was changing fast. Migration of Māori to urban centres created a set of circumstances in Panguru that impacted disproportionately on the elderly. In the 1960s Father Wanders, the resident priest in Panguru, publicly criticised the state's policy of integration for causing the unnecessary migration of elderly people out of the area. The young were leaving in droves, mainly to find work in Auckland.[46] Normally only one child stayed back to assist parents and work on family farms. Tina had already taken this role up for Tamati, but eventually Tina had to choose between following her daughters who were moving to the city or remaining home and keep the home fires burning for them. Many parents did follow their children, even for short periods,[47] and Tina was one of them: in about 1967 she moved to Auckland.

From the outset, Tina's family relied on each other for accommodation and financial support in Auckland. Rapata, who had already established

The photograph on the left shows Tina (left) with her youngest daughter Hoana at Whakarapa, c.1965–66. The photograph on the right is of Tina in front of her state house in Mangere, Auckland, c.1967–68. Author's collection

himself in Auckland, supported his two younger sisters; he took them in while they found jobs in the city. By the time Tina came to Auckland they were settled. Therese helped her get a state rental house in Otara, which became home for Tina and her three daughters.[48] This type of whānau support network existed in every whānau that migrated to Auckland, and was further supported by a range of Catholic groups established by Māori migrants to the city. Within this supportive environment Tina addressed her health needs. She had major dental work done, and acquired a shiny set of false teeth (with a gold insert); she also had an operation for cataracts and thereafter wore her signature thick-lensed glasses. Aside from the need for her 'water pills', she was fit and in good physical health.

Tina was also financially secure on her widow's benefit (or possibly by this stage her old-age pension). She moved to a state house in Mangere to be closer to her daughter Elizabeth, and adopted two companion cats, Betty and Robbie. Her son and daughters may have initially helped her settle in Auckland, but eventually Tina continued to care for them in her home. It was where whānau could meet, get a good meal and stay over. After Elizabeth married Stuart in 1968, Tina provided them with 'meals on wheels', sending them 'lifesaver' meals on the bus.[49] When Elizabeth and her family went to live near Wellington for a short time, Tina moved again – to a two-bedroom state unit in Avondale, one door down from Rapata; he recalls that it was good having 'Ma' next door.[50] She was still very independent at the time: she had a garden and was close friends with Belle, her next-door neighbour. Every pension day she would pull her wicker trundler to the Avondale shopping centre to do her shopping.

It was at this home that I overheard my mum and aunty talking about Nan's occupation. In the 1970s they were both independent-minded young women who played different roles in the family. Therese worked at the Central Post Office in the tolls exchange and was in the process of building a home in West Auckland for herself and her partner. She was lesbian and out. She was also financially stable and eager to experience new cultures and places. She learned Japanese, took up photography, and enjoyed fine dining and overseas holidays.[51] She seldom spoke te reo to anyone in the whānau, even her mother, but she was undisputedly Nan's favourite child. Therese showed her care for 'Mother' by organising her business affairs, applying for housing and ensuring she wanted for nothing. My mother worked in a

Tina at Elizabeth's wedding to Stuart in 1968. From right, Therese, Rapata, Tina, Elizabeth, Stuart, his parents Edith and Kenneth, and his best man.
Author's collection

factory and had less cash to spare, but she gave Nan the cultural support she needed, and they would regularly kōrero in te reo. My mother also provided Nan with mokopuna. Hoana had left for Timaru and then Christchurch, so it was to our home that Nan would come every Christmas Day. Everyone lived in separate homes but close by each other. Yet looking after their mum intimately, in the same way that she had looked after Tamati and others, was not part of their life equation, at least at that time.

It is ironic that around the time my aunty and mother were attempting to define my grandmother's occupation, Nan was looking after me and my siblings after school while our parents worked. Nan's home was like a little haven; she always had nice things for us to eat, and to tutu (meddle) with, and the sameness of her daily routine and rules made us feel safe and secure. She was more kind than stern, but was quick to give us a little slap if we were naughty, like when I lit a Little Lucifer firestarter in her vegetable garden and unsuccessfully tried to extinguish it with soil. Nan also had a good relationship with her four mokopuna one door down, Rapata's children, who were in their late teens and early twenties by then. They called her 'Ma', like their dad did.

Going back-home

It's unclear when Nan started planning to go back-home[52] to the papakāinga. She took me and my siblings back there for the winter school holidays of 1979. It was our first visit to Panguru and the papakāinga. I suspect this was when she decided she wanted to return permanently. One of her brothers was living at the papakāinga at the time, with his wife and mokopuna. When her brother passed away, she made arrangements to return. But it was not easy. Rapata found the ensuing conflict difficult to accept: 'The time I really got hurt [was when] I took her home, and I keep asking her, "Everything alright Mum?" "Yeah." We got there, I think, before seven in the morning. Down the creek, up [the driveway], nobody answered [the door]. And I said to her, "Well, Mum, better have a talk."'[53]

Talking could not resolve differences within the whānau about who should live at the papakāinga. On 1 July 1980 Tina made an application to the Maori Land Court to 'determine ownership'. There, she gave evidence that she had 'lived at the papakainga for more than fifty years' and 'on the death of her mother in 1926' had 'looked after her father until he died in 1957'. She stated that she was 'promised the house' before her father's death, and was 'duly awarded' the house by her family when he passed away. She explained that her move to Auckland was semi-permanent and that she sought to return in 1980.[54]

It took a lot of courage for Nan to take her claim to the Maori Land Court, even with the support of her children. It was an unpleasant experience for all parties involved. There was much mamae (pain and hurt) and the whānau became embroiled in raruraru – rifts and resentments – that rippled down to my parents' generation. But to Tina, the papakāinga was worth fighting for. The Maori Land Court made an order in her favour, awarding her lifetime ownership of the papakāinga. In 1981 she returned home.

Once she was home, with the help of whānau Nan began repairing fences; she acquired a milk cow and chickens, and she started gardening. She also got a mokopuna to stay with her in 1983 – myself. Essentially we looked after each other. Nan was in charge – she organised my schooling, my meals and purchased everything for the house, and I kept her company, entertaining her with my news of the day, playing cards at night and having midnight snacks of takakau bread and cups of tea. We both did chores

Nan at the papakāinga with her mokopuna Quentin and Thirza, 1981.
Author's collection

around the house, but I usually did the harder things like lawnmowing and washing the clothes in the agitator washing machine. Others in the family showed their love and support with special parcels, usually delivered by my uncle Rapata and my aunty Therese. My cousins worked in confectionery and pharmaceutical factories, so Uncle Rapata brought me lollies and Nan got huge bottles of Dettol and other cleaning supplies. Aunty Therese was a bit more flamboyant: one drizzly day an appliance truck crossed the creek to deliver a brand new television for us, and on Nan's birthday she drove the five hours from Auckland to surprise us with Kentucky Fried Chicken for lunch. We wanted for nothing.

My time with Nan was similar to Tamati's time spent with his mokopuna. Nan lectured about living – not holidaying – at the papakāinga. She sent me for baptism lessons, suggested I join the kōmiti wahine of Waipuna marae, and would tell me stories about the old days. She was planting my feet firmly in the whenua. I stayed with her for a year, and returned again in 1985–86. In the interim Nan wrote a letter to her sister Terehia, expressing her loneliness. On 30 April 1984 Terehia responded: 'Dear lonely Sister, Kia ora ano e hoa... what a life my dear. We are pulling out of big families ano, you none, I only one he mokopuna atawhai. Never mind, one person knows.'[55]

Nan's oldest daughters Therese and Elizabeth died in the mid-1980s. The emotional toll on the whānau was tremendous. After Therese died in 1984, my mother Elizabeth moved back-home and built a house next to the papakāinga. Nan considered applying for a partition of the land under the Maori Affairs Act 1953. The application stated:

> As I am on my own I require the land for the construction of a dwelling house for my daughter to provide care as I am no longer able to walk to the Post Office and shops and am now dependent on family members. The existing dwelling is in need of substantial repair being far too small to accommodate my daughter, husband and 3 children.[56]

Constructing a house back-home was not easy. As many others who returned to Panguru found, it was expensive, and the lack of employment made it near impossible to get a bank loan, even under the Papakainga Scheme run by the Department of Maori Affairs. The sale of their house in Auckland barely covered their debts and the cost of a kitset house. In the end my father returned to work, travelling to and from Auckland, while my mother, siblings and I lived in the unfinished house. These types of conditions were not uncommon. Within a year my mother was forced to move back to Auckland with kidney failure. She died in Auckland Hospital in December 1988.

My mother and aunty left us before they were able to care for their mother in the same way she had cared for her father. They never had the opportunity to experience the long-term personal commitment of giving their time and care to our most important whānau member. Looking after our kaumātua and kuia was empowering, not disempowering, but only if the whānau unit was strong and, as Durie noted, had the capacity to provide the ongoing level of care required. But just when Nan needed the same type of care she had given to her father, our whānau was at its weakest point. The loss of a generation of our women had come too fast and too early. The remaining whānau unit was too small to create a cohesive blanket of care around those who needed it the most. For a time, we were all living in a blur of grief and instability in separate homes in Auckland, raising young babies, travelling between Auckland and Panguru where my Nan was still grieving for her daughters. The only continuity of care she could rely on at that time was from our wider whānau back-home and a number of our whaea (aunties), who were paid to provide Nan with a set number of hours of 'home help' every week.

Caring for Tina

A formal meeting was called to discuss Nan's care in 1992. Although she was still fiercely independent she was now on her own and needed someone to help her full-time with daily meals and personal care. It was a difficult whānau meeting at which it became clear that Nan did not want to come to Auckland (she was not present at the meeting), and no one at that time could go back and look after her. Everyone had commitments in Auckland – work, health issues, homes, young families. There was no work back home and anyone moving back to the area was declined social welfare benefits. Ultimately, I visited Nan and she agreed to let me look after her in Auckland for a while. So we packed a few of her clothes, her dog and some personal things and we took a road trip to Auckland.

On reflection I was ill equipped to care for her. She needed help with everything by this stage and it was difficult juggling childcare with Nan care. There was a lack of information about where and how to access any form of professional support. Other whānau members visited regularly, but Nan was reluctant to live anywhere else. It isn't surprising. I let her smoke cigarettes in the house, and do and eat anything she liked. She often requested the great-mokos dance and sing for her, and she talked on the phone to relations for a good part of the day. Eventually, though, the time, energy and skills required to ensure she was receiving adequate physical care led to her going to stay with her son Rapata. But by now he was in his sixties and Delia was unwell, and they too struggled. Nan's health had been slowly deteriorating and eventually it was suggested that she required constant professional care. Carnarvon Hospital, close to my home in West Auckland, was selected as Nan's new home.

Nan did not like it at Carnarvon. And I did not like her living there. The patients and staff were nice enough, but she was the only Māori resident and the environment and routines were culturally alienating and stifling. We all rationalised that she needed proper medical care, and that was right. But the fact that she was in a 'hospital', not an old people's 'rest home', did little to shift my belief that we, her whānau, were failing her. She wanted to go back to the papakāinga and I feared she was losing her mind. The whenua and papakāinga was always about more than having a place to live. Being home provided a much broader sense of oranga or wellbeing that nourished Nan's worth, being and identity. Good physical care was almost pointless while Nan was forcibly separated from the papakāinga. It was a distressing situation and in my view, at that time, there was no solution to it.

Who cares?

Caregiving is universally practised and it should be acknowledged that many New Zealand families have negotiated difficulties in the care of family members – a role that is dominated by women and undervalued by society. The reasons for and implications of a 'crisis of care' are currently a major topic of concern overseas and in New Zealand.[57] Nancy Fraser argues that the 'present strains on care are not accidental' but are the result of systemic inequalities that are built into a capitalist economy, where the gendering of work places men in the primary role of economic production (wage earner), and relegates women to 'a newly institutionalised "domestic sphere" where its social importance [is] obscured'.[58] Fraser highlights the entrenched injustices of this gendered sphere – a situation that Susan Moller Okin argues can only be addressed by applying a political 'ethic of justice' to all social institutions, including the family.

Fraser and Okin's arguments are strong, but they need to go further. Justice in care is not just about gender. The systemic inequalities Māori face in their attempts to care for their whānau were – and still are – both gender and race based. Caregiving may be universal, but the impacts of a capitalist system and its supporting policies are not felt and experienced in the same way or on the same scale by everyone in New Zealand. Māori had little choice but to commit to the requirements of a capitalist economy when they migrated to the cities for paid work. By the mid-1900s many Māori women were expressing their aspirations through the Maori Women's Welfare League, whose aims to improve the welfare of whānau positioned women within the home as homemakers and caregivers.[59] Yet as an organisation, the league's concerns and influence extended – and continue to extend – beyond the home into the world of cultural politics. Caregiving was and is not merely about mirroring the ways Pākehā cared for their families, it was about upholding and practising care in a Māori way and according to Māori values, whether that meant lobbying for te reo to be taught in schools[60] or controlling how Māori homes and ways of caregiving were presented to the public.[61] Māori women fought to define and control what care meant in their world.

To our whānau, and to many other Māori families, the challenges we experienced extended well beyond an undervaluing of women's caregiving roles and work to an undervaluing of our people, values and practices. The changing landscape of caregiving in our whānau was heavily impacted by a capitalist system and assimilative policies that were never designed to support the ways in which we cared for each other, nor the reasons for providing such care. By the 1980s almost our entire whānau were a part of the 80 per cent of the Māori population living in urban centres. The communities our whānau left were kept alive by the elderly and a skeleton crew of hau kāinga (home people) who worked hard to maintain the tūrangawaewae of those who were absent. The neoliberal policies of the 1980s and 1990s further squeezed whānau wellbeing on many levels – financially, jobs in newly established state enterprises were lost or threatened and attempts to return home to care for the elderly were thwarted by social welfare policies,[62] home lending criteria, unemployment and a lack of housing. There was no flexibility in the system.[63] In turn, the capacity of Māori to return to their whenua to undertake customary caregiving practices of some of their most valuable and vulnerable – the elderly – suffered.

Taking Nan back-home

Nan's desire to go back to the whenua and papakāinga was so strong that towards the end she began imagining she was home. One day she looked out the window onto the Carnarvon carpark and described the creek below her home. I took my children to visit her daily and we talked about her life back-home. It was there that I recorded her memories of her wedding day with George. Sometimes we went for a drive in my car, visiting people. She enjoyed it and I remember us laughing as we left one relation's house: 'Thanks for coming,' Nan said as we drove down the driveway. Not once did Nan complain or accuse any of her family members of failing to look after her.

Me and Nan (centre) with family on Christmas Day, 1992. Author's collection

This just shows how she continued to serve our needs for care and wellbeing as we attempted to do the same for her. Nan spent Christmas Day of 1992 with my family. She was confined to a wheelchair by then, but she enjoyed what was to be her last Christmas Day celebration.

In July 1993 Nan died at Carnarvon Hospital at the age of 84. We took her back-home to Whakarapa, Panguru where she was laid to rest next to my mother. It was a relief to get her home. We went to the papakāinga straight after her burial and it was a deeply sad time as we walked through the tiny house she had loved so much. All of her belongings and photos of us mokopuna were still on the walls. The papakāinga was a place of so much whānau caring. The whenua nourishes us and it is an inextricable part of our caregiving history. The feelings and understandings Nan had about the papakāinga have transferred to me and my siblings. To us, that place represents her, our whakapapa and our place on this earth. Our wellbeing is connected to it. She would be pleased to know that she taught us that.

Notes

1 'Our Family History', personal papers of Melissa Matutina Williams.
2 I refer to my grandmother as Nan and Tina throughout the chapter. I have chosen to refer to her as Tina when discussing her early life in Whakarapa and Auckland. I refer to her as Nan during the period of her life in which I was present.
3 Annette C. Baier, 'What do women want in a moral theory?', *Nous* 19, 1985, reprinted in Mary Jeanne Larrabee (ed.), *An Ethic of Care: Feminist and interdisciplinary perspectives* (New York & London: Routledge, 1993), 19–32.
4 Maori Land Court records state that Pipiana and Tamati had 10 children. Whakapapa papers in possession of author identify 11 children.
5 Baptism certificate of Matutina Tamati Peita, personal papers of Melissa Matutina Williams.
6 John (JP) Peita, interviewed by Melissa Matutina Williams, Waihou, 20 July 2005.
7 Atholl Anderson, Judith Binney & Aroha Harris, *Tangata Whenua: An illustrated history* (Wellington: Bridget Williams Books, 2014), 366.
8 Ibid.
9 Melissa Matutina Williams, *Panguru and the City: Kāinga Tahi, Kāinga Rua: An urban migration history* (Wellington: Bridget Williams Books, 2015), 42; Michael King, *Whina: A biography of Whina Cooper* (Auckland: Hodder & Stoughton, 1983), 81.
10 For an indepth account of the economic and social condition in the Panguru area during this period see Williams, *Panguru and the City*, 43–59.
11 As recorded on a rosette received by Matutina at the closing ceremony of the school in 1982. Personal papers of Melissa Matutina Williams.
12 Karora (Charlie) Thomas, interviewed by Melissa Matutina Williams, Auckland, 21 January 2008.
13 Mason Durie, 'Introduction', in Pania Te Whāiti, Marie McCarthy & Aroha Durie (eds), *Mai i Rangiatea: Māori wellbeing and development* (Auckland: Auckland University Press with Bridget Williams Books, 1997), 10.
14 Ibid., 2.
15 See, for example, Joan Metge, *New Growth from Old: The whānau in the modern world* (Wellington: Victoria University Press, 1995), 79–105.
16 Direct quotation from James Belich, 'Myth, race and identity in New Zealand', *New Zealand Journal of History* 31, no. 1 (1997), 14. For a range of historical views, debate about the reasons underpinning them, and how state policies developed over time, see: Alison Jones & Kuni Jenkins, *He Korero: Words Between Us: First Maori and Pakeha conversations on paper* (Wellington: Huia Publishers, 2011); Anderson, Binney & Harris, *Tangata Whenua*, 140; John Stenhouse, '"A disappearing race before we came here": Doctor Alfred Kingcome Newman, the dying Maori, and Victorian scientific racism', *New Zealand Journal of History* 30, no. 2 (1996), 124–40; Bronwyn Dalley, 'Moving out of the realm of myth: Government child welfare services to Māori, 1925–1972', *New Zealand Journal of History* 32, no. 2 (1998), 189–207; Angela Ballara, *Proud To Be White? A survey of Pakeha prejudice in New Zealand* (Auckland: Heinemann, 1986).

17 Kuni Jenkins & Helen Mountain Harte, *Traditional Maori Parenting: An historical review of literature of traditional Maori child rearing practices in pre-European times* (Auckland: Te Kahui Mana Ririki, 2011), 22–24.

18 Karora (Charlie) Thomas, interviewed by Melissa Matutina Williams, Auckland, 21 January 2008.

19 Rapata (Bob) Thomas, interviewed by Melissa Matutina Williams, Auckland, 13 August 2007.

20 Karora (Charlie) Thomas, Auckland, 21 January 2008.

21 Rapata (Bob) Thomas, 13 August 2007.

22 Ibid.

23 Ibid.

24 Paul Diamond, *Makereti: Taking Māori to the world* (Auckland: Random House New Zealand, 2007), 23.

25 Certificate of Marriage between Hori Maui and Tina Tamati Peita, Personal papers of Melissa Matutina Williams.

26 As described by Matutina Murphy at Carnarvon Hospital, Auckland, 1993. Recorded by Melissa Matutina Murphy in 'Our Family History', personal papers of Melissa Matutina Williams.

27 Rapata (Bob) Thomas, 13 August 2007.

28 Ibid.

29 The Liberal Government introduced a pension for widows in 1911.

30 Delia Thomas, interviewed by Melissa Matutina Williams, Auckland, 5 September 2008.

31 Ibid.

32 Karyn Okeroa McRae & Linda Waimarie Nikora, 'Whangai: remembering, understanding and experiencing', Intern Research Report 7, *MAI Review* 1, 2006, 1.

33 Ibid.

34 Ibid.

35 Ibid.

36 Ibid., 2.

37 Ibid.

38 For a very good discussion about the principles and practice of whāngai or atawhai, and how adoption and other laws impacted on the process, see Metge, *New Growth from Old*, 140–41 & 210–57.

39 McRae & Nikora, 'Whangai', 2.

40 Metge, *New Growth from Old*, 25.

41 For more on the nature of concerns and media coverage of this issue see: www.stuff. co.nz/national/politics/90228202/Back-to-the-table-over-controversial-whanau-first-clause-Government-to-soften-stance

42 See the announcement by the New Zealand Human Rights Commission about their request to have the United Nations call for a New Zealand government inquiry into the abuse of children, predominantly Māori, while in state institutions: www.hrc. co.nz/news/call-inquiry-state-abuse-reaches-united-nations/

43 See the Mana Ririki website for more information: www.ririki.org.nz/
44 McRae & Nikora, 'Whangai', 3.
45 Rapata (Bob) Thomas, 13 August 2007.
46 Williams, *Panguru and the City*, 62.
47 For an indepth discussion about family arrangements arising from urban migration, see Williams, 58–63.
48 Rapata (Bob) Thomas, 13 August 2007.
49 Stuart Graham, interviewed by Melisa Matutina Williams, Auckland, 16 August 2009.
50 Rapata (Bob) Thomas, Auckland, 13 August 2007.
51 Nganehu (Nessie) Whatu, interviewed by Melissa Matutina Williams, Auckland, 26 April 2007.
52 The term 'back-home' is commonly heard in conversations among Panguru whānau and among Māori migrants generally when referring to their original homeplace. Its use here is a variant of that used in Patricia Grace's novel *Tu*. Grace uses the term 'backhome'. See Patricia Grace, *Tu*, Penguin, Auckland, 65.
53 Rapata (Bob) Thomas, 13 August 2007.
54 Judge A.G. McHugh, 'Formal Decision pertaining to Tina Murphy, application to determine ownership of house', Maori Land Court, Tai Tokerau District, 16 October 1980, personal papers of Melissa Matutina Williams.
55 Letter from Terehia Davis to Tina Murphy, 30 April 1984, personal papers of Melissa Matutina Williams.
56 Tina Murphy, Application for Land Partition (not submitted to court), personal papers of Melissa Matutina Williams.
57 Nancy Fraser, 'Contradictions of capital and care', *New Left Review* 100 (2016), 99.
58 Ibid., 100–02.
59 Anderson, Binney & Harris, *Tangata Whenua*, 393–94.
60 Ibid., 394 & 408–09.
61 For a discussion about the latter see: Barbara Brookes, 'Nostalgia for "innocent homely pleasures": The 1964 New Zealand controversy over *Washday at the Pa*', in Barbara Brookes (ed.), *At Home in New Zealand: Houses, history, people* (Wellington: Bridget Williams Books, 2000), 210–25.
62 The 'Remote Areas' policy, for example, made people living in remote areas ineligible for the unemployment benefit if they were technically able to work. The rationale was that individuals on an unemployment benefit could not expect to live in areas where opportunities to gain paid work were limited. This policy continued beyond the 1990s under the 'Limited Employment Location' policy. For an overview of the policy see Gabriel Luke Kiddle, 'Spatial constraints on residency as an instrument of employment policy: The experience of limited-employment locations in New Zealand', MA thesis, Victoria University of Wellington, 2005, 17–19 & 47–87.
63 The Whānau Ora policy, developed by the Māori Party and introduced by the National Government in 2011 as part of a coalition agreement, goes some way to addressing the needs of individuals in a much more holistic and whānau-based approach.

4

IN THE DARKNESS OF NIGHT:
Traversing worlds through
the concept of ayah care

Jane McCabe

The earliest memories of Abanindranath Tagore ... revolved around the 'dark skinned', 'gentle-hearted' Padmadasi in whose company and care he spent his early years. In the artist's own words, his maid was 'as black as the darkness of the night'. She would sit by his side while putting him to sleep but would remain invisible in the darkness. Abanindranath could not see her but could feel her gentle touch. He would also hear her munching puffed rice and driving the mosquitoes away. If Padmadasi knew Aban was awake she would gently remove the mosquito net and put a morsel of coconut-ball in his mouth.[1]

The Tagores were a quintessential 'Bengali elite' family. Abanindranath was the nephew of Rabindranath Tagore, the Nobel prize-winning poet, and was himself a noted artist and writer. In his fond reminiscences of Padmadasi, his ayah, Abanindranath draws attention to an aspect of daily life in these elite families that was born of the specific cultural, social and political encounters that British rule in India effected. Here was a form of care that traversed cultures, social worlds and oceans, in bodies and in minds; and, as Abanindranath's memories so evocatively describe, one that ushers us into the hushed world of night-time care. These precious interactions are not specific to British Indian homes but conjure a universal human experience: of care performed in the quiet, dark space on the cusp of waking and dreams, where there is time for reflection on the day and thoughts of tomorrow. It is a vulnerable space where the senses are at once muted by the approach of sleep and heightened by stillness, by fear of the dark and by the magic of the night. Every noise is amplified, whispered interactions make memories that are deep and enduring, bodies are close, breath is tangible and eyes reflect in the dark.

Here I want to explore the practice of night-time caring, a phenomenon embodied in the role of the ayah and thus captured as a relationship that can be usefully discussed in relation to other kinds of caring. This exploration travels across time and space, across cultural and national borders, and across generations. I do this by virtue of the extraordinary lifeways of a community that I have dubbed the 'Kalimpong Kids' – mixed-race children of British tea planters in northeast India who experienced ayah care in their early lives on plantations before being sent to St Andrew's Colonial Homes ('the Homes') in Kalimpong. The Homes was a Scottish missionary's solution to these 'problem' children. His 'grand vision' involved the children being housed and educated at Kalimpong for 10–15 years in preparation for emigration to settler colonies as adolescent workers.[2] One of these emigrants was my grandmother, Lorna Peters, who arrived in Dunedin in 1921. For Lorna, and for most of the Kalimpong women, work in New Zealand meant caring for children of colonial families and thus following an unusual life trajectory – from *receiving* attentive ayah care on the plantation, to robust self-sufficiency at the Homes, to then *providing* something akin to ayah care for settler families.

What aspects of the Kalimpong women's early care experiences were expressed in performing this familial role in New Zealand? Did their time at the Homes erase the early feeling of safety and closeness engendered by ayah care? Tracing this genealogy of night-time care affords a new understanding of the transmission of cultural practices across institutional and national boundaries. Schemes that separated children permanently from their mothers in order to erase native culture from their minds and their bodies were widespread in the colonial period and have attracted sophisticated scholarly attention. But these studies have focused primarily on power and intimacy in household and institutional domains.[3] Here I am instead looking at an aspect of caring that was supposed to be removed by sending the children away – namely a 'native' mode of caring – and speculating on the ways it may have persisted. In doing so I highlight the process by which all carers are at the end of a chain of caring that has passed through multiple sets of historic hands, despite the rocky terrain of cultural encounters, social shifts and divergent gender roles. As Heather Devere notes, theorist Annette Baier described individuals as 'essentially successors, heirs to other persons who formed and cared for them'. Not only across generations but across cultures, we are all passing it on.

Throughout this chapter I aim to decentre Western perspectives, as several chapters in this collection do – most notably Melissa Matutina Williams' exploration of her grandmother Tina's caregiving role, deeply situated by the author in the Māori world Tina was born into. In the existing scholarship on care, even when it proceeds from a stated awareness of the cultural specificity of familial configurations and dynamics, non-Western social practices are often relegated to an interesting side comment or case study, the 'periphery' to the Western 'core'.[4] To counter this Eurocentrism, I foreground ayah care, beginning with an outline of the historical dynamism by which South Asian women came to inhabit a routine space in the night-time worlds of British and middle/upper class Bengali families. I then turn to northeast India, a region marginalised in the history and historiography of South Asia, and to the specific and privileged space of tea plantation bungalows. In this and each subsequent section I sketch the close spatial world within which night-time care was experienced: from plantation bungalow to residential cottage at Kalimpong, to settler households in New Zealand. In that final destination – where the Kalimpong women cared for other families and later raised their own children – I paint some broad strokes that relate a plethora of eventual life outcomes back to their early care.

The archive for this chapter is as muffled as the spaces it occurred within. The interracial relationships that produced the Kalimpong children were illicit and a taboo subject, and hence are barely recorded. No official documentation such as marriage or birth certificates exists, and planters did not write home about these children nor reminisce about them in their plentiful memoirs.[5] In later life the Kalimpong emigrants themselves rarely spoke of their Indian heritage or childhoods; indeed they often refused to answer questions about their past from their own children. Within this structural, transgenerational silence, the ayah relationship – itself a matter of contention and privacy – is almost impossible to detect. I cannot say for certain that all of the Kalimpong children were cared for by ayahs on the plantations. But my search for these traces is integral to my argument. Rather than brush over the aspects of daily (and nightly) life of which it is not customary to speak, I magnify what has come through in the record. Bringing some rare voiced early memories to these pages directs readers to the protective and evocative space where women (and men) have sat quietly in a dark room while the cared-for drift in and out of sleep. What follows is an examination of the senses, of the feeling of being cared for, and of caring for others. This chapter invites the imaginative engagement of the reader.

Standing in the shadows: The figure of the ayah

The term ayah is generally assigned to the 'native nursemaids' who cared for the children of British families in India. Yet the linguistic origins of the term – from the Hindi and Urdu *āyā*, the Portuguese *aia* and the Latin *avia* – reveals the complex cultural encounters that culminated in this role solidifying as a historically specific presence in British Indian families. From these fluid origins the term appeared in other colonial contexts too. It has been used to refer to nursemaids in Africa and Singapore, and the related *amah* carries the same meaning in China and Southeast Asia. Both terms, ayah and amah, have come to carry an essentialised meaning that ascribes a certain type of care to non-European women: a gentle, untaught, natural capacity to nurture.[6] In the written record this capacity has been portrayed positively in the nostalgic memoirs and literature of British childhoods, and negatively in household manuals that derided the native proclivity to spoil the child.[7] This assumption – that indigenous women are inherently suited to caring for babies and children – needs to be interrogated in the same way as this volume engages with the question of women's capacity and motivation to care, inside and outside the family, paid and unpaid.[8]

From this broader context of colonial racial anxieties, it is useful to consider the ayah's presence in middle-class Bengali families. These families were not exclusively Hindu. The new elite forged under British rule comprised a substantial Muslim population as well, and so we must acknowledge the role of both class and caste sensibilities. The long-standing coexistence and syncretism of Hindu and Muslim communities in Bengal challenges any assumed trajectory from precolonial 'tradition' to changes brought about by the colonial encounter. Tracing our ayah figure to her deeper historical origins reveals the persistence and transformation of a form of care that reaches far back into the precolonial period. As historian Swapna Banerjee notes, unlike in other colonies where 'domestic service emerged as a colonial institution', in India the practice of employing household servants has existed as far back as the written record goes.[9]

Ancient literary and religious texts contained detailed descriptions of various household roles. The ayah and similar female servant figures often occupied a central position – and a position of moral teaching – in mythical stories of love and attachment. The powerful symbolic information associated with the very real figure of the ayah has thus passed from the imagination of one generation to the next, from storyteller to storyteller.[10] A fitting example is the character of the nurse (*dhāī*) in a sixteenth-century text called *Mrigāvatī* or *The Magic Doe*. According to its translator, the characters in texts like *The Magic Doe* are 'emblematic types' in 'fictional universes' where they exemplify 'abstract qualities such as love, wisdom, mystical absorption and spiritual guidance'.[11] In this Sufi romance the nurse 'as usual' performs the role of 'Sufi pīr or guide' to the central character – she is confidante to the prince as he deals with the grief of a lost love, and an intermediary in the 'cultivation of a sympathetic understanding among lovers, Sufis and listeners'.[12]

From this setting of ancient inscriptions and persistent practices, substantial changes to domestic service did occur in the colonial period. British administration of India transformed aspects of local society but it also brought opportunity – particularly in the realm of class and caste. Caste was an important organising feature of Hindu social structure, and its fluidity is exemplified in the way individuals and groups took advantage of the British presence.[13] The British, meanwhile, sought to concretise 'traditional' roles; they took advantage of a highly stratified society and the prevalence of low-cost labour to perform a multitude of household and other daily tasks.[14] At the higher end of the South Asian social spectrum, the scholarly class and administrators – whom the British relied on heavily – along with the landowners, forged a new middle class in Bengal, known as the *bhadralok*.[15] The emergence of the ayah role as a feature of both British and bhadralok families exemplifies the complex legacy of these cultural and political encounters. By the mid-nineteenth century, having a retinue of servants and a non-kin ayah to nurse their children became a key indicator of respectability for middle-class families in colonial Bengal.[16]

Perhaps surprisingly, given their intimate relationship to high-status families, ayahs for British and Bengali families alike were drawn from the lowest sectors of society. The reason for predominantly low-caste women performing this role for British families was that Europeans were without caste and thus were a source of pollution to those who associated closely with them.[17] As with all such concerns about purity, the lower the caste, the less there was to lose. While this same concern did not apply to ayahs working for high-caste Bengali families, certain aspects of infant and child care – toileting, for example – were off limits for any other than the lowest castes.[18] In addition, in both British and Bengali families there was an element of self-sacrifice for ayahs performing this role, given that night-time service took a woman away from her own children; and, of even greater consequence, the common scenario where an ayah stayed with a family for a long time – in Bengali families often for a lifetime – precluded them from having their own family.[19]

For the bhadralok families who employed ayahs, the fear of pollution operated in reverse: while the ayah did not risk losing caste through close contact with them, the family feared crossing certain boundaries with the ayah. Bengali parents were wary of the possibility that the low-class ayah might taint their children, and they strictly policed this. Their anxiety mirrored British concerns that their children would be contaminated by close contact with the 'native' women whom they placed in an intimate role at the heart of their families. Fuelling these fears was the association of lower-caste/lower-class women with darker skin – as expressed in the potent language of sin, night-time, sensuality and the mythical. These anxieties were intricately bound up in the sensitive nature of night-time care and its contradictions: the intimacy and physical proximity of the ayah in the vulnerable world of sleeping children, versus the vulnerability of the ayah in the family *because* of this proximity and the parental concern about her tainting influence. It was and is a world of secrets.

Memoirs of Bengali childhoods like the one cited at the start of this chapter reveal the multiple dimensions of relationships between ayahs and Indian children. Swapna Banerjee included excerpts of writings from middle- and lower-class families in her work on domestic service in colonial Bengal. Many speak of the tense relationship between adults and ayahs; they contrast this with the children's closeness to the ayah, and recall with fondness their mutual secrets, how they were mesmerised by fairy stories and lullabies, and how they felt protected from their parents' rage.[20] Not all accounts are positive or nostalgic, however. Like the relationships between the British and their

Indian servants, the bond between a child and an ayah was often fraught and frequently violent, in both directions.[21] For Rabindranath Tagore, uncle of Abanindranath, the lingering memories of servants from his childhood were of the 'subordination and intimidation that he and his siblings suffered at the hands of servants'.[22] His niece, Sarala Debi Chaudhurani, lamented that 'immediately after our birth, we lost direct touch with our mothers ... our maid's lap became our mother's lap. I never knew what a mother's affection was.'[23] For Abanindranath, nostalgic recollections of his ayah Padmadasi were perhaps affected by his empathy for her. Padmadasi left the family abruptly when he was young, and he 'waited and longed for her every day'. Later, he pondered her life and surmised that 'perhaps nobody in the whole world except me has any impression left of her'.

Night-time in the plantation bungalow

These records of the relationships between Bengali children and their ayahs help us to understand the ayah's place in tea plantation families in the neighbouring districts of northeast India. Many Bengalis, from clerical workers to servants, were enticed to work in the tea districts.[24] This 'frontier' was relatively late to be brought under British administration, and such was the ethnic and cultural fragmentation of the region, imperial control was never fully established. An 'inner line' was drawn to protect the areas where tea plantations were established, and the boundaries of plantations, too, were strictly guarded, confining thousands of workers on large, self-sufficient estates. Tea planters' bungalows were imagined and constructed to be imposing and detached, indicative of the planters' position at the top of a hierarchical labour force organised around race and class.[25] The bungalow, like the ayah, had its origins in local (Bengali) forms but was adapted by the outside ruling class and became an icon of the British era. Initially one-storey but increasingly grand and multi-levelled, the bungalows in flood-prone Assam were sometimes elevated on stilts. A thatched roof, verandas and pillars were characteristic features. There are many historic photographs of these bungalows, usually taken from the outside, invoking a dark space within. Some show servants lined up outside the bungalow (see photo); others feature the planter relaxing on the veranda, often with other planters, and almost always with a servant in attendance.

Egerton Peters' bungalow in Cachar, Assam, c.1900 – where my grandmother spent her early years. Author's collection

I am interested, however, in the space *within* the bungalow – a privileged world in which the Kalimpong children spent their early years. What would we find if we could peer through those windows darkened by the bright light of day? Rare photographs of living rooms, in tandem with the recorded memories of those who grew up in tea bungalows, portray interiors that blended familiar items from 'home' with necessities and luxuries that moved from exotic to familiar as planters became immersed into local life – large fans, draped textiles and hunting trophies. In the children's sleeping quarters one imagines a relatively sparse room: wooden floor, a small bed, minimal bed coverings for the hot climate, a mosquito net, and a chair or a bed for the ayah. But what did it feel like in the night, where outside was dark and inscrutable and inside was safely lit? Did the night magnify a soundscape of animals calling in the surrounding forests, scurrying noises from under the house, and imaginings of magical jungle creatures fuelled by ayah tales?

While the planters were reasonably prolific at recording their 'Assam adventures' in diaries, letters and memoirs, none who fathered mixed-race children in this era wrote home or published any words about family life within the bungalow.[26] The Kalimpong emigration scheme does, however, provide glimpses into bungalow life through several sources: the Homes personal files, which contain application forms for the children and regular correspondence from the planters; the notes written by the scheme's founder about his visits to plantations; and the memories and stories passed on by the emigrants. The letters from the planters to the Homes are an invaluable source since they are perhaps the only occasion where the planters were required to commit the existence of their families to the written record. Not surprisingly, few mention ayah care. But the application forms and the letters do make it clear that their children lived in a manner that British commentators regarded as highly dangerous: growing up in the close company of 'natives', mimicking their behaviour, learning local languages, and all the while bereft of education or religious training.

In this quest to trace the genealogy of night-time care we must also consider the heritage of the planters. Many were born into 'empire families' for whom India had been a place of work for generations.[27] The accepted norm for raising British children in these families was to have them in India until the age of four or five; they were then sent 'home' to escape the proximity of 'natives', to be educated, and to be immersed in British social and familial structures.[28] All of these British youngsters had ayahs in India, and many later wrote of the bitter shift from acquiescent ayahs to the boarding school experience that awaited them in England.[29] They were very likely to return to India as adults, which saw this pattern repeated over generations. Thus the tea planters often brought their own early memories of being cared for by an ayah – and of that experience being sharply broken – when they made decisions about the way their own children would be raised.

A second consideration regarding the newly arrived tea planter is his relationship to household staff. These workers were the only close human company he experienced on a daily basis. In a workforce that numbered in the thousands, comprised of diverse ethnic and language groups, planters were socially isolated on their estates and often physically cut off by monsoon flooding from other plantations or local towns for months at a time. It is unsurprising to learn that, anecdotally, one common way of initiating a sexual relationship with a woman on the plantation was to cross the line of intimacy with his housekeeper. When children were produced from these relationships, either the mother raised the child, or an ayah might be brought in – reflecting the status both of the child and of the mother as the planter's 'wife'. This slippage between the figure of the ayah and that of the mother – which cannot be resolved by the archive – raises interesting questions about the ambiguous place of indigenous women in colonial households and their role as carers for the men as well as the children. The murky boundaries of night-time life within the bungalow are made even murkier by the fact that the planters' mistresses were often of the same low social strata as the ayahs, and for the same reason: an intimate relationship with a European man meant a loss of caste. Such low-status women were almost always voiceless in the historic record.

The Reverend Dr John Anderson Graham, the Scottish founder of the Homes, was a missionary in Kalimpong for 10 years before he opened the institution in 1900. The notes he wrote about his visits to tea planters' bungalows provide more detail here. Although he was shocked by the discovery that planters were routinely cohabiting with South Asian women, he noted that the relationships were often 'real and tender', and he sympathised with the planters who wanted to take responsibility for their children but had limited options for doing so.[30] He also wrote, however, of his disapproval of the 'local policy' where the women were paid a sum of money when the planters inevitably returned to Britain. Furthermore, he was disparaging of cases where women who were engaged in a sexual relationship with a planter were essentially treated as 'servants'. Here he is referring to the scenario mentioned above, where a housekeeper became a mistress and then acted as ayah to her own children.

More detail can be gleaned from the letters written by the planters to Graham. When my great-grandfather, Egerton Peters, sent his oldest child Lorna from Cachar (in Assam) to Kalimpong in 1906, he begged Graham to show some kindness to his daughter, aged four, and his son George, aged two. 'They have been mostly in the hands of natives,' he wrote, 'do not know a word [in] English and will I'm afraid be difficult charges.'[31] The application forms show that their mother was alive when the first two children were admitted to the school; she died five years later when a third child, Alice, was 18 months old. Alice was sent to Kalimpong several years later, which suggests that she was cared for by an ayah in the interim. And indeed Peters, in his letter asking Graham to admit Alice to the Homes, made a similar claim as he had for his other two children – that she could not speak a word of English – but this time he specified the nature of her care up to this point:

'the poor child has necessarily been left very much in charge of her Ayah'.[32] As his sentiment makes plain, this was a form of care that the British regarded as inferior to the care of a (white) mother.

Other tea plantation children were sent to Kalimpong from a variety of familial circumstances. In one case the father had died and an associate arranged for the children to be sent to the Homes. In another family the mother had died, and a woman from the local Lepcha community was looking after the children (all seven of them) at the planter's behest.[33] Dane Kennedy, in his study of British settlements in the Himalayan region, notes that the British regarded Lepcha women as highly suitable ayahs.[34] His assertion again points to the way that women (or men) from some cultures have been regarded as embodying a greater propensity for care work than others. The British in India were particularly disposed to ascribing certain 'useful' traits to entire communities who were then motivated to nurture these apparent propensities for their own economic and social benefit – thereby internalising and perpetuating the stereotype.[35] In another family the mother, a Khasi woman, had left the plantation (and the planter) and was struggling to raise her children after her family refused to support her because she had converted to Christianity. The woman's only option for supporting her children was to find work but, as the local missionary's wife wrote on her behalf, 'she can't go out to earn money [as she would] have nobody with whom to leave her children'.[36] These diverse scenarios reflect the social fragmentation in the northeast wrought by the tea industry labour migrations, and the complex history of the region. What the children all had in common was that none were raised by white women, and all were immersed in the daily life of their mother's and/or their ayah's families during the early years of their childhood.

More direct evidence of ayahs on tea plantations has come to light via the testimony of two women who emigrated to New Zealand from Kalimpong shortly after the organised scheme ended. The first, Isabella Leith, was the younger sister of Fred Leith, who had been a member of the last group that was sent to New Zealand in 1938. Isabella emigrated to New Zealand independently of the Homes in 1947. Her children interviewed Isabella in the twilight of her life about her childhood in India. When they asked about the moment of separation from her mother when she was sent to the Homes, her immediate answer was that she was closer to her ayah; and, speaking in a generalised way that indicated how commonplace this relationship was, she added, 'you spent more time with ayahs ... played with their children and all that, you mixed with them.'[37] For Isabella, separation from her ayah affected her more than parting with her mother.

Ruth Nicholls' situation was very similar to Isabella's. Her oldest sister was also in the final group sent to New Zealand. After the New Zealand government closed the door to any further groups from the Homes, Ruth's father took matters into his own hands: he bought a farm in New Zealand and escorted his remaining three children over one by one as they reached working age. When I interviewed her on several occasions, Ruth spoke at length about plantation life and her relationship to the workers out in the gardens and in the household. These were very close relationships. The Nicholls family had the usual retinue of indoor and outdoor household staff, including an ayah; Ruth remembered the regularity with which the ayah and the watchman arrived in the evenings. She did not speak specifically about this relationship, but she did state that her mother did not live with them, so her ayah was her primary caregiver. She spoke of tearful goodbyes to the staff when she was sent to the Homes. Unlike most tea planters' children at Kalimpong, Ruth went home to the plantation for holidays, so the ritual of the staff all lining up outside the house and sadly saying goodbye was repeated on many occasions.[38]

A different kind of care: Kalimpong

Ruth's memories of arriving at the Homes were visceral. She recalled being taken to nurses in the hospital there, being poked and prodded, and feeling utterly alone in the first few weeks.[39] Fred Leith's son referred to his father's difficult memories of this time that saw him wrenched out of the 'cosseted life' of his father's bungalow to the institution.[40] When they arrived the children were quarantined in the hospital for a few days or weeks – a frightening environment and their first experience of falling asleep and waking up alone. As a Homes graduate of the 1970s recalled, 'I didn't know what hit me to be honest. I looked for my mother and she wasn't there ... I'm falling out of the bed and she's not there to get me ... Dragged off here, dragged off there, and you just didn't know where you were.'[41]

The journey to get to the Homes no doubt added to the trauma of the experience. Egerton Peters did not travel with his children to Kalimpong.

Woodburn Cottage group, Kalimpong, c.1916. Lorna Peters standing far right, Alice Peters (her sister) front row, third from right. Both girls spent 15 years at the Homes in Kalimpong. Author's collection.

Like many of the tea planters, he had managed to discreetly carry on his interracial relationship on the plantation, and would not risk exposing his secret for the peace of mind that accompanying his children on the journey might have brought. Lorna and George were sent off by boat with a 'reliable man' from a nearby mission. It was a challenging journey that required travelling over flood-swollen rivers, then by train for several days. At a station close to Kalimpong they were passed over to a kind of human they had never seen before – a white woman. If they were under five years old (many were infants) the children would then be placed in Lucia King Cottage, known as the babies' cottage. Those five years or older were sent to their cottage for the rest of the time at Kalimpong; for Lorna it was Woodburn Cottage that was to be her home for the next 15 years.

The cottages at the Homes were large, two-storey roughcast buildings. There were 20 in all, each named after a sponsor, such as Woodburn (see photo), Fraser, Hart, and so on. They each housed 30–40 children and were staffed by one housemother and one auntie. All the children slept in a single dormitory room upstairs. The layout is the same today as it was a hundred years ago: 40 small wooden beds side by side in a stark room with a wooden floor and no cupboards or other furniture. For children from the plantations this was a substantial physical change to night-time life.[42] There may have been some gentleness shown towards the new arrivals, but they were quickly absorbed into the bustling routines of cottage life. Bullying, hunger, and harsh discipline were all part of the challenge of this existence, and the children simply had to find a place for themselves over time. Their sudden shift from close, attentive care in the bungalow to a kind of wild negotiation among children from a variety of circumstances must have felt vastly more unruly and frightening than the life they were accustomed to – the life that Graham derided as 'wild' and 'injurious'.

A crucial sensory change for the children was the sound of the English language spoken by all staff at the Homes. In time the children picked up English, but at first they were immersed in the hybrid language that developed in the cottages, and communication with housemothers would have been minimal.[43] At night, the soothing sounds of the ayah were replaced by the enforced silence of the British dormitory. One imagines that the only night-time adult presence in the Homes sleeping quarters was the housemother or auntie occasionally storming in to order the children to sleep, administering some physical punishment or putting the fear of God into them. The sound of shoes coming up the stairs, and going down the stairs (leaving them to fend for themselves), must have been a daunting one. The children who came from the plantations perhaps closed their eyes and heard their ayah's (or mother's) voice, dreamt of her, remembered her.

Interviews with descendants of the Kalimpong emigrants and with later graduates indicate that the children's relationship with the housemothers dictated much of their experience of growing up at the Homes. If they got on the wrong side of a housemother at an early age, they faced years of harsh treatment. Discipline was meted out in the way expected of most institutions at the time.[44] Even if a housemother was kindly and wanted to help a new arrival, she would have little time to spend with individual children, and coddling from a housemother would not have helped a child trying to find their way among peers. Of course we cannot discount the possibility that some of the housemothers were kind and nurturing. Dorothy McMenamin has interviewed several Anglo-Indian women in New Zealand who grew up in India (although not at Kalimpong). One woman remembered her tears at leaving home for boarding school; but she countered this with a memory of a housemother appearing when she woke from a nightmare and taking her back to her room and cuddling her – a memorable moment of comfort.[45]

Despite the richness of the Homes archive, there are few details about the women who volunteered as housemothers and aunties. As with the ayahs on the plantations, the Homes women's caring roles, although absolutely crucial, were not made visible in a way that enables us to explore their individual motivations and experiences. The New Zealand emigrants, in their letters to John Graham, often asked him to pass on their regards to the housemothers or expressed their gratitude for the strict discipline they received which, they believed, set them up well for the challenges of life in New Zealand.[46] Housemothers were also referred to in the *Homes Magazine* when they acted as a support person for the emigrants, after they had finished volunteering at Kalimpong. Mary Kennedy, for example, travelled to Kalimpong from Dunedin in 1908 to volunteer as an auntie and, during her time there, accompanied at least one emigrant group on their journey to Dunedin. When she came back to Dunedin in the 1920s and got married, she welcomed the emigrants, old and new, into her home. These visitors included my grandmother, with whom Mary retained a life-long relationship. Like an elderly ayah, Mary was part of my grandmother's extended and slightly unusual family life in Dunedin – her tea planter father had followed his children to New Zealand several years after they emigrated, and lived out his days with Lorna and her young family.

There was another key role of the housemothers at Kalimpong: they modelled care and provided training for the young women in residence, who were destined to perform care duties for settler families. This training incorporated a full range of domestic skills that corresponded to the ethic of self-sufficiency and, conveniently, saw their labour contribute enormously to the daily functioning of the cottages (as did the boys'). Each child was assigned a role in the cottage that increased in responsibility as they grew older, tasks that kept them busy from early morning until late at night. Some girls received additional instruction in 'nursing' duties by caring for the infants in Lucia King Cottage. This work was often undertaken by those who were set to go to New Zealand, as it was a useful way for them to spend the months (and sometimes years) it took to arrange their emigration. It was an uncertain time and, considering their own past, a troubling task for them to be dealing with very young children separated from their parents, but the Lucia King nurses were inculcated with a sense of pride and professionalism in the roles that awaited them in New Zealand.

Performing care in settler households

Tracing a culture of care to New Zealand is complicated by the diffuse experiences of the emigrants there. The Homes propaganda suggests a predictable and organised pathway for the women: all were placed with families, usually Presbyterian, and entered the Dominion as 'domestic servants'. But these positions varied according to the individual relationship with the family, and encompassed a wide variety of duties, reflected in the terminology used to describe them – which included 'nanny', 'nursery nurse', 'mother help', 'companion help' (for elderly people) and 'domestic help'. Most of the emigrants were placed in suburban homes, but some were on the outskirts of town in semi-rural settings, and others were placed in rural areas and wrote 'home' to Kalimpong about milking cows and feeding chickens. Many of the women did write about caring for children; but never is there any reference to the women as ayahs. Naming was a crucial way of creating colonial distinctions and the Kalimpong scheme constantly reinforced the status of the women graduates as respectable and educated imperial citizens, trained in the duty and discipline of child rearing. This distanced them from the figure of the 'natural' ayah despite the fact that their roles entailed very similar work.

Among the emigrants who wrote about childcare was Nellie Savigny, who was placed in Dunedin in 1913. In an excerpt from a letter published in the *Homes Magazine*, Nellie sent a photograph of herself with the child she cared for. She wrote that although they lived in a 'lovely house' she did sometimes feel like 'throwing the baby out the window'.[47] Nellie explained that she shared a room with the child and seldom had an undisturbed sleep. This clearly invites comparison to an ayah role. While the architecture of settler colonial life and the cool climes of Dunedin made for a sensory world distinct from that of a tea plantation, 'sharing a room' surely brought echoes of a distant but familiar feeling for the Kalimpong women: of drifting off to sleep with a presence close by, knowing that she would be there all night. Sitting quietly in this role created an apt space for contemplation of their own early experiences.

We might also consider the Kalimpong women themselves as being cared for in these New Zealand placements. They were teenagers when they arrived and their employers were meant to become another in-lieu family and to ease the emigrants' transition into settler colonial society. Again this invites comparison to the situation in India where ayahs were often destitute and consequently vulnerable to the embrace (or otherwise) of the employer family. This comparison is particularly appropriate for those Kalimpong women who remained with New Zealand families for their whole lives. My grandmother's best friend Mae Sinclair, a 1913 Kalimpong emigrant, had a position with the Hazelwood family in Dunedin. The Hazelwoods owned a tearooms and Mae worked in the business and as their housekeeper and lived in separate quarters in their comfortable home in an affluent suburb until she passed away in 1984, aged 88 years.

The majority of the Kalimpong women married, however, and presumably the most meaningful performance of care in their lifetime was for their own children. A letter from Isabella Leith to a staff member at Kalimpong expressed the new and difficult perspective that parenting gave her. She reported a conversation with her brother Fred, whose son John had just turned five, in which Fred asked Isabella if she could imagine sending John away at this age. This caused both siblings to reflect on their own childhoods and their father's actions.[48] Fred's question points to one that many descendants have pondered: how did the Kalimpong emigrants' early experiences affect the way they raised their own children? I have heard a spectrum of answers to this difficult question. The most common response is that the lack of close family while they were growing up made the Kalimpong emigrants (men and women) especially focused on the families they created in New Zealand. They cherished home life and seldom wanted to be away from it.

For my grandmother, life in Dunedin began with her placement with Reverend J.M. Simpson and his family at Port Chalmers Presbyterian Church. According to letters from her father to the Homes, she received scant reimbursement for her heavy household duties, which included care for 'five grown boys'.[49] The only testament from Lorna regarding this role is her son's (my father Don's) belief that the Simpsons were very good to her. This assessment was based on Lorna's continued visits to the couple during Don's childhood, and fond recollections of her lively banter with 'Simmy' (Reverend Simpson). Lorna's two sons, Bill and Don, grew up knowing nothing of her upbringing at Kalimpong or the circumstances that brought her to New Zealand. But like the many children who were cared for by

Lorna McCabe
(née Peters) and her
son Bill at home in
Pine Hill, Dunedin,
c.1940.
Author's collection

Kalimpong women, they were at the end of a chain of care that included a form of child bonding that would be unknown to them in any conscious, named way, but which, I suggest, was not without a legacy in their lives.

Two memories that were passed on to descendants stand out for their association with the night-time realm, with storytelling, and with care in a different sense – that of healing. Mary Milne remembers only one story that her mother Kate Pattison, a Kalimpong emigrant of 1915, told about *her* mother on the plantation. It was of an incident that occurred when her tea planter father was away from the plantation. Kate fell ill, and because her father was away and could not stop her, her mother called in the 'witchdoctor'. Kate vividly recollected to her daughter in New Zealand a night-time scene with the witchdoctor and other locals present, a large fire being lit, and herself being passed around the shoulders of those present. The memory was frightening, and thrilling, as was the memory of the tea planter returning and being extremely angry with Kate's mother.

The second memory is my own, from when I was a small child and my dad told me something he remembered Lorna remembering to him. As he told me, he ran his fingertips very gently down the outside of my arm. This is what the doctors did in India, he said. Lorna told him that they would run their hands over the skin like this, barely touching it, until the illness would start to gather under the skin like a big bruise. All of a sudden the doctor would reach in and grab the badness out. I was mesmerised by this one memory – a memory of a memory – that had made it all the way from the night-time of India to the night-time of my bedroom in my house in Mosgiel, far across the big black ocean.[50]

The ayah care that travelled with the children to Kalimpong and then to New Zealand moved along a rugged cross-cultural and transcolonial pathway. It was performed within the bounds of a relationship that was hidden away, and to unearth it in any meaningful sense we need to be attentive to kin relations, cultural diversity, social practice and family formations. All caring occurs at an endpoint of a genealogy of care, moving through families and cultures, and across shifting social contexts. In colonial settings, these shifts have often been abrupt, forced and institutionalised. The Kalimpong children's migration illuminates the chain of night-time care across generations *because* of their placement at the Homes and the attendant paperwork it created, but that rupture simultaneously obscures our view because of the silence that has constrained the transfer of knowledge and memory. Perhaps that silence, that difficulty in asking and answering questions, has in fact allowed cultural forms – a more powerful force than confessions or trauma or details – to persist. Perhaps that is the real resilience here: the movement across time and space of ancient night-time stories and the practice of storytelling, surreptitiously binding us to what came before.

Notes

1　Swapna M. Banerjee, *Men, Women and Domestics: Articulating middle-class identity in colonial Bengal* (New Delhi: Oxford University Press, 2004), 57.

2　Between 1908 and 1938, 130 adolescent Anglo-Indians were sent to New Zealand via the scheme. See Jane McCabe, *Race, Tea and Colonial Resettlement: Imperial families, interrupted* (London: Bloomsbury Academic, 2017).

3　See, for example, Ann Laura Stoler (ed.), *Haunted by Empire: Geographies of intimacy in North American history* (Durham: Duke University Press, 2006) and Victoria K. Haskins & Claire Lowrie (eds), *Colonisation and Domestic Service: Historical and contemporary perspectives* (New York: Routledge, 2015).

4　Nancy Fraser, for example, while briefly highlighting the exploitation of colonised peoples, uses this terminology of 'core' and 'periphery' and seeks 'universal' answers in new models firmly grounded in Western principles. See Nancy Fraser, 'Contradictions of capital and care', *New Left Review* 100 (2016), 107–08 and Nancy Fraser, *Fortunes of Feminism: From state-managed capitalism to neoliberal crisis* (London: Verso, 2013), 123–35.

5　A close reading of the correspondence and memoirs of tea planters who fathered Kalimpong children reveals no admission or discussion of their interracial families: this attests to their concerted attempts to conceal them. See McCabe, *Race, Tea and Colonial Resettlement*, 22–23, 159.

6　Indrani Sen, 'Colonial domesticities, contentious interactions: Ayahs, wet nurses and memsahibs in colonial India', *Indian Journal of Gender Studies* 16, no. 3 (2009), 314–15.

7　Many scholars have explored the racial ambivalence apparent in the colonial desire for distance between ruler and ruled despite indigenous women occupying a crucial role in the most intimate spaces in their home lives. See for example Sen, 'Colonial domesticities', and Ann Laura Stoler, *Race and the Education of Desire* (Durham: Duke University Press, 1995), 112.

8　Sen points to the infantalising of Indian women by their British employers – children took to ayahs because they were childlike. See 'Colonial domesticities', 301. Julia T. Wood's question 'How do we explain who the caregivers are?' could be broadened to include the presence of non-Western women caring for 'white' households: Julia T. Wood, *Who Cares? Women, care and culture* (Carbondale: Southern Illinois University Press, 1994), 86.

9　Banerjee, *Men, Women and Domestics*, 34.

10　I am indebted to Samia Khatun for sharing her thoughts on her own experience in the care of ayahs in a Bengali Muslim family, as well as for pointing me to Aditya Behl's work.

11　Aditya Behl, *Love's Subtle Magic: An Indian Islamic literary tradition, 1379–1545* (New York: Oxford University Press, 2012), 110.

12　Ibid., 117.

13　Sociologist M.N. Srinivas coined the term 'Sanskritisation' in the 1950s to describe this process and to refute Western assumptions about the fixity of Hindu society.

The term has been widely used (and modified) by historians of the British era. Susan Bayly, *Caste, Society and Politics in India: From the eighteenth century to the modern age* (Cambridge: Cambridge University Press, 1999), 13.

14 Ibid., 80–85; Banerjee, *Men, Women and Domestics*, 43.

15 Banerjee, *Men, Women and Domestics*, 4–6.

16 For an excellent example of the way that this status had purchase in colonial government policing of women activists in the Gandhi era, see Banerjee, *Men, Women and Domestics*, 14.

17 Sen, 'Colonial domesticities', 303.

18 Some colonial families had two ayahs – one from the *mali* (gardening) caste, who would perform all duties other than dealing with toilet waste, which would be left to the ayah from the lower *mehter* (sweeper) caste. Sen, 'Colonial domesticities', 303.

19 Banerjee, *Men, Women and Domestics*, 78.

20 Ibid., 131–35; Swapna M. Banerjee, 'Blurring boundaries, distant companions: Non-kin female caregivers for children in colonial India (nineteenth and twentieth centuries)', *Paedagogica Historica* 46, no. 6 (2010), 781–86.

21 Banerjee, 'Blurring boundaries', 783; Shireen Ally, 'Domesti-City: Colonial anxieties and postcolonial fantasies in the figure of the maid', in *Colonisation and Domestic Service*, 54.

22 Banerjee, 'Blurring boundaries', 782–83.

23 Ibid.

24 George Barker, *A Tea Planter's Life in Assam* (Calcutta: Thacker, Spink & Co., 1884), 103–04.

25 Thomas R. Metcalf, *Ideologies of the Raj* (Cambridge: Cambridge University Press, 1995), 177–79. For the establishment of the tea industry in northeast India see Jayeeta Sharma, *Empire's Garden: Assam and the making of India* (Durham: Duke University Press, 2011).

26 Unlike the earlier period in British rule of India, by the late nineteenth century interracial relationships were absolutely unacceptable for Britons wanting to retain respectability.

27 McCabe, *Race, Tea and Colonial Resettlement*, 23.

28 Elizabeth Buettner, *Empire Families: Britons and Late Imperial India* (Oxford: Oxford University Press, 2004).

29 From the adults' point of view, this simply reflected the problem of the child 'spoiled' by the attention of native servants, which needed correction. The popular novel *The Secret Garden* (1911) is a classic example of this message in literature. For a discussion of the psychological impact of this break from early care, see Cora L. Diaz de Chumerceiro, 'The Secret Garden: On the loss of nannies in fiction and life', *Journal of Poetry Therapy* 16, no. 1 (2003), 45–57.

30 John Graham, typed notes, Kalimpong Papers, 6039:15:1, National Library of Scotland (NLS).

31 E.G. Peters to John Graham, 22 April 1906. Peters family file, Dr Graham's Homes Archive (DGHA), Kalimpong.

32 E.G. Peters to John Graham, 18 December 1914. Peters family file, DGHA.

33 This information has been compiled from family files at Kalimpong, with their permission.

34 Dane Kennedy, *Magic Mountains: Hill stations and the British Raj* (Berkeley: University of California Press, 1996), 68, 190.

35 Sharma, *Empire's Garden*, 58–59.

36 A.V. Jones to John Graham, 21 September 1916. Mortimore family file, DGHA.

37 Video recording, family interview with Gavin and Isabella Gammie, 2000, Gammie private collection, Wellington.

38 Ruth Nicholls, interviewed by Jane McCabe, Auckland, 2012.

39 Ibid.

40 Personal communication with Martin Leith, Wellington, 2012.

41 Interviewee in *We Homes Chaps*, DVD, directed by Kesang Tseten, Kathmandu, Nepal, Filmmakers Library, 2001. While the migration scheme to New Zealand ended in 1938, the Homes continued to operate as a school for Anglo-Indian children until the 1970s and still operates today as a school for children from all over India.

42 Shurlee Swain discusses the sensory experiences of entering orphanages in 1950s Australia, in 'Institutionalised childhood: The orphanage remembered', *Journal of the History of Childhood and Youth* 8, no. 1 (2015), 17–33.

43 The 'Homes slang' is a fascinating combination of English boarding school colloquialisms with frequently used Hindi terms. Simon Mainwaring, *A Century of Children* (Kalimpong: Dr Graham's Homes, 2000), app. 5: 'Homes Slang', 191–98.

44 Ibid., 13, 20.

45 Dorothy McMenamin, *Raj Days to Downunder: Voices from Anglo-India to New Zealand* (Christchurch: Dorothy McMenamin, 2010).

46 Excerpts of these letters were printed in the *St Andrew's Colonial Homes Magazine* (SACHM).

47 'For the Old Boys and Girls,' SACHM, vol. 14, no. 2, 1914, 29.

48 Isabella Leith to James Purdie, 22 August 1951. Purdie letters 1951–52, Kalimpong papers, 6039:14:2, NLS.

49 E.G. Peters to John Graham, November 1921. Peters family file, DGHA.

50 I refer here to my childhood imaginings of the large ocean between India and New Zealand as black; and to my knowledge now of *kala pani* (lit. dark water) – the taboo about not crossing the ocean for fear of losing caste.

5

HELEN SMAILL'S PHOTOGRAPH ALBUM:
Traces of care in the mission archive

Antje Lübcke

For my thirtieth birthday my mother gave me a photograph album she had compiled using an online template that was then printed and sent to her home. She had spent hours looking through old photographic prints that she keeps in a cupboard in her study and in large sealed plastic tubs under her bed as well as digital images she stores on an external hard drive. The photographs were scanned and copied and then lovingly ordered, juxtaposed and captioned to tell the story of me, my place in my family and my adventures out in the world. I was living in Australia at the time, working on my PhD dissertation, and the arrival of this book of personal and shared memories moved me to tears.

While the album I discuss in this chapter differs in significant ways to the album my mother made for me in 2011, like my album it was produced by a mother from photographs that were taken, collected, gifted and then lovingly kept safe over the years. In both albums we see the work of women as transmitters of family memory, taking care to preserve images that connect past and present.

Helen Smaill, a Presbyterian missionary wife and fellow worker in the mission field, lived and worked on Epi in the New Hebrides (present-day Vanuatu) between 1890 and 1906. A servant of God – unlike the role performed by Melissa Matutina Williams's grandmother or the ayah figure described by Jane McCabe – she found her raison d'être on the mission field. At the time, women who embarked on mission work found a usefulness for their talents that may have been unavailable at home. Missions have since come under severe historical scrutiny for the disruption they caused to indigenous communities, but in 1890 service on the mission field was held in high esteem. That service by missionary wives, which was often central work to the enterprise, reflects the injustice of the invisibility of women's work. Susan Moller Okin suggests this injustice resides in traditional family structures. Missions were structured on the idea that women performed caring work in the family and the community and did not require payment; the work was its own reward.

Unlike the other New Hebrides mission albums I encountered while undertaking research in 2008, in which the photographs were typically ordered and captioned to tell a succinct story of mission success, Helen Smaill's album caught my attention because of the haphazard composition of its contents and because of the many photographs that included her daughter Nellie, who was born in November 1899. At first it seemed a random assemblage of pictures compiled merely to prevent the loose prints from going missing or being damaged; but the very act of keeping and then selecting and cropping the photographs to fit into the pages' precut windows showed how important they were to Helen and the story she wanted to tell.

The conversations sparked by individual images in the pages of Helen's album and others like it in the mission archive have now become 'suspended', to use Martha Langford's description; all that is left for the historian is to 'look closely at [these] object[s] and ... imagine [them] in use'.[1] My analysis of the album constitutes an act of archival recovery and speculation on meaning. What I demonstrate is that the ways in which we engage with photographic archives influence the stories we read out of them. In the case of the mission archive, the work and the lives of missionary wives have too often been overshadowed when the textual archive is given precedence over the visual sources to be found there.

Helen travelled to Epi from New Zealand in 1890 with her husband, Presbyterian missionary Thomas Smaill, to assist in the work of converting the New Hebridean 'heathen'. She worked alongside Thomas until 1902 and, during that time, gave birth to four children – only one of whom survived. Helen returned to New Zealand with her daughter for a brief period after Thomas died. However, she found it a struggle to be away from the islands and the work they had left behind, so she and Nellie went back to Epi to work alongside Thomas's replacement before they finally returned to New Zealand in 1906.

I do not know exactly when Helen compiled her album, for whom, or exactly how she engaged with it. But when her correspondence is read alongside the album and critical attention is turned to its contents, it tells us of the way Helen valued the work she undertook in the New Hebrides. A close examination of the album further exposes the blurring of the boundaries between a 'public' form of care that was integral to the mission work she undertook and the family or 'private' care embodied in her relationship with her daughter, as represented in the numerous photographs of Nellie inserted in the album's pages.

Introducing Helen Smaill and her photograph album

While white male missionaries, particularly missionary pioneers, were often memorialised in celebratory biographies written by their colleagues, missionary wives received limited attention in the published literature of the church.[2] They are also conspicuously absent from the mission archive because, unlike their 'missionary husbands', missionary wives were not expected to correspond with the Foreign Missions Committee (FMC) in New Zealand or to submit annual reports for the work they undertook. Brooke Whitelaw, in her study of single women missionaries stationed in the New Zealand Presbyterian Church's mission field in India between 1910 and 1940, notes the difficulty of tracing the life and work of missionary wives as 'their participation was unofficial and often went unrecorded'. Their single female colleagues, on the other hand, reported to the FMC as 'part of their missionary duty' and 'occupied a rare and privileged position in the church as paid workers'. From 1906, the Presbyterian Women's Missionary Union (PWMU) began publishing a bimonthly periodical, *Harvest Field*, that frequently contained letters written by missionary wives.[3] Helen Smaill, however, was no longer active in the mission field in the New Hebrides by 1906. For her, compiling, displaying and safeguarding her photograph album was therefore the means through which she was able to leave a record of the story of her life and work in the islands alongside her husband, and then with Nellie at her side after Thomas died.

The album is held in the archives of the Presbyterian Research Centre (PRC) in Dunedin, which is where I first encountered it (Figure 1).[4] When I was shown the album by the photographic curator Donald Cochrane there was no information about the compiler.[5] It had been assigned an accession number, A-S18-85, and 'Smaill, T. Rev.' is the sole entry in the 'Provenance' column for the photographs in the online databases, accessible through the PRC's website.[6] The album has 30 thick card pages with four precut windows on each page: it contains a total of 121 small-format and cropped photographic prints. The photographs date from the 1890s to at least 1911, and the album itself most likely dates to sometime in the first two decades of the 1900s, judging by the distinctive art nouveau design on the cover. However, dating the album, while it is useful in establishing the date of compilation, does not provide clear evidence of this, as the album might have been purchased by or presented to Helen several years before the images where placed into its pages.[7] As for the subjects in the individual photographs, the photographic database at the PRC lists the contents of the album as: 'Images of New Hebrides, people and places'. This lack of contextualising information is unsurprising, as it is common practice in archives to describe and catalogue individual photographs rather than the entire album. Thomas took several of the photographs contained in the album's pages, which accounts for the provenance recorded in the PRC database.

Thomas and Helen had been married only five months when they landed at Nikaura on Epi on 3 July 1890. They quickly set to work establishing their mission station with the help of New Hebridean teachers from the Tongoa and Nguna districts, where the New Zealand missionaries Oscar Michelsen and Peter Milne, respectively, were stationed. The district that was to be Thomas's, which included the neighbouring islands of Paama and Lopevi, was notorious for cannibalism and for deadly wars between the various villages. As in most parts of the New Hebrides, malaria and other sicknesses were a constant burden. The people of Epi, for the most part, welcomed the new white residents and the message they preached, as there was an expectation that the missionaries would bring about peace. By 1897 Thomas had built another outstation on Lamenu Island and the Smaills were able to report a 'flood tide' in worshippers and Bible scholars. By 1900 only three 'heathen' villages were left in their district.[8] This was in no small part aided by the work Helen undertook alongside her domestic duties, establishing and running an English school for children and teaching Bible classes.

Helen and Thomas suffered their share of setbacks, including the death of three of their children and repeated bouts of malarial fever over the years. During one such period of sickness in April 1902, when both he and Helen were run down by fever, Thomas was called to provide medical assistance to a woman in another village who had sustained injuries during a hurricane that swept through the district. Already weak from the fever, Thomas spent a night on the floor of a village hut in his damp clothes as he could not make it back to Nikaura before dark. When he finally made it home the following day his condition had worsened, and he passed away several days later, on 12 April 1902.[9] Helen wrote to his siblings to tell them of his death: 'My darling laddie has gone home after a week's illness.'[10] Maurice Frater, the missionary on Paama at the time, wrote a letter to accompany a 'biographical sketch' of Thomas Smaill published in the missionary periodical *The Outlook*, in which he noted that Helen had suffered a 'heavy, heavy blow' and that she was 'very loath to leave Nikaura'.[11]

The Smaills in many ways epitomised the model missionary couple. Thomas undertook the public work of itinerating and preaching, opening up new areas in which to spread the Gospel, building outstations and reporting back to the FMC, while Helen tended to the home and spent the time she had left teaching English and Bible classes and giving sewing lessons to the local women. Several scholars have drawn attention to this particular aspect of the division of labour in European missions, in which women's and, in particular, missionary wives' duties were bound to the mission home and family while the men did the primary work of 'missionising'.[12] In the British evangelical worldview, as Cathy Ross observes, 'the role of the missionary wife was clear – to serve in the home, to help her husband and then if there was any time left over, to be involved in other areas'.[13] These 'other areas' were predominantly in the sphere of education: running schools for the indigenous women and children and equipping the women with the domestic skills required of a 'civilised' Christian wife. Such work 'was perceived to fall within the nurturing and caring aspects of women's nature and was considered as suitable missionary involvement according to the evangelical worldview'.[14] The centrality of the domestic realm in Helen's New Hebridean life is signalled on the first page of the album, which contains two

Figure 1. Helen Smaill's album, 27 x 22.5 x 3.5cm. A-S18-85, 3/100 Smaill T. (Rev.) and H. (Mrs), New Hebrides Photo Album, PA 42001/56, Presbyterian Research Centre Archives, Dunedin

photographs of unidentified infants in baskets (one European and one New Hebridean in each), a group portrait of mission girls whom Helen taught European domestic skills and who assisted her in the home, and a still life of a tropical plant arranged in a vase on the porch of a mission house (Figure 2).[15]

In letters to his mother and his siblings in New Zealand, Thomas painted a picture of a partnership in marriage and in work. He acknowledged the toll the work took on Helen in mid 1897, when she continued her daily English classes despite feeling unwell and exhausted. 'Now she has begun her daily

Figure 2. Page 1.
A-S18-85, Presbyterian Research Centre Archives

English school from 9 till 1 o'clock, but today the [children] spun it out to 1.30 and that together with her housework, and her not over strong makes too big a day.'[16] On 7 January 1902 Thomas wrote that he and Helen 'have been much too busy to have time to get sick', and in November 1900, when Nellie was just one year old, he informed his siblings that Helen had not been well but that 'she would still put to shame most of her sisters in law'.[17] Presumably this was in reference to the travel and work Helen undertook in addition to her domestic and motherly duties. Indeed, as Ross has argued,

Figure 3. Pages 18 & 19. A-S18-85, Presbyterian Research Centre Archives

Figure 4. Page 15. A-S18-85, Presbyterian Research Centre Archives

Figure 5. Page 5. A-S18-85, Presbyterian Research Centre Archives

Figure 6. Page 3. A-S18-85, Presbyterian Research Centre Archives

Figure 7. Page 6. A-S18-85, Presbyterian Research Centre Archives

Figure 8. Pages 26 & 27. A-S18-85, Presbyterian Research Centre Archives

given the multitude of tasks that fell on missionary wives – as mother, nurse, cook, seamstress, laundress, hostess and teacher – 'their workload was even heavier than that of their husbands'.[18]

The burden of the emotional, mental and physical investment of missionary wives' work in such places as the New Hebrides begins to crystallise out of such traces in the mission archive. But the rewards were great: by 1900 Helen's school had become a 'useful agency in preparing teachers' and '[had grown] in status into a training school' for candidates for the official Teachers' Training Institute on Tangoa, which Thomas had helped to establish in 1894.[19] Helen's pride in this achievement and the vital part her school played in the growth of the indigenous church in the islands is displayed in the portraits of New Hebridean students and teachers in her album. The teacher standing in a relaxed posed in the portrait in Figure 3 is Supabo. Thomas Smaill mentions Supabo in his correspondence with the London Missionary Society, and he appears in at least one other portrait in another of the Smaills' photograph albums held at the PRC.[20] Supabo was converted at the age of 13 and attended Helen's school before transferring to the Teachers' Training Institute in 1898.[21] He became Nikaura's most prominent leader and stories about him were told in the village for many years after his death.[22]

Compiling the album: Enshrining acts of care

Mission albums have been and still are a crucial site for the construction of narratives of the church's work in New Zealand and abroad. While at first glance Helen's album may appear to be yet another collection of standard mission images of converts, colleagues and mission stations, if we look closely at its contents and the way the individual photographs are framed within its pages it becomes clear that the album tells a distinctive story of Helen's experiences in the New Hebrides. Susan Stewart identifies the resonance of the handcrafted object as a result of 'its connection to biography and its place in constituting the individual life', and argues that 'it becomes emblematic of the worth of that life and of the self's capacity to generate worthiness'.[23] Like the letters of the single women missionaries in India which, Whitelaw argues, constitute the women's 'attempt to make sense of experience through the means of selection and arrangement', for Helen the act of compiling her album' was, we might speculate, a way of enshrining the public and private acts of care that defined her life.[24]

The album belongs to an important subset of photograph albums in the Presbyterian Church's archives in that it allows the historian access to a missionary wife and mother's construction of life and work in the islands. Its way of telling is less ordered than the public presentation albums compiled by the FMC and the PWMU that are also held in the PRC, in which the photographs are arranged geographically and thematically and convey a story of mission progress.[25] It contains many of the same official images as the public albums, such as portraits of missionaries, New Hebridean converts and mission workers neatly posed before the camera, as well as views of mission stations. However, the photographs in Helen's album are in no apparent order and are often in different orientations and odd juxtapositions on the pages, so that no clear narrative can immediately be deduced from them (see Figures 3, 4 & 8). There are few captions, and those that do appear are in ballpoint pen and were almost certainly added later than at the original compilation of the album.[26]

What immediately stands out in Helen's album, aside from the disorganised appearance of its contents, is the scope of subjects contained in its pages. This may be explained by the fact that this album was compiled after Helen had left Epi in 1906. Over the years, the photographs that she and Thomas took would have been added to as Helen collected pictures and was sent them by friends still working in the islands. The resulting pool of images available to her when she began compiling would, therefore, have been made up of a broader range of subjects. Helen's connection with the islands remained strong throughout her long life (she passed away in Hastings in 1966 at the age of 99).[27] In 1932 she ends a letter to the FMC secretary with the comment: 'We are always deeply interested in anything from the New Hebrides.'[28] Graham Miller noted that when he first met Helen in 1944, 'she was grateful for news of Epi ... and retained to the end her prayerful interest in Epi'.[29] These traces of Helen's voice in the archive and in the remembrances of subsequent mission workers testify to the 'level of emotional investment [mission] work demanded' and imbue the album with further significance for the reconstruction of her experiences in the New Hebrides.[30]

Images of mission colleagues and friends appear regularly throughout the album, but one face in particular dominates the photographs: that of Nellie, who appears in 39 photographs. Nellie was Thomas and Helen's fourth child, born on 18 November 1899. They had already lost three infants, so her birth and the first few months of her life must have been an anxious time for them. In most of the photographs she appears to be around three or four years old – or, at least, older than the 18 months she would have been when Thomas died in 1902. Several of the images also include Thomas Riddle, the missionary who replaced Thomas. This would suggest that Helen took many of the photographs in the album herself after she returned to Epi with Nellie in 1903 to assist Riddle as his housekeeper. Indeed, given the demands of her work as a teacher as well as the time she spent fulfilling her domestic duties, she might well have taken most of her photographs in the few months before she and Nellie returned to New Zealand in 1906. On 27 September 1905 Helen wrote to the FMC secretary: 'We do not go at once to New Zealand but are to spend some months here with our friends in the islands before going up. The fold here have been coming in great crowds to take farewell of us & bringing large presents of yam, they wish to do something to show their love.'[31]

In a family portrait on page 5 of the album, taken when Nellie was a newborn, a mixture of exhaustion, concern and cautious joy can be read on her parents' faces (Figure 5). Their first daughter did not survive the birth and two sons died during malaria epidemics in the Smaills' mission district.[32] The remaining photographs on this page of the album are all of Nellie at around four years old, very much alive and playing with mission friends. Although she is not always the primary focus of the photographs in the album, she is a persistent presence among the subjects. She was photographed alongside friends from other mission stations, such as Isobel Milne and Nettie Frater, as well as with groups of islanders and with the New Hebridean housegirls who assisted Helen in her domestic duties and helped care for Nellie (see, for example, Figures 3, 5, 6 & 7).

Nellie's frequent appearance in the album requires little explanation given that she was the beloved daughter and constant companion of Helen, particularly during the three years she spent on Epi after Thomas's death. She was a sickly child, and a health scare in late 1900 meant the Smaills had to take an unplanned trip back to New Zealand early the following year. Nellie was nursed 'back from the grave', but Helen's concern for her daughter remains a theme in letters she wrote once she was back in New Zealand after

1906.[33] In one instance, she reported to the foreign missions secretary that Nellie was 'laid up' as a result of 'over work at school'.[34] It might have been the case that Helen and Nellie sat down together to compile the album during such periods of fatigue or, at least, looked through old photographs of their island home and the many friends they left behind. It was with heavy heart that Helen left the islands, and she and Nellie no doubt remained homesick for Epi for many years.[35]

Images of missionary colleagues posed in groups, as well as individual portraits of Helen's co-workers and friends, make up 35.5 per cent of the album. When you add the many photographs of island helpers, villagers and converts, around 70 per cent of the images are of people. The photographs of missionary colleagues linked Helen to the community of carers she worked alongside for 15 years. Although it may be difficult to view the work of missionaries from this perspective today, in the evangelical worldview mission work was, at its core, centred on caring for 'heathen' souls and improving their lives through evangelism.[36] According to Whitelaw, 'a maternal concern for the world around them' often shaped the work of missionary women with indigenous populations, and they would write of their interactions with potential female converts in a manner that 'closely resembled a mother and daughter relationship'.[37] Infantilisation is well documented in the paternalistic rhetoric of nineteenth and early twentieth-century missions in which 'heathen races' were regarded as 'children' in need of guidance from their civilised Christian 'guardians'.[38]

Not long after Helen and Nellie returned to live in New Zealand permanently, increasing numbers of single women were sent to work as missionaries overseas. In 1902 the FMC resolved to look into extending women's work in the mission fields, and consulted with the home churches to provide more financial support to this end.[39] Until Thomas's death, Helen's role as a missionary wife was clear: she supported her husband's work by tending to the domestic duties of the home and participated in the mission work in her capacity as a teacher. She was not paid and she was not officially acknowledged as a missionary, although the FMC did give her £130 to 'assist' her on her husband's death.[40] When Helen insisted on returning to the work she knew and loved, the church found itself in an awkward position. While the FMC was committed to facilitating mission work for single women, Helen's status in December 1902, when she wrote to the FMC convenor with her request, was not 'single' but 'widow'. It seems that she was acutely aware of this and, in her petition to William Hewitson, she stressed the assistance she could give as a caregiver to the 'natives' and to the missionary who had temporarily taken over the work on Epi until a permanent replacement was found:

> I have a great desire to go back to the work until the new missionary is got. I have been praying much about it & feel there is nothing to hinder me going if the Committee will give their consent. It is hardly fair for Willie Milne [missionary from Nguna] to be their [sic] alone for he will have everything to do for himself as the natives are very little use unless there is some one to guide them. If he takes fever or anything else there will be no one to care for him the natives are just helpless at such times & then I know I could be a great help to him & the natives & would be far more useful there than here … I would not be a burden to you. I could quite well take my little girl back with me. I would not be in the way of the new missionary when he arrived for I have no doubt he might not care to have me about but I could go over to Paama for a time & be near if I could help him in any way.[41]

That Helen believed she might be a 'burden' on the FMC is a sad indictment of the church for its lack of recognition of the work that missionary wives did alongside their husbands. By the 1910s the situation was improving, however, and in October 1912, Hewitson's wife Margaret published a letter in the PWMU's *Harvest Field* in which she noted the heavy workload under which the wives often struggled: 'I sometimes wonder if we enter as sympathetically and understandingly into the life and work of our missionaries' wives as we should … [T]hese women are not only wives of missionaries but are missionaries themselves, and take their full share in the work.'[42]

The church finally granted Helen permission to return to Epi after she entered into a 'private agreement' with Riddle that she would go as his housekeeper. The mission report of 1903 further stated that Helen would 'also take some part in mission work'.[43] She resumed the work she had begun in the New Hebrides with Nellie at her side and in 1905 was put in charge of the Lamenu mission station when Riddle took a short furlough. When Helen finally made the decision to return to New Zealand at the end of 1905 the committee offered her an honorarium of £50.[44] In a letter to the FMC dated 27 September 1905, in which Helen thanks the FMC for their 'generous gift', she writes: 'I neither looked for nor wished for any recognition for the work

I have been doing. My one great desire was to be allowed to come back to the work & that was granted.'[45] Her apparent gratitude was at odds, however, with her private view that she had been undervalued and underpaid. She felt her situation was unjust and she criticised the mission organisation for not providing her with a stipend, which meant Riddle had to pay her out of his own wages:

> I may be worth the money to Mr Riddle but am I not doing the Church's work? I think they ought to have paid me from the first. Mr Hewitson's excuses seemed very poor at the time but I could not say anything. First of all he said if they paid & we did not get on it would mean they would have to stand by their missionary. Isn't that risk taken with all assistants? Then the other about complications with Mr M. I don't see it at all. The Church is paying Mrs Neil 30 a year. She is assisting Mr M. I think I can say without boasting that I do far more for them than she does … Mr H said something about them not wishing to have me working for them without payment & that they would do something, give me a present of some thing. I don't like that. If I am worth being paid why not pay me? I would gladly do anything I do down here for my food & home but I know that would not be allowed. Well why not the Church pay me if I am to be paid? I think I do more for them than for Mr Riddle.[46]

To underline the statement that her contribution to the mission work outweighed her work as a housekeeper, Helen included a cutting from the previous year's annual report written by Riddle:

> In closing this report I should like to testify to the great help I have received from Mrs Smaill. Her knowledge of the natives and her experience of the work and language have prevented much blundering. Throughout the year she has conducted the children's English school, and the sewing and Bible classes.[47]

Helen's photograph album provided a window of remembrance of these tasks when she was back home in New Zealand. The album contained the faces of the many people Helen cared and worked so hard for. It is easy to imagine her recounting the hardships and triumphs of the mission field and the particular part she played in evangelising.

That Helen's album gives a glimpse of her life and work in the New Hebrides, as opposed to an official narrative of mission progress such as in the FMC and PWMU albums, is further evidenced by the inclusion of photographs that on technical grounds or artistic merit might otherwise have been omitted.[48] As Patricia Holland writes: 'the photographs we keep for ourselves are treasured less for their quality than for their *context*, and for the part they play in confirming and challenging the identity and history of their users'.[49] The badly discoloured and faded portrait of a woman standing on a garden path on page 19 is a good example of Helen's everything-included selection process (Figure 3): the desire to include the image of a friend (most likely Mrs Annand, the wife of Joseph Annand from Nova Scotia who was stationed on Santo) was of far greater importance to Helen than the quality of the image.

Aside from portraits of missionaries and New Hebrideans, the images that stand out in the album are those that depict leisure activities or recreation. Around 10 per cent of the photographs are of activities that are not immediately related to mission work, such as scenes of missionaries having picnics together. These outings were likely connected with the annual Synod meeting, an event that was eagerly anticipated by the missionaries who often had very little contact with the workers on other islands. In a letter printed in *The New Zealand Presbyterian* in 1891, Thomas Smaill wrote:

> I cannot tell you what benefit the annual meeting of Synod is to us. If it were nothing more than to get a real good laugh, its worth would not be small, for owing to our isolation one seldom gets a real good laugh – at least we rarely hear a good story; our own stock gets run out.[50]

The strains of mission work and the importance of such events for the mental health of missionaries are evident in such statements. Scenes of missionaries reclining in cane chairs or sitting on the ground drinking from china cups also provide a counterpoint to the formal Synod portraits that are more common in the photographic output of the mission, and they give valuable insight into the social life of missionaries in the New Hebrides.

While Nellie's constant presence and the many photographs of mission colleagues and New Hebridean converts in the album are easily explained in relation to Helen's position as mother and mission worker, there are several images that, at first sight, do not appear to sit comfortably alongside them. Helen inserted a small number of photographs of ethnographic subjects in the album – for example, Figures 4, 7 & 8 – but with no captions to assist the contemporary viewer, her reasons for including these images are not immediately apparent. Given the prevalence of ethnographic, or quasi-ethnographic, representations in the photographic output of other mission fields of the late nineteenth and early twentieth centuries, what is striking about her album is the relative lack of such subjects. The private albums compiled by missionaries in Papua that Max Quanchi analyses in his book, *Photographing Papua*, were 'overwhelmingly focused on ethnographic documentation, to a lesser extent on mission life, and hardly at all on picnics, husbands and wives, social or domestic activities, visitors, gardens or views from the veranda'.[51] The picture of the New Hebrides presented to New Zealand audiences in the church's periodicals, postcards, publications and magic lantern slideshows also catered to ethnographic curiosity, but not to the same degree as that identified by Quanchi for Papua.[52]

Ethnographic subjects are rare in Helen's album, and where they do appear, they are often juxtaposed with photographs that render the images more complex and ambiguous. For example, on page 6 of the album she included a photograph of *kastom* stones with human skulls placed on them alongside images of Nellie and a friend in dress-ups, Nellie with a dog on a garden path, and a portrait of herself and Thomas with another missionary couple (Figure 7). When the album is opened out to pages 26 and 27, the two photographs inserted into the one window stand out, as does the photograph on page 27 of the New Hebridean youth standing in front of three carvings in an outdoor setting (Figure 8).[53] The two photographs in one window are from India: one shows washermen in what looks to be a studio portrait; the other is of potters on a street. These photos look remarkably out of place alongside images of people Helen knew, the house they lived in on Lamenu Island and the housegirls who worked on the mission station. However, they comprise a part of the story of Helen's life as a mission worker, and they relate to the theme of care, as she might have known the boy posed in front of the carvings, and it is even possible he was a student at her school. As for the photographs from India, Riddle could have sent these to Helen after he transferred to the Punjab mission field in 1911 and they may therefore have signified the enduring ties established between missionaries who worked in the church's overseas fields.[54]

The use of an album to 'explore, construct, and confirm identity',[55] both in terms of community and individual identity, is evident in Helen's album. The many photographs of missionaries in the New Hebrides, as well as of Nellie, link her in an intimate way to these people as well as to the islands. By including picnic scenes and other photographs of leisure activities, interspersed with Synod groups, indigenous helpers and portraits of prominent missionary celebrities, Helen was showing the viewer the wider missionary community she was a part of, and the people they cared for and worked to bring into the Christian faith.

Encountering the album: Visual and material traces of care in the archive

Helen Smaill's album functioned first and foremost as a personal memory storehouse – an object closely tied to the past and necessary for its rejuvenation through the telling of stories prompted by the individual photographs on the pages. As Rosemary Seton and Robert Bickers observe, 'the first things records tell us concern the people who created them'.[56] In my discussion of the album, the attempt to answer the question of why it appears as it does brings us closer to the compiler of the album. This is a valuable line of enquiry, and reveals a little of Helen's personal experience in the New Hebrides and of her recollection of it once back in New Zealand. The next step in the engagement with the album is to consider its trajectory before it was deposited in the PRC archives.

As albums are both a collection of photographs and a narrative, ideally, the album requires Helen's presence to reanimate the story she was trying to construct in its pages and to make sense of the uncaptioned images.[57] In Helen's possession, the album might have been placed on the lap or in the hands of a relative, friend or parishioner to be discussed, gazed at and pointed to as Helen recounted her stories. In this manifestation the photograph album is an aide-mémoire or, as Langford argues, 'an oral-photographic performance' in which individual images jog the memory of its presenter, refreshing connections with the past as each page is turned.[58] Helen kept the album with her in her home and it is easy to imagine it being brought out to display to family members and friends curious to know more about her and Nellie's life in the New Hebrides. When the pages were turned and the viewers were confronted with images such as the kastom stones and the boy with the carvings, Helen had the opportunity to act as cultural intermediary, explaining the complex customs of the New Hebrides to her audiences. More importantly, displaying the album gave Helen the chance to assert her identity and worth as a mission worker in her own right.

Helen's album bears the 'physical traces [that] are manifestations of the presence of, and the relationship between, maker and reader'.[59] These are visible in the bent corners, loose binding, and the tears in some of the pages. It is uncertain whether the majority of the wear happened while it was still in Helen's possession. She no doubt viewed the album often for, as Alfred Lichtwark notes, 'There is no work of art in our age so attentively viewed as the portrait photography of oneself, one's closest friends, and relatives, one's beloved.'[60] This album and two other photograph albums that Helen and Thomas compiled of their time in the islands were among Helen's most treasured personal possessions.[61] Following Nellie's death in around 1940, Helen is likely to have looked through them on many occasions.[62] They remained with her until the mid-1960s, when they were entrusted to the care of Graham Horwell, the missionary on Epi at the time. Helen was moving into a rest home in Lower Hutt, and after family members had deliberately destroyed her husband's diaries, she feared her photograph albums would suffer a similar fate.[63] She therefore contacted Horwell, who was more than happy to accept the Smaills' albums which, he noted, 'had been their own record of activities on Epi in the New Hebrides, and they are a fine collection.'[64] Unlike the contemporary viewer of the album, Horwell had the privilege of experiencing these albums in Helen's presence as she presented all three to him while he was on furlough in New Zealand. He writes that he 'spent some time with Mrs Smaill at Lower Hutt', during which he may have looked through the album with her and compiled the index sheet that is kept with it in the archives.[65]

In Horwell's care, it seems Helen's album was maintained almost in its original form, with some extra wear and tear bearing testimony to continuing viewings, and the index sheet indicating a desire to preserve as many details of her story before she forgot them and before she died. By this time some of the faces had faded in her memory, but throughout its life the album remained a treasure worth safeguarding until it was deposited in the archives of the PRC in 2000 to be cared for and preserved for years to come.

When I first encountered the album, its significance as a container of memories and a testament to Helen's mission work in the New Hebrides was in danger of being overshadowed as a result of its location alongside presentation albums compiled by the church for propaganda purposes, as well as collections of loose photographs that had been amassed by the FMC and other church organisations. Photographs were regularly sent from the overseas fields of the church to be reproduced in mission periodicals, pamphlets, histories of the mission and biographies of individual pioneer missionaries. As already mentioned, Helen's album does contain similar and, in some cases, the same photographs (or duplicates) as in the presentation albums and other forms of propaganda disseminated by the church. However, after spending some time with the album, it became clear that it was not originally intended as a propaganda album for the New Hebrides mission. The narrative contained in its pages and the uses to which it was put while it was in Helen's care emerged as more intimate, familial and domestic.

The current context in which the album exists frames it as a cultural and historical document, whereas it was once an 'instrument of collective show and tell' and/or a 'repository of memory'.[66] In so far as its original function was to prompt stories of life and work in the New Hebrides, and thereby connect its compiler/narrator and viewers in an environment of faith sharing, in its afterlife in the archives the album has become a 'new' object. The afterlife of albums is closely tied to, and shaped by, the practices and role of the archives in which they are housed.[67] As Edwards and Hart note, archives 'are active environments for participating in the histories of objects, active environments that ultimately shape histories, through the preserving contexts that they themselves constitute'.[68]

The images contained in Helen's album, once it was deposited in the PRC, thus became part of the story of the New Zealand Presbyterian Church's work in the New Hebrides mission field. From the point of view of the collecting practices of the PRC this is its meaning and significance. However, Edwards and Hart write that albums are 'natural' objects that 'remain in [archives] as discrete singular entities'.[69] This is in contrast to, for example, a box of ethnographic photographs in a museum that has been arranged, rearranged, accessioned and described over the course of its life. Helen's album was exposed to similar treatment during its time in the PRC archives. While its physical form has not been radically changed, the process of accessioning, numbering the pages and photographs, as well as describing them for the photographic database, constitutes a reinscription of meanings onto the album-object. Edwards and Hart claim that this is 'simple taxonomic description', but considering that these processes have enabled the digitisation of the photographs in the album (making it more widely accessible and preserving the physical object), the album, like the box of photographs, has begun to move 'into a set of changing values ... into a framework of policies, strategies and practices'.[70]

Conclusion

In 2000, Helen's album was finally deposited in the PRC archives, far removed from its original context. This could have been where her personal narrative was lost. Even before the age of digitisation, albums such as this one in public archives were most often mined for illustrations. However, by looking closely at the album, it is possible to get a little closer to Helen Smaill and to the story of this portion of her life that she wanted to tell. What emerges is a picture of a woman dedicated to the work of evangelising in the New Hebrides and to maintaining her record of the past for herself and for her daughter. As Andrew Walker and Rosalind Moulton observe, 'for ordinary people, collections of photographs are more significant than are singular photographs'.[71] Therefore, no matter how 'disorganised' Helen's album may appear, it nevertheless represents her ordering and understanding of her experiences as a missionary wife, a mission worker and a mother. The theme of care weaves through the story of the album: from its compilation and display through to its preservation and safeguarding in the face of destruction. The photographs contained in its pages tell a story of mission work and of Helen's connection to a community of evangelists, and her daughter's persistent presence in the images reveals the extent to which public/mission and private/family care were intertwined for Helen in the mission field. Her love of God and her care for the children, women and men she worked with and, of course, the continual love and care of a mother for her daughter brought Helen's album into existence and ensured its survival in the archives today.

Notes

1   Martha Langford, *Suspended Conversations: The afterlife of memory in photographic albums* (Montreal & Kingston, London, Ithaca: McGill-Queen's University Press, 2001), 18.

2   See, for example, Alexander Don, *Peter Milne: Missionary to Nguna, New Hebrides, 1870 to 1924 from the Presbyterian Church of New Zealand* (Dunedin: Foreign Missions Committee, 1927).

3   Brooke Whitelaw, 'A message from the missahibs: New Zealand Presbyterian women missionaries in the Punjab, 1910–1940', MA thesis, University of Otago, 2001, 2, 19–20, 66, 67. The paucity of sources by or about missionary wives across denominational boundaries is noted by several scholars: see Whitelaw, 'A message from the missahibs', 3, 67; Cathy Ross, *Women with a Mission: Rediscovering missionary wives in early New Zealand* (Auckland & London: Penguin Books, 2006), 18; Regina Ganter & Patricia Grimshaw, 'Introduction: Reading the lives of white mission women', *Journal of Australian Studies* 39, no. 1 (2015), 4; Patricia Grimshaw, *Paths of Duty: American missionary wives in nineteenth-century Hawaii* (Honolulu: University of Hawai`i Press, 1989), xxi; S.J. Goldsbury, 'Behind the picket fence: The lives of missionary wives in pre-colonial New Zealand', MA thesis, University of Auckland, 1986, i.

4   Antje Lübcke, 'The photograph albums of the New Zealand Presbyterian mission to the New Hebrides', MA thesis, University of Otago, 2009.

5   A-S18-85, 3/100 Smaill T. (Rev.) and H. (Mrs), New Hebrides photo album, PA 42001/56, Presbyterian Research Centre Archives, Dunedin (PRC).

6   www.presbyterian.org.nz/archives/missions/photodatabases/ pre1900nhimages.htm; www.presbyterian.org.nz/archives/missions/ photodatabases/1900to1909nhimages.htm; www.presbyterian.org.nz/archives/ missions/photodatabases/1910to1920nhimages.htm

7   In letters dating from 1914 Helen noted that her eyesight was failing, which further points to a compilation date between c. 1906 and 1915: Helen Smaill to Alexander Don, 12 November 1914, GA0146, New Hebrides Mission Staff Files, H.J. Smaill Staff File 1902–1932, AA 13/5/2, 1984/18, PRC.

8   J.G. Miller, *Live: A history of church planting in the Republic of Vanuatu. Book 5* (Port Vila, Vanuatu: Presbyterian Church of Vanuatu, 1987), 340, 388, 395, 398.

9   Ibid., 400, 401–02.

10 Helen Smaill, transcribed unsigned letter, 17 May 1902, Smaill family: Letters and obituary notices, Misc-MS-0440, Hocken Collections, University of Otago, Dunedin (HC).

11 *The Outlook,* 24 May 1902, pp. 33–34, Misc-MS-0440, HC.

12 See, for example, Regina Ganter, 'Helpers–sisters–wives: White women on Australian missions', *Journal of Australian Studies* 39, no. 1 (2015), 7–19; Emily J. Manktelow, 'The rise and demise of missionary wives', *Journal of Women's History* 26, no. 1 (2014), 143–49; Dana Robert, 'Evangelist or homemaker? Mission strategies of early nineteenth-century missionary wives in Burma and Hawaii', *International Bulletin of Missionary Research* 17, no. 1 (1993), 4–12.

13 Ross, *Women with a Mission*, 14.

14 Ibid., 173.

15 Given the particular focus of this paper, I have not been able to include a discussion of the pivotal work undertaken by New Hebridean 'house-girls' or domestic servants. For more on this, see Margaret Rodman, Daniela Kraemer, Lissant Bolton & Jean Tarisesei (eds), *House-Girls Remember: Domestic workers in Vanuatu* (Honolulu: University of Hawai`i Press, 2007).

16 Thomas Smaill, letter to 'Bob & Aggie', 7 June 1897, Misc-MS-0440, HC.

17 Thomas Smaill, letters to 'Bob & Aggie', 7 November 1900 and 7 January 1902, Misc-MS-0440, HC.

18 Ross, *Women with a Mission*, 175.

19 Miller, *Live*, 399–400.

20 See Helen Smaill, letter to Alexander Don, 2 August 1918, AA 13/5/2, PRC. Helen's letter contains transcribed sections of Thomas Smaill's letters and diaries.

21 Helen Smaill, letter to Alexander Don, 2 August 1918, AA 13/5/2, PRC; Miller, 399.

22 Michael Young, *One Hundred Years of Christianity in Nikaura 1890–1990* (unpublished manuscript written at the request of the Centenary Celebration Committee: October 1990, held at Vanuatu Cultural Centre Library, Port Vila, Vanuatu), 8.

23 Susan Stewart, *On Longing: Narratives of the miniature, the gigantic, the souvenir, the collection* (Durham, NC: Duke University Press, 1993), 139.

24 Whitelaw, 'A message from the missahibs', 66.

25 The narrative of mission progress, conveyed in images of converts and churches, is necessarily tempered somewhat in these albums by, for example, photographs of hurricane damage, as the compilers no doubt wanted to ensure that viewers not get the impression that the work there is complete and there is therefore no need for further funds for the mission. See A-L-2, Foreign Missions Committee, New Hebrides Mission Album, PA 496/34, PRC; A-S3-9, Foreign Missions Committee, New Hebrides Mission Album (Presbyterian Women's Missionary Union), PA 496/37, PRC.

26 The ballpoint pen did not come into common usage in New Zealand until at least the 1950s, possibly even the 1960s.

27 Miller, *Live*, 408.

28 Helen Smaill, letter to Rev. Mawson, 20 September 1932, AA 13/5/2, PRC.

29 Miller, *Live*, 408.

30 Whitelaw, 'A message from the missahibs', 1.

31 Helen Smaill, letter to Chisholm, 27 September 1905, AA 13/5/2, PRC.

32 Thomas Smaill, letter published in *New Zealand Presbyterian,* April 1891, 186, GA1 FMC, Published letters, Thomas Smaill, 2008/197/17, AC 10/3, PRC. See also Miller, *Live*, 389, 391.

33 Thomas Smaill, letter to 'Bob & Aggie', 13 July 1901, Misc-MS-0440, HC; Miller, *Live*, 400.

34 Helen Smaill, letter to Alexander Don, 12 November 1914, AA 13/5/2, PRC.

35 The sources I have consulted in the archives do not state why Helen returned to New Zealand indefinitely in 1906, but Nellie's education was likely a factor.

36 Whitelaw, 'A message from the missahibs', 1.

37 Ibid., 20, 122.

38 See, for example, Nicholas Thomas, 'Colonial conversions: Difference, hierarchy, and history in early twentieth-century evangelical propaganda', *Comparative Studies in Society and History* 34, no. 2 (1992), 377.

39 Whitelaw, 'A message from the missahibs', 45.

40 Miller, *Live*, 403. The 'problem' of Helen's status is reflected in her entry in the 'Roll of Presbyterian missionaries to the Central Islands, 1881–1920' that appears as an appendix in Miller's book. Here Helen is listed as 'Honorary asst. to 1906' (Miller, 445).

41 Helen Smaill, letter to W. Hewitson, 26 December 1902, AA 13/5/2, PRC.

42 M. Hewitson, *Harvest Field*, 8 October 1912, i–ii, quoted in Whitelaw, 'A message from the missahibs', 68.

43 Miller, *Live*, 404.

44 Ibid., 407.

45 Helen Smaill, letter to Chisholm, 27 September 1905, AA 13/5/2, PRC.

46 Ibid.

47 Ibid.

48 Max Quanchi, *Photographing Papua: Representation, colonial encounters and imaging in the public domain* (Newcastle: Cambridge Scholars Publishing, 2007), 140.

49 Patricia Holland, '"Sweet it is to scan ...": Personal photographs and popular photography', in Liz Wells (ed.), *Photography: A critical introduction*, 3rd edn (London: Routledge, 2004), 117 (italics in original).

50 Letter dated 5 June, *The New Zealand Presbyterian*, August 1891, 23 (cutting included in GA1 FMC, Published letters, Thomas Smaill, AC 10/3, PRC).

51 Quanchi, *Photographing Papua*, 134.

52 See Max Quanchi, 'The power of pictures: Learning-by-looking at Papua in illustrated newspapers and magazines', *Australian Historical Studies* 35, no. 123 (2004), 37–53.

53 This photograph was almost certainly taken on Epi, as the two carvings on the right closely resemble drawings done by the Russian anthropologist Nikolai Miklouho-Maclay in 1879 on the island: see Joël Bonnemaison, Kirk Huffman et al. (eds), *Arts of Vanuatu* (Bathurst: Crawford House Publishing, 1996), fig. 15.

54 J.S. Murray, *A Century of Growth: Presbyterian overseas mission work 1869–1969* (Christchurch: Presbyterian Bookroom, 1969), 28.

55 Patrizia di Bello, 'Albums', in Robin Lenman (ed.), *The Oxford Companion to the Photograph* (Oxford: Oxford University Press, 2005), 21.

56 Robert Bickers & Rosemary Seton (eds), *Missionary Encounters: Sources and issues* (Surrey: Curzon Press, 1996), 6.

57 Andrew L. Walker & Rosalind Kimball Moulton, 'Photo albums: Images of time and reflections of self', *Qualitative Sociology* 12, no. 2 (1989), 169.

58 Langford, *Suspended Conversations*, 20.

59 Stephanie Snyder, *Snapshot Chronicles: Inventing the American photo album* (New York: Princeton Architectural Press, 2006), 33.

60 Quoted in ibid., 26.

61 A-S17-79, 3/100 Smaill, Rev. T. and Mrs H., New Hebrides Album, c. 1900, PA 42000/33, PRC; A-S17-78, 3/100 Smaill, Rev. T and Mrs H., New Hebrides Album, c. 1895–1902, PA 42008/53, PRC.

62 Miller, *Live*, 400.

63 This information comes from the copy of a letter written by Rev. Graham Horwell to Misses C. and A. Smaill, dated 1 July 1976. Horwell writes: 'You may know that Mr. Smaill's diaries and other valuable historical material was lost forever'. (Letter to C. and A. Smaill, 1 July 1976, 'Dunedin' section, GA0101 Joint Interim Board for Missions, folder no. 1976/6, AC 4/2/3, PRC). In discussions with Donald Cochrane and Yvonne Wilkie at the PRC archives about this reference, I was told what Rev. Horwell had told them (i.e. that the diaries and other documents had been destroyed by the family members who were shifting Helen's belongings to the rest home).

64 G. Horwell, letter to Lewis Wilson, 24 March 1976, 'Dunedin' section, GA0101 Joint Interim Board for Missions, folder no. 1976/6, AC 4/2/3, PRC.

65 Horwell, letter to Misses C. and A. Smaill, 1 July 1976, AC 4/2/3, PRC.

66 Langford, *Suspended Conversations,* 20; Martha Langford, 'Speaking the album: An application of the oral-photographic framework', in Annette Kuhn & Kirsten Emiko McAllister (eds), *Locating Memory: Photographic acts* (New York & Oxford: Berghahn, 2006), 223.

67 For discussions on the roles and influence of collecting institutions see, for example, Bickers & Seton (eds), *Missionary Encounters*; Joan M. Schwartz, '"Records of simple truth and precision": Photography, archives, and the illusion of control', *Archivaria* 50 (2000): 1–40; Joanna Sassoon, 'The politics of pictures: A cultural history of the Western Australian Government Print Photograph Collection', *Australian Historical Studies* 35, no. 123 (2004): 16–36.

68 Elizabeth Edwards & Janice Hart, 'Mixed box: The cultural biography of a box of "ethnographic" photographs', in Elizabeth Edwards and Janice Hart (eds), *Photographs, Objects, Histories: On the materiality of images*, (New York: Routledge, 2004), 49.

69 Ibid., 49.

70 Ibid. Photograph albums have also frequently been taken apart on their arrival in museums, archives and in the possession of private collectors. The pages and images were removed for display as well as storage purposes: see Glenn Willumson, 'Making meaning', 72–74; Holland, 130, footnote 6 text.

71 Walker & Moulton, 'Photo albums', 158.

6

FEEDING THE FAMILY:
Pākehā and Māori women in rural districts, c.1900–1940

Katie Cooper

'What shall we have for dinner?' This is the constant cry of the housewife who feels that housekeeping would be relieved of one of its greatest bugbears if someone else would undertake the planning of the meals. And yet this is a burden not so easily shifted on to another's shoulders. Menus may be written, but they seldom fulfil requirements exactly as they stand. The foods designated are not in the market, or the family does not like them, or there are 'left-overs' to be disposed of, and the problem remains unsolved. In fact, the one who is entrusted with the feeding of the family has a responsibility not lightly escaped.[1]

This excerpt comes from an article written by the Home Science Extension Bureau in 1930. In it the author provides advice on producing well-balanced meals and mastering the principles of dietary health. The provision of three meals a day, 'so appalling in [its] inevitability', required a great deal of planning and preparation, and this 'burden' of care fell heavily on the women of New Zealand. Entrusted with feeding the family, wives and mothers had responsibility for the physical and spiritual welfare of every member for, as the author of the article goes on to suggest, there could be 'no life of the spirit without sustenance for the body'.[2]

In *Hearts of Wisdom*, an expansive study of American women caring for kin in the decades between 1850 and 1940, Emily K. Abel demonstrates that the content and context of the work of care have changed dramatically over time. She argues that the essential components of care – instrumental, spiritual and emotional – are all culturally conditioned, and can be analysed to reveal broad social issues such as the relationship between knowledge and power.[3] Building on Abel's analysis, this chapter historicises one particular type of care –the work of feeding – in order to illuminate the range of visible and invisible responsibilities that have at various times been considered 'women's work'.

The processes involved in feeding a family, writes sociologist Marjorie L. DeVault, are partly determined by the material conditions of household groups, including 'the organization of markets, supply and distribution of energy, and typical arrangement and accoutrements of dwellings'.[4] The way women encounter the work of feeding is thus specific to their time and place, and those charged with the nourishment of the family in the early decades of the twentieth century had to manage their responsibilities in a broad range of material situations. Furthermore, DeVault continues, 'the work of feeding others is also shaped by, and in turn expresses, beliefs and customs of the society at a particular time. More than just the provision of edibles, feeding work means staging the rather complex social events that we label meals.'[5] So while the provision of meals may have seemed like an unchanging and appalling inevitability to the writer from the Home Science Extension Bureau, in fact the process was conditioned by a complex set of constructed expectations that were constantly in flux.

For women in New Zealand, the physical, intellectual and emotional labour inherent in the work of care changed dramatically in the early decades of the twentieth century. In particular, the feeding of the family was transformed by the introduction of new domestic technologies and ideologies in the 1920s and 1930s. Women experienced this transformation in diverse ways, as Melissa Matutina Williams demonstrates in her chapter. Their experiences depended, among other things, on their financial circumstances, access to service networks, their religion and cultural values. I have chosen to focus in this chapter on Māori and Pākehā women in rural districts and to explore the challenges they faced in meeting new standards for physical and emotional care, often without the benefits of modern technology and transportation. Under these circumstances the work of feeding the family demanded a particularly heavy investment of time and energy, and this in turn shaped how rural women interacted with the various welfare institutions looking to rationalise and supervise their work. The care of the family was a responsibility not lightly escaped, and the wives and mothers of New Zealand's country districts were expected to demonstrate their care at every meal.

The ministering spirit

Recent historical analyses of caring have forced us to reassess what was once regarded as an innately feminine propensity to nurture, and to recognise that caring for others is a socially constructed idea. Julia T. Wood identifies three separate but overlapping explanations for the genesis of women's tendency to care in Western cultures: family psychodynamic processes that encourage empathy in females and independence in males; sex-role socialisation through a variety of social institutions that define caring as constitutive of femininity; and the social subordination of women which forces them to care for those with more power in order to secure their own safety and comfort.[6] For the purposes of this chapter it is sufficient to note that, whatever the genesis, Pākehā women had primary responsibility for familial care in the early twentieth century, and few thought to question that construct. The traits considered essential to caregiving – 'responsiveness to the needs of others, patience, and an ability to adapt to change' – were part of a cultural definition of womanhood that most Pākehā women accepted and enacted.[7]

The preparation of meals – considered women's work in almost all cultures – was central to this definition of femininity.[8] According to one food specialist in the 1930s, meal planning, cooking and serving accounted for 70 per cent of the time New Zealand women spent on housework, and for many women it was the primary way of 'doing' gender and displaying recognisably feminine ideals.[9] Some women expressed the view that they had an intrinsic capacity to carry out the work of feeding others, and they drew on religious rhetoric and the teachings of Christianity to explain their role within the family contract.[10] In 1934 Mrs Pollock of Waihi wrote:

> Man's brain has worked miracles in producing food, making the wilderness blossom like the rose, blazing trails through pathless wastes, building exquisite homes of supreme comfort, and has harnessed the forces of nature to work his will. But the ministering spirit lags behind the brain in organisation, so little mouths are not fed, little limbs lack clothing in the midst of plenty. Women must arise, complement man's labours, distribute the fruits with justice and mercy and so conserve the life she bore.[11]

Other women, too, conflated the bearing of children with the capacity to care, and suggested that that most sacred of responsibilities imbued their daily work with a spiritual significance. 'Surely each honoured mother may feel she has not lived in vain,' wrote the mother of a large rural family in

Preparing to serve a meal at a tangi in the Stratford region, Taranaki, c.1930.
John Reginald Wall, ref: 1/2-017655-G, Alexander Turnbull Library, Wellington.

1938, 'when she holds in her arms this most precious of all fruits and hears that unspoken command, "Take this child and nurse it for me."'[12]

In Māori society women are referred to as te whare tangata (the house of humanity), and venerated for their ability to provide life and nurture future generations.[13] Until the twentieth century, however, communities tended to share caring responsibilities, and 'individual Maori mothers were less tied to their children's immediate needs' than their Pākehā neighbours.[14] That said, from the late nineteenth century, Māori women were increasingly encouraged to take responsibility for family meals, and in 1904 the government's Māori health officer, Dr Māui Pōmare, called for girls' cooking classes to be established in every native school in the colony. 'Latin and geometry may add culture to our modern lasses,' he wrote, 'but in my humble opinion more time should be devoted to the art of cooking a good wholesome meal. Have this done, and the girls will be of more use to society.'[15]

Arapera Blank (Ngāti Porou, Ngāti Kahungunu) wrote in 1974 that this stage of 'weaning into a dual society' raised challenges for many whānau.

It was one thing to survive as a member of a group in which three or more generations of a family nurtured the strong and the weak, as was the custom; it is another and more exacting task to manage as a small unit of father, mother, and children, where the sole responsibility of satisfying its physical needs is that of the parents.[16]

With incomes often at a subsistence level, it required 'versatility in all spheres' to ensure that the physical needs of the family were catered for, and that children could succeed socially and academically.[17] This exacting work was increasingly framed as the 'sacred duty' of Māori women, and in 1939 Mīria Pōmare suggested that the foundation 'of any strong and virile race' lay in the care of a mother for her child.[18]

Good plain cooks and providers

Mrs Pollock of Waihi considered it men's responsibility to 'make the wilderness blossom'. In fact, producing food for strong and virile youngsters also required women in rural districts to perform a variety of laborious tasks. For Pākehā, the qualities of responsiveness and adaptability, so central to the work of care, encompassed a range of practical tasks that would otherwise not have been within the cultural definition of ideal womanhood. As Claire Toynbee suggests in *Her Work and His*, 'the colonial helpmeet, the "really useful" woman, was still an important image of rural femininity' in the early twentieth century – although other scholars have noted that there was a 'tension between the values and needs of rural communities and the growing power of domestic ideology'.[19] Many Pākehā women managed these seemingly contradictory expectations by framing their work both inside and outside of the home in terms of the welfare of the family, enacting a pragmatic form of family care that incorporated a diverse range of roles and responsibilities. Most Māori communities, meanwhile, relied on labour from all members, and Māori women worked indoors and out, at home and away, in order to provide food for the whānau.

The Associated Countrywomen of the World noted in their 1936 publication *Food in the Country Home*:

> In general, the farm wife's interest ranges over the following field: what can she get from the farm, from her kitchen garden, orchard, dairy, poultry-run, or from the stock kept? How can she even it out over the year, so as to have sufficient at all times and not too much at some times? How can she use it and put it on the table?[20]

Two men and a woman butchering a cattle beast on Armstrong's farm at Becks in Central Otago, date unknown.

Unknown photographer, ref: 00.234, Central Stories Museum and Art Gallery, Alexandra

A woman and child sit in a field, surrounded by sacks and kete full of potatoes. Mataatua, Whakatane District, c1920s.

Unknown photographer, ref: PAColl-8841, Alexander Turnbull Library, Wellington

Women in rural districts, in addition to being primarily responsible for cooking, produced, processed and preserved food for domestic consumption. In the photo above, for example, an unknown woman is helping to butcher a cattle beast on Armstrong's farm at Becks in Central Otago – overseeing the business of feeding from paddock to plate. Men and children did intersect with these processes at various points, but it was women who took primary responsibility for household provisioning, planning for seasonal shortages and easing 'the trial of reduced income' by carrying out the 'cutting and contriving that so frets the nerves and tries the brain'.[21]

For those who were unused to rural life and its 'manifest earthiness', feeding the family under these conditions could be a daunting prospect.[22] Teacher and author Mary Scott, who moved to a farm near Te Awamutu in 1914, wrote in her 1966 autobiography that:

> Roads in the King Country were then so bad, land so poor, and settlers so few that you had little hope of obtaining supplies unless you carted them yourself. And when you did bring them home they looked alarming. I had never before seen a hundred-weight of flour, and it dismayed me to know that my own pair of hands would have to turn all that into bread and cakes, and that that seventy-pound bag of sugar would all be needed for jam and bottling which I should have to cope with.
>
> Even more perturbing was the sight of a whole sheep hanging in a safe under a shady tree, for of course refrigerators were unheard-of, and electric power a distant and ever-retreating mirage for at least thirty years of my country life. It was revolting to think we were going to eat all that, and worse to realise that I had to cook every chop of it.[23]

Her neighbour Mrs Griffiths gradually initiated Mary into many of the 'mysteries' of her new life, and by degrees she became 'what is unflatteringly described as "a good plain cook", with the reputation of supplying excellent meals'.[24]

The instrumental work of feeding was physically taxing and required practical skill as well as financial prudence. Relative self-reliance became a badge of honour for many rural women, and 'tin-opener' cooks were much maligned in magazines of the era. A 1932 feature in *The Dairy Exporter* named tin-opener cooking alongside nagging and a lack of daintiness as the three 'virtues' men did not want to see in their wives, although the following year another contributor to the magazine noted that '[t]here must have been moments in the lives of most of us when a tin of tongues in the pantry was worth a dozen running about on the hills'.[25] The 'harried helpmeet' did sometimes need to rely on conveniences such as tinned food but this was not to be encouraged, for, in the words of Te Awamutu woman Pamela Harrington, running to the shops for emergency provisions was 'resorting to city tactics' and letting the whole side down en masse.[26]

For women in rural districts, feeding the family came with a particular set of cultural expectations around self-sufficiency and adaptability that urban women did not necessarily share. They were also isolated from stores and other services, and far less likely than those in towns and cities to have electricity in the home. The introduction of the refrigerator, electric stove, motorcar and sealed roads in the early decades of the twentieth century signalled dramatic changes to provisioning processes, but the effect of those changes would not be fully felt in country areas until after World War II. In the meantime, women continued their work using only rudimentary equipment, hoping that 'the same Providence that provide[d] up-to-date farm implements and costly stock would peep into [their] domain and see the conspicuous absence of anything in the line of modern conveniences'.[27]

In many rural Māori communities, income levels covered only essential subsistence needs and there was little cash available for even basic household amenities, let alone electric ovens and refrigerators.[28] The photo opposite, for example, shows a woman bent over an outdoor cooking fire in the early twentieth century, splashing water onto a steaming container of hot stones. Mihipeka Edwards, born in 1918 and raised in Manakau in the Horowhenua district, recalled in *Mihipeka: Early years* (1990) that she lived in a nice house, according to the standards of the day, although her grandmother still cooked over an open fire and, she could not help but notice, the neighbouring Pākehā houses were nicer still.[29] It was not until 1935 that the Native Housing Act introduced a housing loan scheme for Māori, but although this provided assistance to some, substandard housing remained a serious issue for many decades.[30] The Maori Women's Welfare League, established in 1951, identified housing as a central concern and dedicated a great deal of energy to raising domestic standards, but a decade later the census found that nearly 30 per cent of Māori homes still had no hot water, and 38.1 per cent relied on a coal or wood stove for cooking.[31]

The work of feeding thus demanded of rural Pākehā and Māori women a great deal of time and physical exertion, and they sometimes expressed

An unknown Māori woman cooking outdoors, location unknown, 1910s–1920s.
George Bourne, ref: PH-ALB-327-p10-1, Tāmaki Paenga Hira Auckland War Memorial Museum

resentment when they were denied the conveniences other women enjoyed. The compensation for these difficulties, it was said, was that rural people had greater access to 'the fundamentals of healthy growth', and could raise their children with the fresh air, vigorous exercise and plentiful food that were so necessary to their health.[32] Various surveys conducted by the Department of Health in the 1920s, however, found serious deficiencies in rural diets, attributed not to the availability of good food but to its incorrect distribution and preparation.[33] The 1926 report of the director-general of health noted that 'the struggle of life in the backblocks' took a heavy toll on children, many of whom were required to work long hours, had inadequate rest and were given 'food wrongly balanced, monotonous, and hastily prepared'.[34] Two years later, a survey of rural school children found that 14 per cent were underweight and that 30 per cent suffered from 'subnormal nutrition'.[35] A later study of 213 Māori households noted that the daily diet of most families was 'high in carbohydrate, short in first-class protein, lacking in vitamins, especially fat-soluble ones, and deficient in minerals'.[36]

Health officials were by this time well aware that 'correct nurture is the basis of sound public health', and they therefore concluded that 'maternal efficiency' was of vital importance to the future of the Dominion.[37] There were already some public education programmes on nutrition and diet in place, but the number and scope of these programmes increased significantly in the 1930s and 1940s. Various agencies and organisations set about establishing new channels of adult education; they attempted to reach even the most isolated women and to teach them that feeding the family meant not only producing meals but ensuring that those meals were nutritionally balanced and contained all the elements necessary for good health. If, as philosopher Annette Baier suggested in her later work on the ethic of care, 'persons are essentially successors, heirs to other persons who formed and cared for them', then those tasked with the maintenance of the family faced a new set of challenges in the early twentieth century.[38] What we might term 'nutritive care' became a key component of the work of feeding, as women took responsibility for bequeathing their successors with healthy bodies and minds.

Arming the family for the battle of life

In New Zealand, as in other Western nations in the early twentieth century, there was a proliferation of official health and education services that aimed to standardise health care both inside and outside of the home and to impose the 'rationality' of science on domestic activities. As numerous scholars have noted, the weighty responsibility for family health fell primarily on women, who were subject to 'policing' by a number of newly created professional groupings.[39] Rural women's geographic isolation did not preclude them from this official observation, and the establishment of the district and school nursing services alongside the Plunket Society meant that by the 1920s 'European women with children could expect regular visits from government-sponsored "experts"' offering all manner of assistance and advice.[40]

The Society for Promoting the Health of Women and Children (the Plunket Society), founded by Dr Frederic Truby King in 1907, is perhaps best known for providing information on the feeding and care of babies; but the society's advice to New Zealand mothers also included guidance on infant and child nutrition. 'The child who is fed on suitable food,' Truby King's wife Bella King wrote in 1910, 'will become a more vigorous, better-developed adult than one who, beginning with his birth and continuing throughout the entire period of his growth, is given only food possessing indifferent tissue-building qualities.'[41] The Kings and their supporters, who took the name Plunket in recognition of their founding patron, worked tirelessly to ensure that as many women as possible had access to up-to-date dietary information; and the society, as well as employing a league of dedicated nurses who visited homes all over the country, used the press to spread its gospel. By 1913, Plunket was distributing almost 200,000 copies of the 'Our Babies' column every week, with regular features on topics such as the benefits of brown bread over white, the causes of constipation, and the digestibility and indigestibility of particular foods.[42]

In rural Pākehā communities the work of the Plunket Society was bolstered by the establishment of a Backblocks District Nursing Scheme and a School Medical Service, both of which had a mandate to cast light on dietary deficiencies and to promote healthy homes. Established in 1909 and 1912 respectively, these services provided additional troops 'in a major campaign against national unfitness', using an extensive 'propagandist armamentarium' to target uneducated mothers.[43] One district nurse commented in 1913 that 'the dieting of children is as mismanaged with these people as it is possible for it to be', and the Department of Health seemed to share this attitude.[44] Its 1924 publication *The Health of Children, With Special Reference to Food and Feeding* ends with a note that 'in view of the very grave damage done to the rising generation by faulty food habits, all medical and dental officers, nurses, and school-teachers are expected to do their utmost ... to inculcate better and more rational habits in regard to food and feeding'.[45]

Māori communities had their own band of devoted medical missionaries, employed by the Department of Health to spread the message of scientific motherhood and instill Pākehā ideas about diet, sanitation and child-raising in the Māori home. Māui Pōmare was appointed native health officer in 1901, and in addition to surveying the sanitary conditions of Māori communities he provided education on 'the five great causes of the Maoris' decay – viz., the home, clothes, foods, sterility, and disease'.[46] Pōmare himself acknowledged that the work required 'the dissolution of time-honoured customs, the tearing-down of ancestral habits and teachings, [and] the alteration of Maori thought and idea', but nevertheless he found in many of the communities he visited a real desire to learn.[47] The Pākehā nurses employed under the 1911 Native Health Nursing Scheme did not encounter such a receptive audience, and they quickly learnt that to be successful they would have to 'respect the Tapu of all sects' and see things from 'the other chap's point of view'.[48] They offered practical lessons in cooking and dressmaking, and delivered lectures on topics such as 'how to feed and care for the children' and 'how health must be improved by cleanliness and suitable food'. There was 'no soap-box business at all in them': their goal was to tactfully and gently insinuate their own point of view.[49]

In addition to these health services, from the mid-1920s rural Pākehā women – and to a lesser extent Māori women – had access to a range of dedicated home science education programmes. The 'moving spirit' behind these extension services was Colonel John Studholme, a wealthy Canterbury landowner and a close associate of King's.[50] Between 1905 and 1908 Studholme travelled extensively in the United States and Canada, where he was impressed by the home science courses on offer at many of the agricultural colleges. He provided funds to establish a Chair of Home Science at the University of Otago, and in 1911 the School of Home Science opened under the leadership of Winifred Boys-Smith. Boys-Smith implemented a comprehensive academic course, but when she left in 1920 Studholme looked to replace her with someone who was more devoted to community extension work. His candidate was Ann Gilchrist Strong, an Illinois-born professor of home science who shared his belief that the principles of home science should be implemented in every home. Strong quickly became involved in farm schools sponsored by the Department of Agriculture and the Otago Farmers' Union, and provided vision and support to the founders of the women's institutes and the Women's Division of the Farmers' Union.

Home Science Extension Service staff stand outside the School of Home Science at the University of Otago with a range of their demonstration items, including a dress form, a meat safe and jars of preserves. Dunedin, early 1930s.

Unknown photographer, ref: S15-621f, MS_1517_064, Hocken Collections, Uare Taoka o Hākena, University of Otago

In 1928 Strong applied to the Carnegie Corporation of New York for funds to establish a Rural Extension Service. She explained in the application that

> It is the fate of most [rural women] to have not only to rear their children, and carry on single-handed the whole work of the house, but more often than not to provide meals for hired labor as well as for their families ... With little previous training for the work and inadequate equipment poorly arranged, many break down, become prematurely old, or persuade their husbands to abandon the farm and move to the city. The success of the Dominion depends on the success of its farmers, and the farmers' success depends upon their health and contentment. The responsibility for healthful, sanitary homes, adequate diet and happy family life lies largely with the women folk.[51]

The corporation awarded £1500 per annum for five years. This enabled the school to implement a range of outreach programmes that included biweekly radio broadcasts, a series of 'boxed lectures' containing the written and practical materials necessary for specified home science courses, and an advisory service.[52] Additionally, home science experts contributed informative articles to magazines and newspapers, thereby giving women all over the country ready access to advice and recipes for creating balanced, health-giving diets.

As well as reaching isolated Pākehā women, Strong was committed to extending home science education to Māori families. After touring the rural districts north of Auckland in 1936 she wrote: 'We owe a great debt to the Maori people who have lost their traditional way of living, and have been unable to adjust themselves to modern life.'[53] The Carnegie Corporation provided an additional £100 to subsidise the training of Ngāti Porou nurse Emere Kaa in home science principles, and after she had completed a one-year course she was employed by the Education Department to act as a 'Maori apostle of Home Science'.[54] In 1936 Kaa toured native schools delivering lessons to students and their parents; one principal noted that she aroused more enthusiasm in a week 'than any pakeha would arouse in years'.[55] The reason for this fervour, Elizabeth Mountain Ellis and Helen Mountain Harte suggest, was that Kaa made home science relevant to the environment and resources of Māori communities – for example by substituting Roquefort cheese tarts and asparagus vol-au-vents with kaimoana stews and soups.[56] Despite this success, the scheme did not extend beyond Kaa's tour, and although Māori women could still access home science lessons through the Women's Institutes, many felt 'too diffident or self-conscious to confess the inadequacies of their homes to a group of Pakeha women'.[57] The Maori Women's Welfare League was later founded to address this concern, and as J.C. Sturm wrote in 1954, the organisation was held together 'simply by the feeling, well, here we are, all in the same boat, what can we do about it?'[58]

Women in rural districts, Pākehā and Māori alike, were inundated with advice about diet and nutrition in the early decades of the twentieth century as a variety of state and social reform institutions waged war against the 'frying-pan, white-bread-and-jam brigade'.[59] Letters to contemporary publications suggest that some mothers shouldered the responsibilities of nutritive care with diligence and solemnity, implementing the advice of the experts to the best of their ability. 'Farmerette', for instance, reported to the readers of *The Dairy Exporter* in 1938 that her neighbour, a mother with several small children, devoted all her time to their care, dutifully 'preparing their food in the right way ... cooking it aright, studying vitamins, airing bedding and

'Mrs Wereta' (a pseudonym) photographed in front of the wood range at her home in Ruatoria, 1964.

Ans Westra, ref: O.022142/1, Museum of New Zealand Te Papa Tongarewa. Reproduced courtesy of Suite Gallery, Wellington

This photograph was one of a number published in Ans Westra, *Washday at the Pa*, a book originally published by School Publications Branch of the Education Department in 1964. The publication was severely criticised by the Maori Women's Welfare League for its representation of Māori living standards, and all 38,000 copies were subsequently withdrawn from circulation. New Zealand society in the 1960s equated social worth with domestic modernity, and the league objected strongly to the depiction of Māori as pre-modern. See Barbara Brookes, *A History of New Zealand Women* (Wellington: Bridget Williams Books, 2016), 306–07.

clothing, and keeping a watchful eye on their manners generally'.[60] When the mother was asked about her motivation, she explained that the family was too poor to be able to set the children up in business, but by giving them 'clean, healthy bodies and minds' she felt she was giving them 'a good start in the battle for life'.[61]

In general, however, rural women – Māori or Pākehā – seem to have resisted dietary change and continued to cook meals that were familiar and convenient. In 1935 home science advisor Violet Macmillan wrote that because country women considered themselves good cooks they were often unenthusiastic about dietary instruction. As a result, meals in rural homes were usually lacking in variety and deficient in vegetables. Although country women certainly baked 'splendid cakes and pastry', Macmillan noted, they did not give enough attention to 'general meals'.[62] Similarly, the writer of the Plunket page in *Home and Country* magazine scolded readers in 1939 'for gross ignorance on the subject of proper food and feeding' and bemoaned the fact that 'old prejudices die hard and slowly. [M]any are deaf because they won't hear and blind because they won't see, [and] children continue to be given unsuitable food at unsuitable times from the time they can walk.'[63]

Historian Margaret Tennant argues that, among other concerns, 'nutrition was becoming one area where there were almost too many "experts"', and that this made the discourse on diet and health diffuse and even contradictory.[64] 'Anybody with a nodding acquaintance with dietetics,' wrote a Christchurch medico in 1937, 'rushes into print on vitamines ... diet appears to be one subject upon which anybody can pose as a specialist and "get away with it".'[65] As this suggests, the voice of the expert was not always the loudest, and advertisers were particularly adept at harnessing the prestige of science to meet their own needs.

Katherine J. Parkin explains in her study of advertising and gender roles in modern America that the regulation of patent 'cure-all' medicines at the end of the nineteenth century coincided with the emergence of the convenience food industry, and 'food advertisers adroitly positioned their products as the best solution to the illnesses they claimed were plaguing Americans'.[66] The New Zealand packaged food industry followed suit, offering vague promises about the 'elements of perfect nutrition' contained in their products.[67] In a 1917 advertisement for Milk Oaties, for example, consumers are assured that 'Milk Oaties are richly nutritive and very easily digested'; they are

A 1917 advertisement for Milk Oaties which suggests that providing 'nourishing, health-giving food for her family is the first care of every mother' and that, for that reason, 'thousands of housewives' choose 'richly nutritive' Milk Oaties.

Sun (Christchurch), 8 June 1917, 5. Papers Past, National Library of New Zealand packed in a 'dust-proof, germ-proof package' and are 'absolutely untouched by hand'. Advertisements for Creamoata porridge promised nothing short of every essential for good nutrition in its proper proportion, and Marmite was proclaimed to be 'richer in vitamin-B than any other foodstuff known to science', aiding the digestion and utilisation of other foods in addition to its own 'positive nutritive power'.[68] In this context, the question 'What shall we have for dinner?' no longer implied 'a choice between nothing and something, as under the precarious conditions of primitive life or the equally uncertain chances of extreme poverty'; rather, as a member of the Home Science Extension Bureau wrote in 1930, it indicated 'bewilderment amidst a wealth of materials for man's delectation' such as the world had never seen before.[69]

Contradictory or confusing information no doubt did bewilder some rural women, discouraging them from adopting new ingredients and cooking techniques, but their reluctance to accept dietary reform also reflected their material conditions. Most rural people lived almost entirely on what they could grow or gather themselves, supplemented by a limited range of essentials such as flour and sugar. This left little room for culinary experimentation, and precluded many households from purchasing the more nutritious – but also more expensive – products available. 'V.W.' reflected on these challenges in a letter to *The Dairy Exporter* in 1936, explaining:

> I commenced baking bread over 20 years ago, starting with 50lb. of flour per month, which quantity had to be increased as the family increased and grew, until I used 200lb. of flour in five weeks, and for a number of years it remained at that. The number of loaves consumed by this family must be considerable, and now our food experts tell us that bread is not the staff of life it is commonly supposed to be, but, on the contrary, we would be healthier without it. What a lot of time I must have wasted, but how can one feed a large family, and put up lots of lunches without a good supply of bread, unless one uses scones, cakes, etc. which are more indigestible. I give up the problem and go on baking, supplying plenty of vegetables and fruit to counteract the evil of the acid content of the bread.[70]

Some health professionals, such as Emere Kaa, tactfully adapted their message to suit these challenges, but in general it seems that dietary reform had to wait for material improvement.

The final, and perhaps the greatest impediment to the implementation of home science principles was that advisors prioritised the recipes over the results, and disdained 'the proof of the palate'.[71] This created difficulties at mealtime, as 'Isabella' wrote in 1938:

> dainty food is eyed with distrust by men, while undisguisedly nutritious meals bring disapproving wails from the children ... Is it any wonder that I prepare three square meals a day with as little trouble to myself as possible, vainly hoping that out of a well-mixed diet someone will some day assimilate enough vitamins to generate a ray of appreciation for the poor old cook![72]

Dietary experts tended to speak about cooking as an activity performed in isolation, forgetting that the work of feeding by its very nature implied 'a relatedness, a sense of connection with others'.[73] Part of the work of feeding the family was taking into account individual preferences and household expectations, and interweaving 'the rather mundane business of the food itself with more fundamental aspects of group life'.[74] Food that provided nourishment and nutriment also had to tickle the palate and content the consumer, demonstrating a different but no less important form of care.

Regarding 'her teapot as a mighty force'

In her 1991 book *Feeding the Family: The social organization of caring as gendered work*, Marjorie DeVault argues that the reality of a family 'is constructed from day to day through activities like eating together', and that those charged with the work of feeding are enabling family interaction as well as producing meals.[75] Although DeVault's analysis is based on a contemporary sociological study, there is evidence to suggest that women in the early twentieth century were aware that meals served this function, and considered emotional care an important aspect of the work of feeding. As 'Alter Ego' of Clinton, Southland wrote in 1941, 'love cooks plain meals, and tries to slip in the time for an "extra special" dainty that is somebody's favourite ... Love keeps an open door, [so] all in sundry are welcome to come in and share a meal.'[76]

This comment reflects an expressive form of domesticity that gradually gained acceptance in the early 1900s as a new set of parental expectations stressed the importance of childhood dependence. Children, it was felt, needed to be able to play and learn without having to work, and parents needed to support them emotionally and materially through this vital phase of life.[77] These expectations added a more affective dimension to the ideal of domesticity in which household work was reconfigured as a labour of love and the home as a place for the emotional and physical development of the child.[78] In practice, only the relatively affluent were able to adhere to these new standards; as Rosemary Goodyear explains in her thesis 'Sunshine and fresh air', most rural families could not afford to raise children who did not contribute economically. Although rural people loved their children as much as others did, she argues, 'the style of parenting in the countryside did not promote open affection and indulgence of children'.[79] In this context, the provision of good meals and 'extra special dainties' was a relatively unobtrusive way of demonstrating love and emotional care without disrupting the practical organisation of farm life.

Judith A. Campbell, who moved to Takapuna as a child in 1941, recalled in her autobiography that, for her mother, 'feeding the family was a major task', but that she made the effort to provide family favourites as well as 'normal farm fare':

> as well as six or seven of us, there was the live-in farm boy, the local school teacher, Gwen Rew, who lived with us and, once a month, the herd tester. As we killed much of our own meat, roast mutton and chops were common fare, followed inevitably by shepherd's pie made from the minced-up cold mutton. Pudding was automatic, with junket made from the still-warm milk straight from the shed, swimming in cream and cinnamon sugar; custard; milk jelly; lemon sago; bread and butter pudding and, of course, our favourite – lemon meringue. As a child I remember that I was going to give my husband lemon meringue pudding every night when I was married. On Sundays jelly was a special treat, as was cake for afternoon tea. Normal fare was hot scones, pikelets, rock cakes, fruit loaf and anything that would fill working men during the day.[80]

Mihi Edwards' kui also expressed her caring through food: she enlisted the help of a Pākehā neighbour so she could make Mihipeka the new foods she knew she liked. At one particularly memorable meal the family had roast pork 'cooked like Pakeha kai', followed by pudding and custard, and Mihi enjoyed it so much that she ate until she could barely walk. Then her 'beloved kui' said to her, 'Mihi, I also know how to make cake, so you will have a nice lunch when you go back to school next week. I also have some nice napkins to wrap your lunch in. My friend showed me how to make them.'[81] In that moment Mihi recognised the compromises her grandmother had made in order to express her love: the meal made manifest the extent of her kui's care.

If providing children with their favourite foods was a way of demonstrating affection, mealtimes were even more important for maintaining marital harmony. Regular columnist 'San Toy' wrote in *The New Zealand Dairy Produce Exporter* in 1929 that

> the truly happy woman is she who cheerfully regards her teapot as a mighty force, and whose meal hours provide a regular succession of most alluring mysteries – glad surprises. The most weary and disgruntled of men would buck up at the sight of his guardian angel with a teapot in her hand and care would fly before the seductions of her sandwiches and cake.[82]

Rural wives seem to have given a great deal of thought to this aspect of feeding the family, and countless articles in the women's pages of agricultural magazines reiterated the message that the way to a man's heart was through his stomach. If, as was suggested, 'digestive troubles accounted for 99% of this world's ills', then women, by the careful and wise planning of meals, could set them right.[83]

This applied not only to familial relations but to 'rents in the fabric of friendship'.[84] Just as the dinner table at Manuka Point Station accommodated family and workers, many women were responsible for feeding large groups of friends, neighbours, labourers and extended kin, caring for the health of the community by extending hospitality to all. For Māori in particular, the practice of manaakitanga (hospitality and kindness) was fundamental to the sharing of food, and it enhanced the mana of the provider while ensuring the physical and mental health of the recipient.[85] Tūhoe tohunga Hohepa Kereopa explained in an interview with historian Paul Moon:

> One of the things that needs to be talked about, Paul, when you are talking about food, is the concept of manaaki. We were told to manaaki ... When you saw someone going past on the road, you'd karanga them, and offer them a cup of tea. And when they accepted your offer, you would race around trying to figure out how you were going to get a cup of tea. And our people have always said, even if it's just a cup of water, the most important thing is that you offer it.[86]

In Pākehā communities, meanwhile, a policy of 'open house and loaded board' applied.[87] The breaking of bread together served to establish and cement personal relationships, which in turn facilitated other forms of social and economic cooperation. In this context the provision of care extended

Dinnertime at Manuka Point Station, 1943: (from right) owner Laurie Walker, farm worker Ted Porter, Ted's wife (and the cook) Grace and their daughter Shirley. John Dobree Pascoe, ref: 1/4-045899-F, Alexander Turnbull Library, Wellington

beyond the home to encompass a broad network of people, and mealtimes could be reconstituted as rituals of community formation and consolidation. Women had to plan for these occasions or – in the case of unexpected visitors – adapt to them, making sure everyone present felt welcome and satiated. Through effective use of the teapot, women could indeed wield a mighty force, drawing together the family and community by facilitating a fundamental aspect of group life.

Conclusion

Dan Davin's 1949 novel *Roads from Home* depicts rural Southland in the
1930s and, evoking the personal experiences of the author, provides stirring
insights into the daily rhythms of the rural community. In one scene, sisters
Norah and Nellie sit together enjoying a quiet Saturday afternoon. Nellie
indulges in a moment of self-reflection:

> She spread [her hands] out in front of her, strong and red. Her life, the
> milking twice a day, the pig-buckets stoutly lifted above the squealing
> snouts, the scrubbing-brush driving its daily quota of dirty suds over the
> linoleum, the swing of the axe on the red-pine stump, the clothes-stick
> thrusting at the heavy union underwear that writhed in the open-air Orion
> boiler, the hoe-thinning in the turnip paddock, the knife that sliced the
> swedes when the morning's frost cut sharpest, and the hard tug that had
> pulled children on to the skids of life and shoved them forward to live with
> her own force, all this was worn there ...
>
> They leaned back in their chairs again ... Saturday afternoon was a good
> time for them. This meeting was a weekly routine but it was a break all the
> same, a deliverance from that other and daily routine which ate their lives
> while they used their strength in seeing that others ate and slept.[88]

Davin recognised that the work of feeding others was one of the primary
responsibilities shaping the lives of rural women, requiring from them an
enormous expenditure of physical strength and emotional energy. The
labours highlighted here, worn into Nellie's hands through decades of
drudgery, are the most visible aspects of the work of feeding the family, and
for many women – particularly those in rural areas – these instrumental tasks
changed little in the early decades of the twentieth century. Although a range
of modern domestic technologies and convenience foods were available,
those in the country continued to rely on the resources they could produce
themselves, ploughing any spare cash into the improvement of the land.
Women paid the price for a more hopeful future, persevering with their open
fires and coal ranges while looking forward to the day when the prosperity of
the farm would be reflected in their homes.

The practical tasks of producing food and preparing meals were not the
only types of work involved in feeding the family, however; and the nature
of women's 'shadow labour' changed dramatically between 1900 and 1940.
Modern domestic ideologies burdened rural Pākehā and Māori mothers

with a new set of expectations and anxieties as they took responsibility for the physical health of their children and the social harmony of their families, marriages and communities. The context in which the work of feeding was performed thus shifted significantly, altering the way women thought about their work and the way it was represented to them by others. By noting the 'invisible' elements of the work of feeding – the planning and preparation that daily meals require – these broad changes in the nature of ideal domesticity and family life are revealed, and the complicated responsibilities inherent in the work of care are made manifest.

Notes

1   'Well balanced meals', *Otago Daily Times,* 7 November 1930, 15.
2   Ibid.
3   Emily K. Abel, *Hearts of Wisdom: American women caring for kin 1850–1940* (Cambridge, Massachusetts & London: Harvard University Press, 2000), 60.
4   Marjorie L. DeVault, *Feeding the Family: The social organization of caring as gendered work* (Chicago & London: University of Chicago Press, 1991), 35.
5   Ibid.
6   Julia T. Wood, *Who Cares? Women, care, and culture* (Carbondale & Edwardsville: Southern Illinois University Press, 1994), 88–102.
7   Abel, *Hearts of Wisdom*, 43.
8   DeVault, *Feeding the Family*, 118. See also Phyllis Herda, 'Ladies a plate: Women and food' in Julie Park (ed.), *Ladies a Plate: Change and continuity in the lives of New Zealand women* (Auckland: Auckland University Press, 1991), 151.
9   'Science of meals', *New Zealand Herald,* 8 August 1934, 5. The idea that preparing meals is one of the primary ways women 'do' gender is explored in DeVault, *Feeding the Family*, 118.
10 For more on this see Barbara Brookes' chapter in this volume.
11 'The best means of making the Women's Institute of real benefit to the rural areas of New Zealand', *Home and Country*, 1 September 1934, 6–7.
12 Correspondence, *Home and Country*, 1 March 1938, 9.
13 Rawinia Higgins rāua ko Paul Meredith, 'Te mana o te wāhine –Māori women – Atua and tipua', Te Ara – the Encyclopedia of New Zealand, www.TeAra.govt.nz/en/te-mana-o-te-wahine-maori-women/page-1
14 Barbara Brookes & Margaret Tennant, 'Maori and Pakeha women: Many histories, divergent pasts?' in Barbara Brookes, Charlotte Macdonald & Margaret Tennant (eds), *Women in History 2: Essays on women in New Zealand* (Wellington: Bridget Williams Books, 1992), 45.
15 Department of Public Health, Report of Dr. Pomare, Health Officer to the Maoris, *Appendix to the Journals of the House of Representatives* (AJHR), Session I, H-31, 1904, 58.

16 Arapera Blank, *For Someone I Love: A collection of writing* (Auckland: Anton Blank Ltd, [2015]), 124.

17 Ibid.

18 Department of Health, *The Maori Mother and Her Child* (Wellington: E.V. Paul, Government Printer, 1939), 7.

19 Claire Toynbee, *Her Work and His: Family, kin and community in New Zealand 1900–1930* (Wellington: Victoria University Press, 1995), 92; Kathryn Hunter & Pamela Riney-Kehrberg, 'Rural daughters in Australia, New Zealand, and the United States: An historical perspective', in Ruth Panelli, Samantha Punch & Elsbeth Robson (eds), *Global Perspectives on Rural Childhood and Youth: Young rural lives* (New York; London: Routledge, 2007), 58.

20 Lady Howard & Sholto Watt (eds), *Food in the Country Home: 500 tested recipes from all the World* (London: Associated Countrywomen of the World, 1936), 6.

21 Elizabeth Hollard, Reminiscences, qMS-0989, Alexander Turnbull Library (ATL), Wellington.

22 Elvira Begg, *Low Country Liz: An autobiography* (Mosgiel: John Begg, 1991), 12, q511022, ATL.

23 Mary Scott, *Days That Have Been: An autobiography* (Auckland: Longman Paul, 1966), 98–99.

24 Ibid., 58.

25 'Between ourselves', *Dairy Exporter*, 1 April 1933, 61.

26 Pamela Harrington, 'Programme 100 – You too might make a farmer's wife', recorded 21 February 1965, Open Country Sound Recordings, OHColl-0002, ATL.

27 'Between ourselves', *Dairy Exporter*, 29 April 1932, 74.

28 Blank, *For Someone I Love*, 124.

29 Mihi Edwards, *Mihipeka: Early years* (Auckland: Penguin Books, 1990), 21–22.

30 Angela Wanhalla, 'Housing un/healthy bodies: Native housing surveys and Maori health in New Zealand 1930–45', *Health and History* 8, no. 1 (2006), 115.

31 Barbara Brookes, 'Nostalgia for "innocent homely pleasures": The 1964 New Zealand controversy over *Washday at the Pa*', in Barbara Brookes (ed.), *At Home in New Zealand: History, houses, people* (Wellington: Bridget Williams Books, 2000), 248.

32 Department of Health, Annual Report of Director-General of Health, AJHR, Session I, H-31, 1926, 36; see also Correspondence, *Home and Country*, 1 March 1938, 9.

33 Department of Health, Annual Report of the Director-General of Health, AJHR, Session 1, H-31, 1926, 27.

34 Ibid., 36.

35 'Report on the Health Conditions and Environment of Rural School-Children in Certain Districts of New Zealand,' Department of Health, Annual Report of the Director-General of Health, AJHR, Session 1, H-31, 1928, 76.

36 Maori Health File, Harold B. Turbott Papers, 88-059-2/09, ATL. See also Department of Health, Annual Report of the Director-General of Health, AJHR, Session I, H-31, 1940, 52–53.

37 Department of Health, Annual Report of Director-General of Health, AJHR, Session I, H-31, 1926, p. 36; Department of Health, Annual Report of the Director-General of Health, AJHR, Session 1, H-31, 1936, 27.

38 Annette C. Baier, 'What do women want in a moral theory?', *Nous* 19 (1985), 85, reprinted in Mary Jeanne Larrabee (ed.), *An Ethic of Care: Feminist and interdisciplinary perspectives* (New York & London: Routledge, 1993), 19–32.

39 Margaret Tennant, '"Missionaries of health": The School Medical Service during the inter-war period', in Linda Bryder (ed.), *A Healthy Country: Essays on the social history of medicine in New Zealand* (Wellington: Bridget Williams Books, 1991), 128.

40 Alexandra Helen McKegg, '"Ministering angels": The Government Backblock Nursing Service and the Maori Health Nurses, 1909–1939', MA thesis, University of Auckland, 1991, 138.

41 'Our babies', *Press*, 4 January 1910, 3.

42 Erik Olssen, 'Truby King and the Plunket Society: An analysis of a prescriptive ideology', *New Zealand Journal of History* 15, no. 1 (1981), 11. See, for example, 'Our babies', *Press*, 25 July 1910, 2; 22 November 1910, 5; 26 April 1913, 6.

43 Tennant, '"Missionaries of health"', 131, 130.

44 'A tough year in the backblocks', *Kai Tiaki: The journal of the Nurses of New Zealand*, 1 July 1913, 30.

45 Department of Health, *The Health of Children: With special reference to food and feeding* (Wellington: W.A.G. Skinner, Government Printer, 1924), 16.

46 Raeburn Lange, *May the People Live: A history of Maori health development 1900–1920* (Auckland: Auckland University Press, 1999), 139, 150.

47 Department of Public Health, Report of Dr. Maui Pomare, Health Officer to the Maoris, AJHR, Session I, H-31, 1902, 61.

48 'Maori health nurses', *Kai Tiaki: The journal of the Nurses of New Zealand*, 1 July 1928, 40.

49 Ibid.

50 Ian Carter, 'Most important industry: How the New Zealand state got interested in rural women, 1930–1944', *New Zealand Journal of History* 20, no. 1 (1986), 29.

51 A.G. Strong, quoted in Tanya Fitzgerald & Jenny Collins, *Historical Portraits of Women Home Scientists: The University of New Zealand, 1911–1947* (Amherst, New York: Cambria Press, 2011), 92.

52 Alison Clarke, draft chapter from forthcoming history of the University of Otago, held by the author, University of Otago, Dunedin.

53 Helen Thomson & Sylvia Thomson, *Ann Gilchrist Strong: Scientist in the home* (Christchurch: Pegasus Press, 1963), 158.

54 Elizabeth Mountain Ellis & Helen Mountain Harte, 'The health work of Emere Makere Waiwaha Kaa Mountain', in Sandra Coney (ed.), *Standing in the Sunshine: A history of New Zealand women since they won the vote* (Auckland: Viking, 1993), 102; Department of Health, Annual Report to the Director-General of Health, AJHR, Session I, H-31, 1936, 6.

55 H. Snelling to Mr Ball, 22 February 1936, BAAA 1001/142a, Maori Schools, Archives New Zealand, Auckland, quoted in Ellis & Harte, 103.

56 Ellis & Harte, 'The health work', 103.

57 J.C. Sturm, 'The Maori Women's Welfare League', *Te Ao Hou* 3, no. 1 (Spring 1954), 8.

58 Ibid.

59 Tennant, '"Missionaries of health"', 133.

60 'Between ourselves', *Dairy Exporter*, 2 May 1938, 110.

61 Ibid.

62 'Country Education: Scheme in Canterbury, Home cookery criticised', *Auckland Star*, 5 September 1935, 13.

63 'The pre-school child, "building materials"', *Home and Country*, 1 October 1939, 49.

64 Tennant, '"Missionaries of health"', 147.

65 'Medical notes', *Home and Country*, 1 September 1937, 20.

66 Katherine J. Parkin, *Food is Love: Advertising and gender roles in modern America* (Philadelphia: University of Pennsylvania Press, 2006), 160.

67 Advertisement for Creamoata, *Evening Post*, 21 April 1928, 14; see also Catherine Cooper, 'The business of breakfast: A history of the Flemings "Creamoata" Mill, Gore, 1877–2001', BA (Hons) research essay, University of Otago, 2011.

68 Advertisement for Marmite, *Auckland Star*, 18 May 1926, 17. Advertisement for Creamoata, *New Zealand Herald*, 25 July 1931, Supplement, 7.

69 'Well balanced meals', *Otago Daily Times*, 7 November 1930, 15.

70 'Between ourselves', *Dairy Exporter*, 1 April 1936, 70.

71 Laura Shapiro, *Perfection Salad: Women and cooking at the turn of the century* (New York: Modern Library, 2001), 68.

72 'Between ourselves', *Dairy Exporter*, 1 February 1938, 63.

73 DeVault, *Feeding the Family*, 39.

74 Ibid., 54–55.

75 Ibid., 39.

76 'What makes a house into a home?' *New Zealand Journal of Agriculture*, 15 July 1941, 80.

77 Rosemary K. Goodyear, '"Sunshine and fresh air": An oral history of childhood and family life in interwar New Zealand and with some comparisons to interwar Britain', PhD thesis, University of Otago, 1998, 2.

78 Toynbee, *Her Work and His*, 184.

79 Goodyear, '"Sunshine and fresh air"', 204.

80 Judith A. Campbell, *Between the Kitchen and the Creek,* 2nd edn (Warkworth: Chappell Printing Ltd, 2004), 22.

81 Edwards, *Mihipeka*, 65.

82 'The best advice I can give my daughter to ensure a happy married life', *New Zealand Dairy Produce Exporter*, 18 April 1929, 72.

83 'The perfect wife', *Dairy Exporter*, 1 April 1938, 87.

84 Jean Boswell, *Dim Horizons* (Christchurch: Whitcombe & Tombs, 1956), 108–09.

85 Sophia Beaton, 'A contemporary Māori culinary tradition: Does it exist? An analysis of Māori cuisine', MA thesis, University of Otago, 2007, 127–28.

86 Paul Moon, *A Tohunga's Natural World: Plants, gardening and food* (Auckland: David Ling Publishing, 2005), 84.

87 'Winter is here', *New Nation Magazine*, 1 June 1932, 103.

88 Dan Davin, *Roads from Home,* ed. & introduction by Lawrence Jones (Auckland: Auckland University Press, 1976), 7, 10.

7

STITCHING THE GENERATIONS TOGETHER:
Clothing and care

Barbara Brookes, Katie Cooper, Heather Devere,
Jane McCabe, Bronwyn Polaschek, Margaret Tennant
& Angela Wanhalla

The sun bonnet / HEATHER DEVERE

A garment that symbolises the links to caring through my mother's family is a cotton bonnet. Five generations are connected through the relationships of aunts and nieces, single women, solo mothers and widows. Made in about 1893, probably in India, the bonnet is designed to protect a child's face from the sun. It is beautifully made of white cotton with intricate embroidery around the brim. We do not have a record of who actually made the bonnet, but we do know that the person who originally wore it is my great-aunt, always known as 'Girlie' although her given name was Evelyn Mary Davies.

In 2017 the bonnet was given by my aunt Julie in Britain to my sister Hazel to take back to the United States for my aunt's great-great-niece – and my great-niece – Saoirse, who is pictured here wearing the bonnet at the age of one. The photo was taken by my niece Liefke, mum of Saoirse.

So here is a garment made with care, as a way of caring for a child's health and to protect her from the sun. It is carefully preserved by Girlie's niece Julie, who attached a label with the date and original wearer of the bonnet, and passed on via Hazel at a time when the three of us were together in Britain arranging care for our mother, who was seriously ill in hospital. Hazel carefully packed the bonnet into her case to take it back to the United States to give to her daughter who will care for the bonnet, taking it out of the tissue paper only to take a photo as requested by her aunt (me) in New Zealand, to illustrate a book on care.

But there is more to this story of caring. My great-aunt Girlie never married. Her mother was widowed and was left penniless when Girlie was seven years old. We think that her mother's brother, Uncle Jack, a chemist, may have helped with her education, and when Girlie left school she became a health visitor in London. She saved up to train to become a doctor. Girlie told Julie that she had to pass every exam as they cost £8 each, which was a lot of money in those days. Girlie became the first doctor in our family, and was one of the first 'lady' doctors in London, where she worked with mothers and babies, continuing right through the war when London was being heavily bombed. She died in 1975 at the age of 84.

I'm the next 'doctor' in the family – but my PhD is in politics and does not link me so closely to caring as did my great-aunt's qualifications. I am pleased to have this opportunity to acknowledge Girlie.

The lure of the fabric department

MARGARET TENNANT

'Let's go buy some 'terial': this, I was told by my mother Coral, was the basis of one of my first and most frequent demands for a shopping trip, long before I could properly pronounce the word. The pleasures of the fabric section of Cobbes' department store were early impressed on a little girl of the 1950s, as was my mother's shared delight and her willingness to create pretty dresses for an only daughter.

The smell of new fabrics hanging gracefully on stands, all the better to feel their textures and drape; the promise of the colour and partially obscured patterns of others tightly wrapped on rectangular forms and stacked behind the counter; the colourful button cabinet, with its tubes of shanked and flat buttons; the ribbons and laces waiting to be cut by the yard – all these were part of an experience shared with my mother. For her, as for many women of her time, sewing was an expression of care for family as well as an outlet for personal creativity. With a whir of her Elna sewing machine (a revered new variety with interchangeable disks for embroidery and other fancy stitches) she would translate the chosen Simplicity or Butterick sewing pattern into her own interpretation of the latest junior fashions.

My mother's handiwork found expression in 1950s dresses with gathered skirts and painstaking details such as handmade belts and buckles. I am wearing a typical version in the photograph here, and my brother's cable-knit jersey signals my mother's equivalent prowess with the knitting needles. Hers was a generation of women who had learned to sew and knit for themselves and for others from necessity, but who had access to a far wider range of fabrics and embellishments than their own mothers had, and whose children expected more than one 'good' dress and a couple of others to be worn and reworn day after day. 'Hand-me-downs' were still common, as were garments remade from adults' clothing, but mothers of the 1950s were also likely to be required to make ballet tutus, school uniforms, party dresses and everyday clothes. Their skills enabled their children to participate in a social milieu without standing out in an awkward way. (I was reminded of the democratising effects of mothers' dressmaking skills by the story of a widow whose children attended Remuera Primary School in the 1950s and 1960s. It was, even then, one of the 'better' schools in Auckland. Her strategy was to wait for her children after school, all the better to observe what others were

wearing. She then recreated garments that would enable her own offspring to 'fit in' without revealing the household's limited income.)

Home sewing today is more often a matter of creativity than of necessity, as cheap imported goods minimise the differential between fabric purchases and ready-made garments. Cobbes' department store is long gone, as are many of the specialist fabric shops, but the shared pleasures remain of fabric and pattern selection, of imagined end product – even if imperfectly realised. I more often sew for my mother now, as I have marginally better vision than she does. Shared forays into chainstores such as Spotlight are informed by reviews on sites such as patternview.com. Here the idealised images and elongated drawings on the covers of sewing patterns are countered by photographs of the end product on real women's imperfect and varied bodies: we are forewarned! The interpretation of the pattern takes on a global dimension, as does the sharing of knowledge and sewing tips. More constant is the pleasure of sewing for another, of helping them to feel better about themselves through the wearing of a personally made garment. And now the chance to repay, at least minimally, the care that went into the construction decades ago of the ballet tutu, the fancy-dress costume, the gathered pinafores tied at the back, and the dress with its neat Peter Pan collar.

The craft of bonding / BARBARA BROOKES

I have the top still: a knitted bodice with a lacelike pattern. It is a work of love that my mother Hannah made for me when I was 15. Perhaps I'd seen it in one of the two magazines that came weekly into the house – the *New Zealand Woman's Weekly* and the *English Woman's Weekly*. I must have asked her to make it, and she obliged. It was slightly revealing (gaps between the front buttons) and required a specially bought maroon bra to go under it. Why do I still have that too? Perhaps because it was a particular luxury: to buy an undergarment especially to go with an outer garment. To throw it out would seem to deny the cost of the gift.

My mother made many of my clothes, whether cotton dresses or knitted cardigans and jumpers. She transformed a white, frilly, pintucked bridesmaid's dress that I wore for my cousin's wedding into a simple and daring halter top for a school ball (I worked on my suntan for that occasion).

I have a strong memory of her at the sewing machine by day and with knitting needles in hand at night. And then there were the ballet tutus: managing the tulle and fixing it in place. Was this a competition for the mothers of the ballet-class girls? I was always proud of mine but completely oblivious to the skill involved in wrestling the fabric into the form.

I made some clothes as a teenager, mostly simple muslin 'hippy dresses' with colourful bodices. Mum must have taught me some skills but I would never have attempted anything complicated. In order to keep my connection with my sister (11 years older than me) after she married and had her own home, my mother organised for us to attend a sewing class together. I made my most complicated garment there – a blouse – but I'm not sure I ever wore it (though I remember the fabric).

Mum taught me to knit, and she joked that the only knitted item that she saw my first child wearing in photographs was the one I had made, rather than any of the 10 she had made. It gave her pleasure that my husband wore her knitted jerseys long after her sons had abandoned the trials of washing woollen garments for easy-care fabrics. Apart from my teenage top, I have two warm jerseys of complicated patterns that she made for me. I rarely put them on now but having them in the drawer is a reminder of her pleasure in seeing me wearing something she had lovingly crafted and which, she knew, gave me delight.

Giving warmth to others / ANGELA WANHALLA

Homemade cardigans and jerseys were a ubiquitous part of my childhood. Our family photos attest to their ever-present place in our lives, especially the numerous pictures of us kids modelling the latest creation, usually positioned in the garden or on the front steps of the house, sometimes with our arms outstretched in order to show it off to best effect. This parade of itchy jumpers, as my sister likes to describe them, were usually handed down among the kids, recycled and refashioned into something else or given away.

My mother Coralie knitted daily when I was a kid. It gave her pleasure and enjoyment, as well as time to think and contemplate. But what is often thought of as an ordinary, everyday, domestic and familial practice is rarely recorded on camera. We do have photographs of wool gathered together in a pile in the corner of the living room, or laid on the sofa, cast aside because Mum's attention was called to other domestic matters. But these were not recorded deliberately; instead they sit at the edge of the frame or in the background of an image, offering a salutary reminder of an overlooked aspect of women's caring work.

We have few photos of Mum knitting, so that's why I am particularly fond of this image from the early 1970s of her sitting outside her flat enjoying the sun and knitting what is probably a jersey for my dad, Stan. Mum was expert in crafting plain and patterned jerseys, cardigans and jackets, but she also experimented with different textures, using angora wool for her own cardigans. She liked trying out different styles, too, such as artificial cable knitting. There is this photograph of me – aged about four – wearing a cable-knit cardigan adorned with beautiful gold buttons.

Mum and her sisters were taught to knit by their mother Ngaire, who also taught them how to sew on a treadle machine. But it was knitting that Mum loved, maybe because she grew up watching her mother having to sew items to bring in extra money for the family during the 1950s and early 1960s. Ngaire made mattress and pillow covers for Clegg Brothers, a Christchurch factory. This was heavy-duty, highly skilled work on a large industrial machine that took up much of the space in the family sunroom, which doubled as a bedroom. This machine loomed over my mother's childhood. It was often linked with danger: none of the children were allowed to put their hands near it for fear of getting their fingers caught in the machinery. But it was also an important part of domestic life for

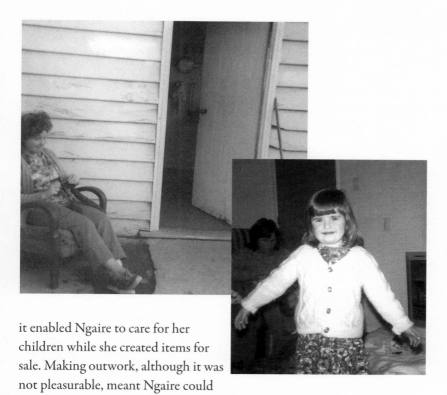

it enabled Ngaire to care for her children while she created items for sale. Making outwork, although it was not pleasurable, meant Ngaire could support her family: it brought in extra money to pay bills and, sometimes, to buy special treats for the kids. A noted dressmaker, she enjoyed designing and making items to fit. In addition to making clothes for her family, on weekends and evenings she designed and made clothes for neighbours and friends measured with patterns she created out of newspaper.

My mother also enjoys creating and designing her own items, or working with patterns and adapting them to suit. Like Ngaire, she made clothes for her children and the wider family – summer dresses on her Bernina sewing machine; booties, woollen hats and other baby clothes, jumpers, cardigans and jackets. Like Ngaire, she gets immense enjoyment from creating practical and beautiful clothing for others to enjoy. That's why I love this picture of her soaking up the heat of the sun while taking pleasure from creating an item that will give warmth to others. Although these days she makes blankets rather than the cardigans and jerseys that were a constant feature of my childhood, knitting remains an important part of her daily routine. And she still prefers knitting in the sun.

Rosemary's teddies / BRONWYN POLASCHEK

After my first child was born, a package arrived. It was from Ringmer, Lewes in England. The handwriting was familiar – I had seen it on Christmas cards for many years, as well as on the much-anticipated £5 cheques that arrived on birthdays when I was a child. Inside the package was a knitted teddy with a smart blue jumper, red trousers, and a red scarf around its neck. The eyes, nose and mouth were stitched on with black thread.

My great-aunt Rosemary knitted this teddy. I imagine her in her living room, surrounded by books and knick-knacks, family photographs on the wall, the television playing her favourite quiz show *Countdown* on Channel 4. She would have the lamp on, a small glass of cider next to her, a sweet evening treat, and she would be knitting, pausing only to fast forward the advertisements (she always videotaped *Countdown* so she could do this). I imagine her days later cycling to her local post office, labelling the package and paying for the postage with coins from her worn leather purse, and sending it off – across the seas to the city of Wellington where her older sister had chosen to make her home many years before. I think of the time taken for the knitting, sewing and sending.

Rosemary knitted many of these teddies for children she knew – my own, my niece and nephews – and for some she did not; she regularly donated them to the Red Cross. The teddies are one small part of a life spent caring for others. Rosemary was a mother and raised her two children, Andrew and Katharine. She nursed her beloved husband Freddie for months before he died of leukaemia at 35. She moved cities to care for her mother Freda for several years before her death, and later looked after her aunty Mar (Margery) when she became ill. In her retirement Rosemary travelled to New Zealand to care for her older sister – my grandmother Betty – during the months before she died.

It was through this act of care that I got to know my wonderful G.A.R. (Great-aunt Rosemary). Over time in Wellington and later in London when I lived there, she taught me many things. Drink the water from steamed or boiled vegetables so as not to waste the vitamins. Wash the pots when they're still warm. Used stamps should be kept. A person should get some exercise every day. Everyone leaves food out for the birds; instead, leave water. Opera is best when it's not sung in English. You're never too old to get a little bit drunk.

Rosemary died on the 3rd of January 2017. A few months before her death my son was having difficulty settling in his first year at school. His kind teacher asked me to email an image of something special for him to look at if he felt unhappy. Ned chose his Rosemary teddy. The photograph I took was pinned up for the rest of the year in Room 7. This object, made for him by an elderly woman he did not get to meet but who loved him all the same, became his reminder of care and home.

A big night out / JANE McCABE

My mother Barbara didn't have a job outside the home when I was growing up. This was an era (late 1970s, early 1980s) when many of my friends' mothers worked part-time, which meant they had more 'bought things'. We had less money and our household was quite old-fashioned: we were the last to get a TV, we cooked on a coal range and did our washing in an old wringer machine. And everything was homemade. We had peppermint slice rather than Toffee Pops, flagons of delicious plum sauce rather than plastic bottles of Watties, and a storehouse packed with preserved fruits and jams. I remember the first time I tasted tinned peaches and realised that some of those storebought items that I had been coveting were actually quite tasteless compared to what we had at home.

Mum made almost all of our clothes (for me and my three siblings), including school uniforms. I went to a Catholic school and she made the pleated pinafore and knitted the jersey. I have many memories of special clothes she made for me; and I also remember the fraught experience of Mum teaching me how to knit when I was seven (the panic of the dropped stitch, the frustration of fingers slow and unable to mimic her smooth click-clacking) and to sew when I was 10 years old.

But my most special memory is of matching outfits Mum made for us to go to the Russian ballet. I started ballet lessons when I was four years old, and for the next eight years Mum undertook the close work of making costumes for competitions. I marvel now at the countless hours she spent sewing thousands of sequins and gathering fiddly nylon netting into shape; and her patience with preparations backstage – stitching me into my ballet shoes, using matchsticks to apply stage makeup around my eyes, and composing a perfect bun.

My father Don took a part, too, making props like the tree trunk in this photograph. He made the trunk from heavy cardboard, but the bark was real: he cut pieces of bark off firewood and glued them individually around the outside. Dad made the little crêpe-paper-and-cardboard vege garden, too. I can still remember the 'aaawww' of the audience when I would crawl out of the trunk at the start of the dance, wiggle my nose and pretend to eat a carrot.

One day when I was about seven, Dad came home from work and announced that his boss had been given two tickets for the Russian ballet at the Regent Theatre in Dunedin and, knowing that I took ballet lessons, the

boss had offered them to us. Mum's response was to get sewing. She made outfits for us both from a fabulous (very seventies) pink and purple paisley fabric, a soft brushed cotton. Mine was a long, sleeveless dress with a bolero jacket. Best of all was the white fur trim around the bolero neckline.

We don't have any photographs from that night, or of those outfits. I must have worn it on other occasions but all I remember is the feel of that fur trim and the thrill of the dimmed lights as we walked into the upper circle of the Regent Theatre. It was incredibly special. Memory tells me that as we took our seats in our matching dresses, we got a similar 'aaawww' response to my 'Peter Rabbit' character appearing out of the trunk.

Homemade to ready-made / KATIE COOPER

My brothers and I grew up with two working parents: my mother Nicki and father Murray met as young teachers in 1982 and they worked together at Gore High School for almost 15 years. Our family routine was shaped around the working day, and my parents called on a range of people and services to provide care and support while they were teaching. As children we had nannies and were enrolled in daycare and after-school programmes. A cleaner came to our house for two hours a week to do some of the housework; and Mum, an excellent cook, was always unapologetic about using shortcuts at dinner time.

Perhaps the convenience she most eagerly embraced, however, was ready-made clothing, for although she was taught the rudiments at high school she was not by inclination a seamstress. Most of the outfits we wore day-to-day were storebought, many of them selected from the mail order catalogue of Pumpkin Patch, a New Zealand clothing company established in 1990. In the photo below, taken on my grandparents' lawn in about 1994, my brother and I are both wearing ready-made outfits in matching white and blue.

For special occasions we did sometimes wear handmade clothing, sewn with great skill and care by my maternal grandmother Yvonne. For her, sewing, knitting and embroidering were a source of pleasure; she was by this time comfortably retired and able to complete needlework projects at her leisure.

This was not always the case, of course: in the 1960s and 1970s Yvonne was a working mother without recourse to commercial childcare,

convenience foods or affordable ready-made clothing. With four children still at home she went back to teaching, and her youngest (later my uncle), who was not yet in school, sat quietly at the back of her classroom while she worked. At the end of each school day she prepared a two-course meal from scratch, and she worked into the evening making dresses, shorts, shirts and jerseys. In the photo above, taken in about 1963, my mother and my uncle are both wearing handmade outfits, and Mum's hair is tied back with leftover scraps of fabric.

The strain of working full time and caring for a family without a broader support network took its toll. Mum still remembers watching a bowl of rhubarb fly across the kitchen as my grandmother, thoroughly exhausted, reached the end of her tether. Soon after, Grandad purchased the family's first automatic washing machine.

Women's participation in paid employment, which grew markedly in the later twentieth century, resulted in a reconfiguration of both the formal and the informal labour force. Gradually, aspects of family care were brought into the marketplace and commercialised, and this allowed women like my mother to prioritise their careers in ways that those of my grandmother's generation could not. Weaving together my mother's experiences as a child and as a parent, these family photographs represent two very different caring contexts and signal a major transformation in the lives of many working women.

8

'PRIVATE SMITH, OF U.S.A., & MISS BROWN, OF N.Z.':
New Zealand's American war children, 1942–45

Angela Wanhalla

With the departure of American forces imminent, an *Auckland Star* journalist took to the streets in June 1944 to survey local women's views of the two-year occupation. Some women said they would miss the relaxed manner, small courtesies and attentiveness of the Americans: '[They] are so appreciative of one's company. They know how much a girl appreciates the gift of a corsage to match her frock, how much she likes having a man stand when she enters a room, and push in her chair at a table. Many New Zealanders are inclined to forget these things.'[1] One 18-year-old referred to the social stigma attached to women who fraternised with US servicemen; she claimed that some New Zealand men refused to date a girl who had been courted by an American. 'I won't humble myself before them in order to be taken out,' she said.[2] Another respondent expressed similar sentiments, but added that she appreciated the new models of intimacy that American men had introduced. New Zealand women now had heightened expectations of how a romance would play out:

> Of course, lots of girls will miss the Yanks! But don't forget that many of us have been loyal to our own boys all the time. That is sometimes forgotten by our men, and it is often forgotten, too, that New Zealanders overseas have broken engagements with girls here and married British and Canadian girls. Most of the girls will be quite happy again with their own men, though they might demand a little more attention and thoughtfulness than they used to, but that is all to the good. Most New Zealanders have something to learn from the Americans in the way of manners and poise, though there are other attributes in which they are better behaved than Americans. And

New Zealanders have this big advantage, for most of us. We know them. We know their background, their customs, their outlook. It will be only natural for us to settle down together, and the American boyfriend of our youth will just be someone about whom we shall tell our grandchildren.[3]

The American forces left a much deeper impact on the lives of some: over 1500 New Zealand women married American servicemen. These couples were further bound together by the children they shared. Additionally, American servicemen fathered an unknown number of children born from a variety of circumstances – as a result of legal marriages, wartime affairs or brief liaisons.[4] Many women, the *NZ Truth* newspaper noted, were 'likely to find that the father of her prospective family is over the seas and far away before the truth of her condition dawns'.[5]

During wartime there were many routes to lone motherhood, including divorce, abandonment, forced separation, widowhood and wartime affairs.[6] Relationships were vulnerable to rupture at any moment. Units were liable to be moved to forward zones at short notice and marriages were made in haste, if at all, leaving couples contemplating uncertain futures. As Susan Moller Okin has argued, within marriage women were emotionally and economically vulnerable, but in international relationships those vulnerabilities were heightened, especially the anticipation of separation and possible divorce.[7] A marriage certificate may have provided legal recognition for cross-border relationships, but it did not necessarily equate with marital security in the future, or even access to financial support as a US war dependant.

This chapter examines the fate of the mothers and children US servicemen left behind, focusing on the financial and social support they were able to access during the war and in the immediate postwar years. It distinguishes between the informal shadow labour provided by families, who formed a vital network of care for lone mothers, and the formal care support available from the government, social welfare organisations and the US military. Patterns of formal care are easier to trace as women were required to submit documentation in order to prove eligibility for financial support from New Zealand government agencies. Their correspondence provides evidence of the limited options available to lone mothers. Unwed mothers were particularly vulnerable. They struggled to obtain financial support from the New Zealand social security system, and their plight was exacerbated by the unwillingness of military authorities to investigate paternity claims lodged against US forces. Military directives, supported by US law, effected gender inequality by enabling soldiers to escape the responsibility of fatherhood, leaving the financial burden and emotional support required for care work to host communities and, especially, women.

American forces in New Zealand

When Japan bombed Pearl Harbor on 7 December 1941, it forced America's entry into World War II. By June the following year New Zealand would become one of the main basing locations for the South Pacific Command Area: a US naval base was located at Devonport on the North Shore in the Waitemata Harbour, several US Army camps were dotted around Auckland, and Wellington and Masterton hosted camps for the US Marines. In total, around 100,000 troops were stationed in New Zealand between 1942 and 1944, although the number of men who passed through the country is likely much larger, given the regular arrival of US naval ships into New Zealand ports that stayed between several days and several weeks.

Military personnel were stationed in the country for days, months or years, and this gave rise to intimate encounters ranging from sexual commerce to romance and love affairs. Couples met at American Red Cross clubs, at chaperoned dances, at hotels and bars, or through friends or family connections. The military authorities encouraged socialising to boost morale, and accepted the reality of intimate relationships, but the prospect of forming any permanent relationship was discouraged. Nevertheless, war heightened emotions and encouraged individuals to think about their future. People 'fell in love very quickly; there was an urgency that gave romance an edge and the instability gave a certain zest to daily life. Virtual strangers made lifetime commitments.'[8] Heightened awareness of life's fragility, and the fleeting nature of the American occupation, inspired fervent declarations of love. US Marine Sergeant Motley wrote passionately about Miss Wilson, for whom he had 'developed an undying love and friendship'.[9] In October 1942, 21-year-old Corporal Dooley, also a marine, sought permission to marry 19-year-old Ellen on the basis that 'I have known Miss Clegg for a period of three months, during which time I have come to love her, so deeply and to such an extent, that I desire, more than anything in this world, to make her my wife.'[10]

Any couple wanting to marry, however, faced the difficulties imposed by the marriage policy adopted by the US Army and Navy in June 1942 (Circular No. 179), which was formulated in response to the mobilisation of US forces to British colonies in the Caribbean where mainly white troops were stationed among predominantly African host communities.[11] Permission to marry was required from a commanding officer, and this system for governing intimate relations 'soon became the norm for American troops stationed across the globe', including New Zealand.[12] When representatives of the US Army, US Navy, US Marines and American Red Cross met at the US Consulate's Auckland office in mid-November 1943 to discuss the marriage policy, hundreds of marriages had already taken place in New Zealand, mostly involving Pākehā women. At that meeting it was agreed the marriage policy would be adhered to, including its racial restrictions, which meant 'permission to marry would not as a rule be granted to American servicemen desiring to marry Maoris predominantly of Maori blood'.[13] This policy was applied unevenly: sympathetic commanding officers sometimes gave their official endorsement to couples, and government directives for churches and registrars to refuse to marry a couple unless the serviceman could produce evidence of his commander's permission were sometimes ignored.[14] Other couples simply cohabited and were regarded as husband and wife by the community. From their arrival until the end of 1944, when the majority of the bases had been closed, 1396 New Zealand–American marriages had taken place.[15] By the end of 1945, 1588 couples had tied the knot.[16]

Although more than 1500 couples legalised their relationships, not all of New Zealand's American war children were born within marriage. During the brief period of American occupation of New Zealand, children were born from a variety of relationships and there were multiple pathways to lone motherhood, including widowhood, desertion and divorce as well as ex-nuptial pregnancy. A lack of statistical data makes it difficult to know exactly how many children American servicemen fathered during their time in New Zealand.[17] Staff at the US Consulate (Auckland) and American Legation (Wellington) who assisted war brides and fiancées with entry permits and transportation to the United States did maintain records on the number of wives and children who took passage, but little is known about the long-term prospects of these wartime marriages, the extent of divorce, or how many women returned to New Zealand with their children.[18] It was not unknown for a serviceman husband to abandon his wife and family in the United States: Sybil, for instance, discovered her ex-serviceman husband 'did not want her' when he failed to meet her and their one-year-old daughter on arrival at San Francisco.[19] With reports of war marriages ending in 'disillusionment' appearing regularly in print media,[20] some brides, already uncertain about how they would be received by their in-laws and anxious about making a new life with a virtual stranger without family support, refused to leave New Zealand.[21] Some husbands failed to initiate the paperwork to enable entry of their wife and family into the United States.

More generally, the divorce rate rose during this period. Among those filing for divorce were increasing numbers of New Zealand men petitioning on the grounds of their wife's adultery; some went so far as to name an American serviceman as co-respondent.[22] Additionally, an unknown number of war brides received American legal papers informing them their American-based husband had instituted divorce proceedings.[23] Divorce was instigated, too, in face of the legal barriers on entry into the United States for those women who were deemed 'racially ineligible' under US immigration laws.[24]

Recognising the difficulties New Zealand women faced in obtaining a divorce from a non-resident serviceman husband, New Zealand's Labour Government passed the Matrimonial Causes (War Marriages) Emergency Regulations 1946, which permitted a woman domiciled in New Zealand to petition for a divorce after a period of six months' desertion or separation. In 1947 the emergency regulations were enacted under the Matrimonial Causes (War Marriages) Act, but the period of desertion or separation was extended to 12 months. As with the 1946 regulations, the 1947 Act also recognised divorce decrees issued in the United States. Politicians were responding to the needs of women like Patricia, whose husband had failed to provide for her and their child for 12 months, nor had she heard from him during that period. While she was concerned about the expense of getting a divorce, Patricia did not want 'to have to wait for three years, as I would, if a separation order were taken out, as I have the opportunity to marry again and make a home for myself and child'.[25]

In addition to those children born within legal marriage there were many who were born outside of marriage. During the period of the American occupation the illegitimacy rate rose: it reached 6.01 per cent of total births in 1944, and fell to 4.93 per cent in 1945.[26] Unfortunately this data reveals nothing about how many of these children had American servicemen fathers. Birth certificates are of little assistance, as an unwed mother was not required to name the father of her child.[27]

Care networks

While it is almost impossible to specify the number of children fathered by American servicemen with New Zealand women from government statistics, other sources provide some insight into the circumstances under which couples met and became parents, as well as the fate of those women and children left behind. In addition to helping unravel what happened to women and children after the Americans sailed, divorce records, newspaper reports on marital breakdown, paternity claims from women and their families now held in US military records, US consular and legation archives and the records of the American Red Cross help make visible formal and informal networks of care. Women had to navigate a number of different organisations: child welfare, social security, the US military, US consular officials and the American Red Cross. The Child Welfare Branch and the Social Security Department were particularly important. They worked closely with the American Red Cross and US consular officials to try to locate men and to 'ensure American servicemen face up to the responsibilities of the children they have fathered in New Zealand'.[28]

In an article in August 1944, *Truth* referred to such couples as 'Private Smith, of U.S.A., & Miss Brown, of N.Z.' The article explained the difficulties women faced in pursuing paternity claims against American servicemen, which involved navigating multiple layers of bureaucracy. First 'Miss Brown' had to write to 'Private Smith' to inform him of her pregnancy or the birth of a child. But in order to undertake a paternity claim, a woman needed to be able to locate the serviceman, who might be 'over the seas and far away'. American consular officials were one source of support, and were regularly called on to trace a putative father so that the paternity claim process could begin. In August 1945, one woman wrote to the American Legation, hoping to track a serviceman in the navy:

> I met him here in my hometown in New Plymouth between Jan 11th and 19th. The affair happened at a party and [I] found that he had got me into trouble, however I didn't realise until it was too late, for he had already left

New Zealand for the South Pacific. Unfortunately I gave birth to a baby girl on Oct. 25th 1944 and he's responsible for her ... Manny was a nice boy but only we fell in love the wrong way.

She had submitted an application to the Social Security Department for financial assistance, but was informed she had to see 'if they could get any information to the father of my child before they could pass a benefit for his child'.[29]

In order to receive financial assistance an unwed mother was required to testify in writing to her circumstances and to name the father. If a woman was unable to obtain confirmation of paternity, she faced considerable barriers to accessing social security. This continued when the Labour Government introduced the universal family benefit in 1946, as children born out of wedlock were not initially eligible.[30] According to historian Margaret McClure, Digby Smith, chairman of the Social Security Commission, believed the father of an illegitimate child was responsible for providing financial support, not the state.[31] Further, it was a woman's responsibility to pursue the father for maintenance – a situation that was made more difficult when he was an American serving overseas at an unknown location, and the military command was little interested in helping to resolve paternity claims against its troops.

On receipt of Miss Brown's letter the serviceman was required to take it to his commanding officer, who then made contact with the American Red Cross to request an investigation. The young woman was interviewed by a representative of the Red Cross and was required to secure a doctor's certificate attesting to her condition. After gathering all available evidence, a report from a Red Cross field investigator was sent to the serviceman's commanding officer. If he admitted paternity, arrangements would be made for a portion of his pay to be allotted to the mother as child support. If the serviceman denied paternity, Miss Brown was advised to seek financial assistance from the Social Security Department, who then liaised with the American Red Cross to make investigations on their behalf.[32]

During the American occupation of New Zealand, the American Red Cross concentrated on providing social services, hospitality and organised entertainment for the troops. After the US forces departed its work increasingly focused on supplying advice and welfare services to local women, initially war brides. In December 1943, William F. Angell, acting field director in Wellington, admitted the US forces had left behind social problems arising from hasty marriages. He noted that the failure of men to adequately provide for their wife and/or child had led to numerous applications for assistance from war brides 'to meet the cost of food, lodging, and other expenses of life'.[33] By the end of 1944 the American Red Cross anticipated an expansion of their role to include paternity investigations where children were 'alleged to have been born of servicemen fathers'.[34] Casework covered deserted wives and lone mothers, and investigations were completed in concert with representatives of the American Consulate in Auckland and the Legation in Wellington, as well as the government's Child Welfare Branch.

Many of the most desperate cases involved young mothers, often without family support. In a letter to the American Red Cross, one woman revealed she was living in a boarding house: 'I have a child 13 months old & am looking for a position where I can have him with me & I find it very difficult to do.'[35] In this instance the US consulate located the errant husband, who refused to acknowledge the child, and nor did he 'desire to have his wife and alleged child come to the United States'.[36] In a separate case Rita had married a US Marine from Oklahoma who 'had not made any arrangements for me to receive any financial support and money was scarce, so I had no choice but to board my precious baby out while I went to work'.[37] One young woman left her husband and child to live with an American serviceman in an Auckland rooming house. In the divorce court she admitted to having a child with her American lover.[38] No further information is available about the fate of her daughter, but it is highly likely she came to the attention of the Child Welfare Branch, which was mandated to ensure the welfare of the mother and child, inclusive of emergency financial assistance, and which provided a range of care options.

During the 1940s child welfare officers took a flexible approach to the 'family', inclusive of unwed mothers.[39] Annual reports of the Child Welfare Branch offer some insight into care arrangements. In its 1944 report, the branch stressed their aim was to 'help the mother keep the infant should she desire', and where possible it turned to relatives to arrange care support.[40] At the end of 31 March 1945, the branch had been notified of 1767 illegitimate births in the preceding 12 months. Of these, 820 infants were in the care of their mothers and 42 were with other relatives, 62 had been placed in state care, a further 280 were in foster homes and 356 had been adopted.[41] Of the 1606 illegitimate births notified to the branch by 31 March 1946, 719 lived with the mother and a further 37 were in the care of other relatives, 62 were in state care, 276 in foster homes and 362 had been adopted.[42] As the data illustrates, although kinship networks were a preferred resource, many women looked to formal adoption.[43]

Although Child Welfare stressed the importance of familial care networks, it was not easy for women to maintain their child alone, especially with limited financial resources. Married and unmarried women called on the services of Child Welfare. A 19-year-old mother married to an American had received no allotment from her husband since March 1945. She had no family living close by, and was 'forced to take up domestic work to support her child whom she has boarded out in a private home at 25/- a week'.[44] Seven weeks after the birth of her child, one unmarried mother placed him in the care of Child Welfare because, as a waitress, she was 'not in a position to assist in maintaining her son'.[45] War brides who later divorced lost access to financial support for themselves and any children as war dependents. One woman had not received an allotment since November 1945: 'I have a small son as well as myself to keep. I am finding it very hard to manage.'[46] 'Unfaithful wives' faced losing custody of their children. As one judge noted in granting custody to the husband, by committing adultery with a US Marine the 'wife as the deserting party was guilty of breaking up the matrimonial home and bringing about the dissolution of the marriage'.[47] For many, adoption may have been the only choice available to them.

Outside of official circles, social organisations provided advice and support, including the New Zealand Eagles Club. Initially established to help prepare war brides for life in the United States, by the mid-1940s it had transformed into an advocacy group for deserted wives. Led by able and energetic women, the club developed a close working relationship with the prime minister, Peter Fraser, and the New Zealand Legation in Washington. By 1947, the Eagles Club 'dealt exclusively with the wives of US husbands who had deserted them': it claimed there were 200 in New Zealand.[48] That year the club appealed for financial support from the public in order to secure legal representation: 'With £2000 we could close every one of our files within three months, knowing every deserted wife who has appealed to us for aid, has been given a fair chance to rebuild her life.'[49] Another important organisation, the Women's War Service Auxiliary, included single mothers within their ambit as well as deserted brides.[50] In the 12 months to June 1946 the organisation successfully obtained financial support for 200 deserted wives and unwed mothers 'from all parts of the Dominion', either from errant husbands or through the family benefit.[51] They served the interests of women like Muriel, who wrote to the American Legation in 1945 enquiring about access to financial support:

> I have been told that single girls in New Zealand who had a child to [a] United States Marine are able to get an allotment from the government to help support the child. If it's true and sufficient evidence in my case could be given I would like to apply for it as I have difficulty in supporting my child. If it is true would you please advise to what I will have to do to get it.[52]

Many of the records cited above showed little interest in the welfare of Māori mothers. During this period the state was expanding its role to encompass Māori whānau, but it focused in particular on monitoring and controlling young Māori women's sexual behaviour in response to their increasing presence in urban centres as a result of the mobilisation of women into wartime essential industries. In the cities Māori women and US servicemen engaged in a variety of intimate relationships, including marriage. Of those couples who married, very few were able to reunite after the war because of US immigration and nationality laws that limited entry to the country on the basis of race. And although Māori women were coming into greater contact with the state during wartime, many whānau remained out of its reach and few women or their families sought consular, military or state support for any US-fathered children. Their absence in the documentary record suggests that they looked to family or friends for support and relied on existing care traditions and practices.[53]

Caring for kin

A young woman in 'familiar' trouble, as a US consular official described it, arrived in his office accompanied by her sister in May 1943. She had kept company with a marine who had promised marriage and 'arising out of this close, confidential and sentimental association, a baby is expected in November or December'. As a consequence the young woman had left her job and was now being supported by her married sister.[54] The shame associated with illegitimacy, abandonment or divorce may have prevented some women from turning to their family for help, but as this case illustrates, others relied on their family for financial and emotional support. Fathers, mothers, siblings, grandparents, aunts and uncles all participated in an informal care economy within intergenerational households. Family members shared childcare and offered security in a time of economic uncertainty and emotional turmoil. One young woman, after the birth of her baby fathered by a US marine, moved in with her aunt who had five children of her own.[55] In another case, after Rita's US serviceman husband deserted her, an aunt supported her through the pregnancy: 'when my daughter was born it was my aunt who took me by bus, train and tram to St Helen's Hospital in Wellington'.[56]

Care was expressed in a variety of ways: it involved accompanying a sibling or daughter to request help from US officials, assistance with the paperwork, and pursuing claims for justice on their behalf. Parents worried about the mental wellbeing of their daughters, and this could prompt them to seek outside assistance. For one mother, her daughter's declining psychological and emotional health was a priority. She had written to the American Legation:

> about 2 weeks ago, about my daughter's allotment, but I have had no reply, I wish you could do something immediately as things are desperate here at the moment, my daughter is talking of going away and leaving the baby, she is getting very depressed and I don't want anything to happen, if you could do something I would be very gratified, please will you reply as soon as you can.[57]

Ivy, who married an American soldier in 1944, had not heard from him since he left for duty in the Pacific shortly after their wedding. In September 1946 her father sought to trace him, as Ivy had had a baby. Although the American Red Cross did obtain his home address in the United States, it had no success in locating him. Ivy was desperately in need of financial support, but her father was anxious about his daughter's emotional and mental health:

> She is making herself ill worrying about him and her future. I would certainly prevent Ivy from going to America now, but if George wishes to come to NZ I would assist him to get a home and a suitable occupation but on the other hand it would be far better if he would take the necessary steps to have the marriage declared void and allow my daughter to make a fresh start in life.[58]

Taking care of family extended to ensuring the financial security of a daughter and her child. Such concerns were at the forefront of parental attempts to secure justice. One father explained to the American consul at Wellington that his daughter had kept company with a US Marine who 'gave her to understand he was very fond of her & I believe he was. They went together some time before she gave way to his desire, eventually finding she was pregnant & he promised to marry her. After a week or two he neglected to come & see her & she heard no more from him.' Unable to locate the serviceman to secure evidence of paternity, and as a single father himself with limited financial resources to provide for his daughter and grandchild, he reluctantly sought help from the consulate.[59]

In the US military and consular records there are many letters from American officials informing women and their families of their inability to provide assistance.[60] In April 1944 a father laid a complaint on behalf of his daughter who had recently given birth to twins fathered by an American serviceman. He contacted the American Red Cross, who informed the American Legation that their communication with the serviceman had not yielded a positive result. The corporal refused to acknowledge paternity 'and wished to consider the case closed'. The young woman's father was informed by the American Legation office in Wellington that if he wanted to take the case further he could write to the commandant of the United States Marine Corps at Washington, DC. 'I suggested this procedure since I have been told both by the Naval Attaché and several personnel officers in the Marine Corps that nothing other than this can be done for persons in the position of this girl, if the serviceman refuses to acknowledge paternity.'[61]

To successfully obtain a military allotment, women were required to obtain documentation to prove paternity. Acceptable evidence included the man's acknowledgement in writing. In addition, a birth certificate had to be forwarded to the appropriate authorities in Washington, DC, along with an application for a dependant allowance. As part of the application, any written documentation supporting paternity had to be supplied, certified by a notary public.[62] Faced with this level of bureaucracy, combined with the difficulties of obtaining evidence of paternity, many women could not pursue their claim. In September 1945 Joyce contacted the American Red Cross seeking their assistance in locating the father of her child. A Red Cross official tracked him down in the United States, but he refused to admit paternity. This information was conveyed to the American consul in

New Zealand, with some regret.[63] 'In these cases we find the tragedy of our helplessness,' wrote the Red Cross official; and he added that in general the serviceman, whether in the United States or in the field, 'is willing to forget his responsibility too easily'.[64]

Families rallied to accommodate the children, and grandparents often took on the role of caregiver. Until she was 13, Lisa lived with her mother and grandparents: 'I had plenty of love. I wasn't short on that,' she recalled.[65] Sandra's Māori grandmother 'raised me right from a baby until she died'; she was 'sent up to my Mum, about a year after my grandmother died', but 'my step-dad didn't want me', so an aunt legally adopted her.[66] Adoption within the family was not uncommon. In another case, Doris, who was Pākehā, 'was adopted by a relative' after the death of her mother.[67]

Whether Māori or Pākehā, the immense social stigma attached to ex-nuptial births, wartime affairs and divorce often generated family silence around paternity, so that many children grew up unaware of the personal cost to their mother of a wartime relationship.[68] Equally, in some cases children were unaware of the difficulties their serviceman father faced in trying to reunite the family.

Servicemen fathers

As far as the US military authorities were concerned, children born of war were regarded as the responsibility of the mother. Underpinning this attitude to American morality is a set of ideals that attached to the US serviceman as a model of American male responsibility, in which American interventionism and presence in overseas territories are imagined and represented as a force for good.[69] Such ideals are aptly represented by Major Gerald Crook (Civil Affairs Division, Department of the Army). He was reported to have said to a 1947 investigation by the Federal Security Agency into social problems arising from the presence of American troops overseas that 'the girls knew what they were doing and that countries need and want increased population as a result of the war'.[70] Children symbolised the virility and strength of the American nation, but they were equally regarded as a social problem and an unwanted economic burden.[71]

Given the fleeting nature of most wartime relationships, combined with the difficulties women faced in locating the servicemen, it is highly likely that many men never knew they had fathered a child. Just as many men who knew they had a child refused to accept responsibility, there were those who did want to marry, especially if their girlfriend was pregnant. In cases where men wanted to play an active role as father to their child, some struggled to return to the South Pacific because of financial constraints. For a small number of couples, race-based immigration and naturalisation laws that deemed that those with less than 51 per cent 'white blood' were 'racially ineligible' to enter the United States severely limited the possibility of postwar family reunification. The American Consulate informed Kitty that she would be ineligible for entry into the United States because she 'was of the Maori Race', but she and Edward still decided to marry, having agreed that on his discharge from the army 'he would return to live permanently in New Zealand'. Edward did not keep his promise: he wrote to Kitty in July 1946 and suggested she petition for divorce, as he was unable to raise the money to obtain passage to New Zealand. 'I will take the blame for it,' he told her.[72] She did so, and obtained a decree absolute in 1949.

American nationality law shaped postwar family reunification, too. Any serviceman father of a foreign-born non-marital child who wished to bring that child to the United States had to meet the requirements set out under the 1940 Nationality Act.[73] According to historian Linda K. Kerber, birthright citizenship (jus soli) is transmitted through the mother, but when an American citizen fathers a child outside of marriage in a foreign territory, in order to obtain US citizenship for that child he must obtain evidence of paternity and agree to provide financial support until the child reaches the age of 18.[74] Furthermore, the serviceman has to meet the requirement of 10 years continuous residence in the United States in section 201(g) of the 1940 Act. In light of these provisions, it has been argued that the 1940 Act reflects a 'construction of fatherhood as legal and motherhood as biological'.[75] Legal historian Manisha Lalwani notes that, in effect, 'Legitimation of paternity was a means by which unwed fathers voluntarily took responsibility for their out-of-wedlock children; in its absence, legitimation acted as a hook by which to burden unwed mothers with care-taking responsibilities'.[76] Given these circumstances it was 'easy for any man to avoid responsibilities', as one mother of a New Zealand woman abandoned by her serviceman husband noted.[77] Equally, a man's opportunity to be a father was constrained by federal law, so that what 'seems like desertion by a father may not have been his choice'.[78] US military regulations and laws, while they constrained opportunities for marriage and placed limits on the possibility of parenthood, also made it possible for serviceman fathers to abrogate familial responsibilities.

Conclusion

For the US military command, wartime intimate relationships were regarded as an inevitable outcome of stationing large numbers of young men in overseas territories for months or years at a time. But for many women in New Zealand, wartime mobilisation changed the course of their lives. Historians have examined the impact of the American occupation on gender relations, noted the effect 'war conditions' had on sexual codes and behaviour, and highlighted the rise in illegitimate births – but the fate of those children and their mothers is still largely unknown. It is with reference to notions of care and care work that their experiences can be uncovered. Paying attention to unwed mothers in child welfare statistics shows that women sought to keep their child and, if they could not, a family member – often the grandparents – took responsibility. When assistance was sought from the state or social welfare organisations such as the American Red Cross and the New Zealand Eagles Club, these organisations sought to respond to the needs of women and their families. But their ability to help was shaped by the willingness of the US military authorities to assist – not to mention the cooperation of the servicemen themselves. Nonetheless, in presenting their cases women demonstrated that they were prepared to make a complaint or to press the issue of American responsibility.

The correspondence surrounding paternity claims brings into relief the enormous difficulties lone mothers faced in obtaining financial support from putative fathers and from a military institution that regarded the social impacts of American occupation as a positive force for good in host communities. Sadly, as the burden of proof of paternity required by military authorities was extremely difficult to obtain and the process was highly legalistic, none of the cases cited in this chapter was successful in obtaining justice. No doubt many women resolved their situation through other means such as adoption, either within or outside the family, or leant on their family for financial assistance and emotional support.

Notes

1 'The Yanks', *Auckland Star*, 26 June 1944, 3.

2 Ibid. This 'sexual sedition' is discussed by Deborah Montgomerie, *The Women's War: New Zealand women, 1939–45* (Auckland: Auckland University Press, 2001), 162–64. See also Sandra Coney, *Every Girl: A social history of women and the YWCA in Auckland, 1885–1985* (Auckland: YCWA, 1986), 230; and Florence Small's account of the prejudicial attitudes she encountered on marrying an American serviceman, in Judith Fyfe & Gaylene Preston, *War Stories Our Mothers Never Told Us* (Auckland: Penguin, 1995), 111.

3 *Auckland Star*, 26 June 1944, 3.

4 It is possible that some pregnancies were the result of coercive encounters. Few sexual assault cases were reported. William Benjamin Miles was court-martialled at the US Naval Base, Auckland, for assault with intent to commit rape and sentenced to 10 years in military prison (*New Zealand Police Gazette*, 8 March 1944, 191). There were likely more instances of gendered sexual violence but the censorship imposed by the government on media reporting of the US forces while they were stationed in New Zealand meant few cases appeared in the press.

5 *New Zealand Truth* (NZT), 30 August 1944.

6 Tanya Evans, 'The other woman and her child: Extra-marital affairs and illegitimacy in twentieth-century Britain', *Women's History Review* 20, no. 1 (2011), 48.

7 See Susan Moller Okin, *Justice, Gender and the Family* (New York: Basic Books, 1989), and Heather Devere's chapter in this volume.

8 Fyfe & Preston, *War Stories*, 13.

9 Edward W. Motley to Commanding Officer, Rear Echelon, First Marine Division, Fleet Marine Force, 12 August 1942, P90-A3, Container 15 in RG313: Naval Operating Forces, South Pacific Area and Force (SOPAC) (Red 179), National Archives and Records Administration, Maryland (NARA).

10 Arthur E.F. Dooley to Commander South Pacific Force and Area, 6 October 1942, P90-A3, Container 15 in RG313 Naval Operating Forces, South Pacific Area and Force (SOPAC) (Red 179), NARA.

11 Harvey R. Neptune, *Caliban and the Yankees: Trinidad and the United States occupation* (Chapel Hill: University of North Carolina Press, 2009), 172.

12 Ibid.

13 Memorandum, 16 November 1943, and Enclosure No. 3 in Despatch No. 127, 5 December 1943, Auckland Consulate Records, Vol. 6, RG84, NARA.

14 For details on these couples see Angela Wanhalla & Erica Buxton, 'Pacific brides: US forces and interracial marriage during the Pacific War', *Journal of New Zealand Studies* 14 (2013), 138–51.

15 *New Zealand Official Yearbook 1946* (Wellington: Government Printer, 1948), 50.

16 Memorandum, Normand W. Redden to Prescott Childs, 12 April 1946, Wellington Legation Records, Part 9, RG84, NARA.

17 A point made by Eve Ebbett in *When the Boys Were Away: New Zealand women in World War II* (Wellington: Reed, 1984), 158.

18 According to Barbara Brookes, one in seven American servicemen deserted their
    New Zealand wife: *A History of New Zealand Women* (Wellington: Bridget Williams
    Books, 2016), 278. In October 1945, US authorities in New Zealand stated the
    divorce rate for New Zealand–American couples was 3.5 per cent: *Evening Post*, 24
    October 1945, 13.

19 'War bride troubles', *San Francisco Chronicle*, 20 April 1946, 5.

20 NZT, 31 January 1945, 5; NZT, 20 March 1946, 2; NZT, 24 April 1946, 25; NZT, 14
    July 1946, 1.

21 For example: 'Vet asks to divorce New Zealand wife', *Portland Press Herald*, 19 March
    1949, 7; 'Bride prefers New Zealand', *Decatur Herald* (Illinois), 4 August 1947, 23. See
    also Ebbett, *When the Boys Were Away*, 162.

22 For instance: NZT, 15 March 1946, 20; *New Zealand Herald* (NZH), 26 May 1943,
    5; NZH, 17 September 1943, 5; NZH, 15 June 1944, 6; NZH, 11 July 1944, 7; NZH,
    30 June 1945, 9. Hayley Brown found that, from 1941, New Zealand men petitioned
    for divorce more often than women: Hayley M. Brown, 'Loosening the marriage
    bond: Divorce in New Zealand, c.1890s–c.1950s', PhD thesis, Victoria University of
    Wellington, 2011, 55.

23 'Divorce laws', *Auckland Star*, 24 October 1945, 3; 'Shocks for American brides
    "dumped" without support', NZT, 7 November 1945, 5; 'Bride's bombshell', NZT,
    20 February 1946, 9; 'Absence made heart grow cooler: Legal history made', NZT, 17
    April 1946, 7; 'Advice to American wives', NZT, 26 June 1946, 11; NZT, 3 July 1946,
    15; 'Divorce under new regulation', NZT, 9 October 1946, 10; 'U.S. Marine divorced',
    NZT, 11 December 1946, 12; 'War marriage', NZT, 23 December 1946, 8; 'Wife's
    rights ignored', NZT, 26 February 1947, 26. 'Marine twotimes his New Zealand wife',
    Long Beach Independent (California), 15 July 1945, 20.

24 See Wanhalla & Buxton, 'Pacific brides' for a discussion of the New Zealand cases.

25 Patricia to Under-Secretary, Justice, 20 September 1946, J1 1575 18/41/13 part 1,
    Archives New Zealand, Wellington (ANZW).

26 *New Zealand Official Yearbook 1946*, 45.

27 In one divorce case the woman had formed a relationship with an American
    serviceman and given birth to a child, but no father was named on the certificate:
    Auckland Star, 16 March 1945, 6.

28 There is a growing scholarship dedicated to children and war, which stresses the legal,
    social and psychological complications experienced by those rejected as 'children of
    the enemy', 'children of collaborators' or designated 'children of the dust', and which
    has examined the high rates of institutionalisation or abandonment, as well as the
    implications of international and often interracial adoption: Kjersti Ericsson & Eva
    Simonsen (eds), *Children of World War II: The hidden enemy legacy* (New York: Berg,
    2005); Brenda Gayle Plummer, 'Making "brown babies": Race and gender after World
    War II', in Emily S. Rosenberg & Shannon Fitzpatrick (eds), *Body and Nation: The
    global realm of U.S. body politics in the twentieth century* (Durham: Duke University
    Press, 2014), 147–72; Yara-Collette Lemke Muniz de Faria, 'Germany's "brown
    babies" must be helped! Will you?': US adoption plans for Afro-German children,

1950–1955,' *Callaloo* 26, no. 2 (2003): 342–62; Sabine Lee, 'A forgotten legacy of the Second World War: GI children in post-war Britain and Germany', *Contemporary European History* 20, no. 2 (2011): 15–81; Lucy Bland, 'Interracial relationships and the "brown baby question": Black GIs, white British women and their mixed-race offspring in World War II', *Journal of the History of Sexuality* 26, no. 3 (2017), 424–43. For the Pacific, see J.A. Bennett & Angela Wanhalla (eds), *Mothers' Darlings of the South Pacific: Children of indigenous women and U.S. servicemen, World War II* (Honolulu: University of Hawai`i Press, 2016).

29 G.B. to American Consulate, Auckland, 20 August 1945, Vol. 8, Box 21, Auckland Consulate General Records, RG84, NARA.

30 Margaret McClure, *A Civilised Community: A history of social security in New Zealand, 1898–1998* (Auckland: Auckland University Press, 1998), 106.

31 Ibid., 107.

32 NZT, 30 August 1944; J.R. Nichols, Assistance Area Director, American Red Cross, Auckland to American Legation, Wellington (undated), Part 14, Box 31, Wellington Legation General Records, RG84, NARA.

33 William F. Angell to Hugo Fischer, Area Supervisor, 13 December 1943, Box 985, Records of the American National Red Cross, 1935-1946, RG200, NARA.

34 Hiram Boucher to J.R. Nichols, ARC, Auckland, 2 November 1944, Part 14, Box 31, Wellington Legation, General Records, RG84, NARA.

35 Mrs B. to American Consulate, 6 May 1945, Part 7, Box 46, Wellington Legation, General Records, RG84 NARA. In her autobiography Sonja Davies wrote of the difficulties she faced as a single mother when the financial support arranged by her American serviceman boyfriend and father of her child suddenly stopped: *Bread and Roses: Sonja Davies, her story* 2nd edn (Auckland: David Bateman with Fraser Books, 1993), 59.

36 Prescott Childs, First Secretary and Consul, to Lt Harold S. Abramson, Army Service Forces, Virginia, 22 August 1945, Part 7, Box 46, Wellington Legation General Records, RG84, NARA.

37 Joan Ellis, *A String of Pearls: Stories from US Marines and New Zealand women remembering World War II* (New Plymouth: the author, 2008), 255.

38 NZT, 6 September 1944, 5.

39 Bronwyn Dalley, *Family Matters: Child welfare in twentieth-century New Zealand* (Auckland: Auckland University Press, 1998), 165.

40 AJHR, E-4, 1944, 4.

41 AJHR, E-4, 1945, 5.

42 AJHR, E-4, 1946, 9.

43 Anne Else, '"The need is ever present": The Motherhood of Man movement and stranger adoption in New Zealand', *New Zealand Journal of History* 23, no. 1 (1989), 47.

44 Superintendent, Child Welfare Department, to Prescott Childs, First Secretary and Consul, Wellington, 12 July 1943; Prescott Childs to Superintendent, Child Welfare, 13 July 1945, Part 7, Box 46, Wellington Legation General Records, RG84, NARA.

45 Superintendent, Child Welfare Department to Director, ARC, Auckland, 10 April 1945, Part 7, Box 46, Wellington Legation General Records, RG84, NARA.

46 Mrs E. to American Consul, 16 February 1948, Box 29, Auckland Consulate General Records, RG84, NARA.

47 NZT, 21 November 1945, 19.

48 *Dominion*, 15 March 1947.

49 'Married trouble', NZT, 3 September 1947, 30.

50 Dominion Secretary, WWSA to Prime Minister's Department, 26 June 1946, EA 1/610 87/12/5 part 1, ANZW.

51 NZT, 26 June 1946, 11.

52 Muriel to Prescott Childs, 16 June 1945, Wellington Legation General Records, Part 7, Box 46, RG84, NARA.

53 For further discussion see Angela Wanhalla & Kate Stevens, '"I don't like Maori girls going out with Yanks": Māori–American encounters in New Zealand', in Bennett & Wanhalla (eds), *Mothers' Darlings of the South Pacific*, 202–27.

54 H.P. Bridge to Field Director, ARC, Wellington, 1 June 1943, Parts 18-19, Box 19, Wellington Legation General Records, RG84, NARA.

55 H.P. Bridge to American Legation, Wellington, 26 April 1945, Part 7, Box 46, Wellington Legation General Records, RG84, NARA.

56 Ellis, *A String of Pearls*, 255.

57 Mrs R. to American Legation, 11 August 1945, Wellington Legation General Records, Part 7, Box 46, RG84, NARA.

58 Mr C. to Minister of Justice, 23 September 1946, J1 1575 18/41/13 part 1, ANZW.

59 Mr K. to American Legation, Wellington, 6 December 1943, Parts 18-19, Box 19, Wellington Legation General Records, RG84, NARA.

60 Plummer, 'Making "brown babies"', 158.

61 Memo by J. Jefferson Jones, III, American Legation, 21 April 1944, Part 17, Box 34, Wellington Legation General Records, RG84, NARA.

62 L.E. Gray, US Naval Attaché to G. V. Hislop, Native Agent, 7 July 1945, Part 7, Box 46, Wellington Legation General Records, RG84, NARA.

63 Clarence V. Lemke, Field Director, ARC to American Consul, New Zealand, 29 January 1946, Part 6, Box 64, Wellington Legation General Records, RG84, NARA.

64 William F. Angell to Hugo Fischer, Area Supervisor, 13 December 1943, Box 985, Records of the American National Red Cross, 1935-1946, RG200, NARA.

65 Lisa, interviewed by the author, 18 February 2011.

66 Sandra, interviewed by the author, 17 December 2011.

67 *New Zealand Woman's Weekly*, 20 February 1984, 95.

68 These silences are discussed by the contributors to Bennett & Wanhalla (eds), *Mothers' Darlings of the South Pacific*.

69 Cynthia Enloe, foreword to Catherine Lutz (ed.), *The Bases of Empire: The global struggle against U.S. Military posts* (New York: New York University Press, 2009), xi.

70 Mabel Coleman, Assistant Director, report of meeting with Miss Pauley, 22 October 1947, Box 1279, Records of the American National Red Cross, 1947-1964, RG200, NARA.

71 Joanne Meyerowitz, 'Louts in uniform', *Journal of Women's History* 26, no. 3 (2014), 134.
72 Divorce File, BBAE 4985/416/1948, Archives New Zealand, Auckland.
73 Linda K. Kerber, 'Birthright citizenship: The vulnerability and resilience of an American constitutional principle', in Jacqueline Bhabha (ed.), *Children Without a State: A global human rights challenge* (Cambridge: MIT Press, 2011), 257.
74 Ibid., 258.
75 Kif Augustine-Adams, 'Gendered states: A comparative construction of citizenship and nation', *Virginia Journal of International Law* 93 (2000–2001), 99.
76 Manisha Lalwani, 'The "intelligent wickedness" of U.S. immigration law conferring citizenship to children born abroad and out-of-wedlock: A feminist perspective', *Villanova Law Review* 47 (2002), 733.
77 Letter to editor, *Auckland Star*, 22 September 1945, 4. Similar sentiments were expressed by another mother in: Letter to editor, *NZH*, 17 October 1945, 14.
78 Pamela Winfield, *Melancholy Baby: The unplanned consequences of the G.I.s' arrival in Europe for World War II* (Westport, CT: Bergin & Garvey, 2000), 36.

9

THE MOTHER ALONE:
Solo mothers in New Zealand cinema

Bronwyn Polaschek

Many of the earliest New Zealand feature films depict unconventional caring arrangements within families. In the opening of director George Tarr's 1914 version of *Hinemoa*, the character Rangi-Uru leaves her husband and children for an extramarital affair, then returns with the child born of that affair to care for her original family.[1] In Rudall Hayward's *The Bush Cinderella* (1928) the heroine's mother becomes pregnant out of wedlock, is banished by her family and dies in childbirth; her daughter is adopted and raised by a poor farming family. Mother characters who become pregnant or care for their children outside of nuclear family units – or, in the case of Rangi-Uru, move in and out of such a unit – are recurring figures in even the earliest New Zealand cinema productions, despite the conservative cultural attitudes to family that prevailed at the time in the rapidly growing colonial population.

This chapter looks at one particular version of these unorthodox mothers: the woman who cares for her children primarily by herself, either by choice or by necessity – the 'mother alone' figure. It explores a group of feature films that include this character, all released since the early 1970s, which represent a distinctive celebration of maternal autonomy compared to other national cinemas. The production of these films coincides with and contributes to changing social attitudes about single motherhood in New Zealand culture. Using various cinematic strategies, the filmmakers highlight the experiences of women who are forced or who choose to mother alone, both historically and in contemporary Aotearoa New Zealand. These films represent alternative possibilities: they replace the injustices of typical heteronormative family structures, as identified by Susan Moller Okin,[2] with female-led and female-centric families. This group of films celebrates the caring work of solo mothers – the responsiveness, sensitivity and patience of these women who are parenting alone, in a neoliberal context where caring as an activity is devalued.[3]

Not all New Zealand films celebrate single motherhood. Indeed, one theme of New Zealand cinema is a deep unease about family relationships, including mothers, expressed for example in the dysfunctional, incestuous family of *Heart of the Stag* (1984) or, more recently, in the tragic coming-of-age film *Rain* (2001).[4] The single mother has been portrayed as destructive, exemplified by the monstrous matriarch Evelyn Cartwright in *The Ugly* (1997), and as damaging, such as the account given by the character Tania Rogers of her negligent mother in *What Becomes of the Broken Hearted?* (1999).[5] Nevertheless the corpus of New Zealand films with sympathetic solo mother figures deserves attention. These films make visible the caring work of mothers who are fulfilling their role alone, thereby challenging conventional understandings of what constitutes femininity, motherhood and care in wider New Zealand culture.

The origins of the mother alone figure:
Gone Up North for a While (1972)

Solo mothers began to feature regularly in New Zealand films in the 1970s, as the second-wave feminist critique of the nuclear family was altering the public discourse around femininity, sexuality and domesticity. The National Film Unit's production *Gone Up North for a While*, directed by Paul Maunder, brought the solo mother to local television screens in 1972: it combined a factual assertion of the statistical reality of illegitimate births in Aotearoa New Zealand in its opening titles with a sympathetic portrayal of the protagonist Patricia, who becomes pregnant outside of marriage but is determined to keep her child despite the many obstacles she faces. From the opening interview in the maternity hospital, as the nurse briskly asks for personal information that Patricia is reluctant to give, to the final questions by an off-screen male interviewer about whether Patricia is being 'sensible', the moralistic concern for the capacity of solo mothers to care adequately

Humanising the solo mother.
Gone Up North for a While, Paul Maunder, 1972, National Film Unit

for their children in wider New Zealand society is clearly expressed. This attitude can be traced historically to nineteenth-century settler society where women, especially mothers, were expected to be supported by men – a legacy that continued into the mid-twentieth century through the lack of government assistance provided to women outside of conventional family units, and the moralising judgements made of such women, with solo mothers remaining at the bottom of what Margaret Tennant has termed the hierarchy of 'deservingness'.[6]

Gone Up North for a While counteracts this social judgement by humanising the abstract notions of 'solo mother' and 'illegitimate child'. It represents the story of one ordinary young woman whom the audience comes to know and like. As Gabrielle Hine argues in her dissertation on popular media, Patricia is portrayed as a 'courageous' woman and a character with 'integrity'.[7] The film challenges the viewer to overturn their perceptions of women who become pregnant and choose to raise children outside of marriage. It depicts the painful consequences of an economic system that fails to provide financial support for women like Patricia. This 'social reform' narrative was an 'audacious, yet timely contribution to the ongoing campaign for women's rights'.[8] Indeed, Maunder has suggested that the nationwide screening of *Gone Up North for a While* contributed to public support for introducing the Domestic Purposes Benefit for single parents the following year, in 1973.[9]

The mother alone and the man alone:
Smash Palace (1981)

A decade later, in 1981, Roger Donaldson's film *Smash Palace* begins with a conventional nuclear family. Al, Jacqui and their daughter Georgie live at the vast, remote Smash Palace car yard. Al is comfortable, and refuses to honour the agreement he made with Jacqui that they would only live at the yard for a few months while he prepared it for sale. Jacqui finds the caryard oppressive: she says the rows of wrecked cars remind her of a 'graveyard'. Eventually she chooses to leave Al, taking Georgie with her.

Donaldson has been identified as one of the new wave of New Zealand filmmakers, a group of male directors born in the 1940s who produced 'action-driven, testosterone fuelled content'.[10] His films and those of directors such as Barry Barclay, John Clarke, Geoff Murphy, Bruno Lawrence and Ian Mune are often based in a rural setting and focus on emotionally inarticulate male protagonists struggling with a sense of dislocation and anxiety.[11] Al in *Smash Palace* is portrayed as an archetypal 'man alone' of New Zealand culture for whom, as film scholar Russell Campbell has said, the dream of fulfilling family relationships is scarcely realisable in practice.[12]

But the film has another narrative thread: its sympathetic portrayal of Jacqui as she tries to communicate with her distant husband, and her terror at his violent response when she moves out. *Smash Palace* depicts the effect of the man alone's behaviour on his family in that his conflicted, interiorised masculinity undermines his capacity to care for his wife and daughter,

The family of the man alone.

Smash Palace, Roger Donaldson, 1981, Aardvark Films, Moviescripts, New Zealand Film Commission

and eventually alienates them.[13] The final shot of the film – of mother and daughter, pushing in to a close-up of Georgie alone – asserts the existence of close family relationships but implies that such intimacy is only possible without the destructive influence of the man alone. It is an image of a mother and daughter bound together by vulnerability, dependence and trust – three core concepts in Annette Baier's philosophical discussion of care.[14] The film concludes with mother–daughter connection, female intimacy forged in spite of male pathos.

The mother alone character needs to be distinguished from the woman alone – a figure represented archetypally in novels such as Robin Hyde's *The Godwits Fly* (1938), Marilyn Duckworth's *A Gap in the Spectrum* (1959), Keri Hulme's *The Bone People* (1983) and in the 1977 film *Solo* directed by Tony Williams. These texts all include female characters whose psychic unease and alienation from society parallels the difficult inner life of the man alone, although the experience of this alienation and its expression are distinctively

feminine.[15] Unlike these woman alone characters, the mother alone figure
– epitomised by Jacqui in *Smash Palace* – highlights the cost to society of
an isolationist culture by showing its effect on those in the domestic setting
– most often, the mother and child or children. In other words, the mother
alone reflects a distinctive version of what film and media scholar Hilary
Radner has described as 'a specifically New Zealand feminine sensibility
conditioned by the hardship and isolation felt to characterise a national
experience that was, at least initially, fundamentally masculine'.[16] But the
mother alone, rather than living out her own version of a solitary life as the
woman alone does, complicates the idyllic myth of 'going bush' by showing
the experiences of those who are left behind. Unlike those individuals, male
or female, who reject a conventional social and domestic setting, the mother
alone is always embedded in social life through her care for and relationships
with her children.

The character of Ada in *The Piano* (1993) is another woman who is
in effect mothering alone, given her alienation from her legal husband
Stewart.[17] Ada cannot choose to exist wholly on the edges of colonial Pākehā
society as her lover Baines does – even if she is viewed by her new community
as strange, and even though her muteness can be interpreted as 'an intuitive
attempt to destroy consensual meaning and meaningful communication'.[18]
Her intimate relationship with her daughter Flora connects her always to
another person. Their closeness – or 'emotional fusion'[19] – is expressed
through their similar costuming and mirrored actions; they even play the
piano alongside each other in various scenes as if speaking with one voice.
Ada's responsibility to nurture and socialise Flora requires her to participate
in community life, such as attending a local play to watch Flora perform.
She is drawn into engaging with wider society through her maternal
responsibilities even though her orientation is to a solitary life. As director
Jane Campion has said, it is Flora who 'maintains a relationship with the
world for both of them'.[20] At the resolution of the film, while Ada's husband/
partner has changed from Stewart to Baines and her beloved piano now lies
at the bottom of the ocean, her daughter Flora remains – the only constant
through the turmoil of her life.

Female-centric families:
From *Ruby and Rata* (1990) to *Apron Strings* (2008)

From the early 1990s solo mothers are portrayed in a number of New Zealand films as actively subverting or rejecting the constraints of the nuclear family: the institution of motherhood premised on a conventional family unit is displaced by a female-centric model of maternal care.[21]

Gaylene Preston's 1990 comedy *Ruby and Rata* features the enterprising and talented solo mother Rata who, in the opening scenes, introduces herself to property manager Buckle as a businesswoman and negotiates assertively for the rent on her new flat to be reduced. After she has secured the deal, we realise Rata's ruse. She moves in, dressed now in far less conservative clothing, and brings her quiet, intense son Willie with her (despite the rule that 'no children are allowed'). Rata's love for her son is clear, particularly in her acceptance of his idiosyncratic personality – for example, his love of light and fire. Rata and Willie work as a team in the film. Rata cares for her son by instilling in him the innovative strategies she uses to get by in a society that creates barriers for solo mothers, especially those like her who wish to pursue creative careers. Eventually Willie learns to 'team up' with the elderly landlady Ruby who lives upstairs, a woman as tough and creative as his mother and one who is also struggling bravely for independence and dignity.[22] Ruby never had children because of a personal tragedy, and she relishes Willie's companionship. The strength of both women, and their caring relationship with Willie, are reinforced when they agree to share a household and the responsibility for Willie after Ruby gifts her house to him. The film resolves with a newly formed family unit of grandmother (Ruby), mother (Rata) and son (Willie) living on the top floor of the house.

Ruby and Rata can be compared to more recent mainstream American romantic comedies such as *Maid in Manhattan* (2002) and *Good Deeds* (2012), in which the protagonists Marisa and Lindsey are both minority working-class solo mothers who clean for a living.[23] However, in these films the heroine eventually marries a wealthy, successful man who cares for her child, thereby reconstituting a nuclear family and implicitly reinforcing an earlier lack in the child's life of a patriarchal role model. Preston's resolution of *Ruby and Rata* is firmly resistant to this conventional fairytale ending, and to the introduction of a father figure. Although the main adult male character in the film, Buckle, does have a short-lived romantic and sexual relationship with Rata, he is conspicuously weak when she needs his support; and while he seems to be helping his great-aunt Ruby in the opening scenes of the film by interviewing prospective tenants, he eventually tries to coerce her into selling her house when she is in hospital. In the final scene of the film Rata has supplanted Buckle in his role as manager of Ruby's downstairs flat: wearing her red business suit from the opening scene, this time it is Rata who interviews prospective tenants as Willie and Ruby watch from above. Without sentimentality, the film concludes with an alternative familial arrangement where the maternal role is shared by two women, one elderly Pākehā and one young Māori, caring for a boy they both love.

The legacy of films such as *Gone Up North for a While* and *Ruby and Rata*, which depict alternative family structures headed by women, is echoed in more recent films. *Topless Women Talk About Their Lives* (1997) ends with Liz, having just given birth, holding her baby surrounded by her closest female friends while, unknown to her, the father of her child (who she has admitted she does not love) is dying peacefully in a field after being hit by a car.[24] In *Magik and Rose* (1999) itinerant fortune-teller Magik arrives in small-town Hokitika and decides to become pregnant by sperm donor.[25] Her friend Rose helps her to advertise and screen possible donors, and she encourages Magik to contact the teenage daughter she adopted out to a local family when she was younger. In *Apron Strings* (2008) three solo mothers are depicted: Lorna and Anita both have adult children, and Lorna's daughter Virginia gives birth during the film.[26] Lorna and Anita both have a difficult past that continues to affect their lives: Lorna's husband committed suicide and she fears her adult son will do the same; and Anita's traditional Indian family, including her sister Tara, rejected her when she became pregnant outside of marriage. As the intertwined narratives are resolved, two female-centric families are formed. Pākehā Lorna finally stands up to her son, who has been taking advantage of her generosity for many years, and overcomes her prejudices to accept her mixed-race granddaughter. The film ends with four generations of women under one roof in the closing scene – Nan (Lorna's mother), Lorna herself, Virginia, and Virginia's daughter. Intercut with this sequence, Anita reconciles with Tara after a prolonged estrangement, and the two sisters reconnect with Anita's son Michael.

Women sharing the maternal role.
Ruby and Rata, Gaylene Preston, 1990, Preston-Laing Productions, New Zealand Film Commission

These films reflect a demographic shift in Aotearoa New Zealand throughout the 1990s and into the 2000s, with the rapid growth of single-parent families headed by the mother.[27] The films suggest, too, that motherhood is a role some women will – and should – choose to perform outside of a conventional family unit, with a different form of support network and extended whānau consisting of close female friends and relatives. For the characters in these films, motherhood is not the patriarchal institution imposed on women that Okin so carefully deconstructs. Rather, their experience is of motherhood minus patriarchy – a philosophy of mothering developed by pronatalist feminists such as Jane Alpert and Elizabeth Gould Davies that holds that women should liberate their maternal and creative energies from the restrictive institution of motherhood and bond with other women by sharing the care work of the maternal role.[28] Through these films, then, New Zealand filmmakers Gaylene Preston, Harry Sinclair, Vanessa Alexander and Sima Urale assert the potential for a redefinition of maternal care and motherhood within a female-centric family.

Heroic solo mothers:
From *Once Were Warriors* (1994)
to *River Queen* (2005)

A key theme of the diverse representations of the mother alone since the 1990s is the compassion, even admiration with which she is treated by filmmakers. This depiction of solo mothers contrasts to other mainstream cinema where the nuclear family continues to be valorised. For example, film and media scholars Niall Richardson and Sadie Wearing argue that the figure of the housewife and the lure of the domestic 'maintains a strong hold on the representational regimes of American drama' even if it has also been thoroughly critiqued by those same regimes.[29] As a result, in mainstream American film and television the household and mothering that a single mother can offer is often presented as inadequate. Films with sympathetic solo mother protagonists – epitomised by *Maid in Manhattan* and *Good Deeds* as well as *Jerry Maguire* (1996), *One Fine Day* (1996), *As Good As It Gets* (1997), *Labor Day* (2013) and *The Single Moms Club* (2014) – conventionally end with the reformation of a nuclear family (or families in *The Single Moms Club*) of husband, wife and child.[30] By contrast, in New Zealand films the mother alone is regularly figured as a heroine. Consider Beth's choice to leave Jake at the end of *Once Were Warriors* (1994).[31] Jake – a Māori man alone, as literature and film scholar Alistair Fox has argued, who is alienated from his culture and trapped in a cycle of violence – is a diminished figure by the resolution of the film.[32] He is still physically strong, but his inarticulate rage contrasts with Beth's strength of character and calm resolution as she tells him she is leaving with their children. Barbara Brookes links the character Beth to historically important Māori women leaders in New Zealand history such as Te Puea Herangi and Whina Cooper: Beth Heke, she says, 'fictionally represents the role of strong women who act as leaders and nurturers of cultural tradition'.[33]

There are numerous examples of heroic mother alone characters in recent New Zealand cinema. In *Fracture* (2004), solo mum Leanne is the humanising force of the film: her angry outburst at the arrogant businessman Howard, who inconsiderately lands a helicopter in a public park and scares her son, becomes a catalyst for him to change his ruthless capitalist ideology.[34] Similarly, in *Show of Hands* (2008), Jess's commitment to her disabled

The antipodean new woman.

River Queen, Vincent Ward, 2005, Silverscreen Films, The Film Consortium, Endgame Entertainment, Invicta Capital, New Zealand Film Commission, New Zealand Film Production Fund, UK Film Council.

daughter and her optimistic view of human nature challenge her competitor Tom to examine and reject his cut-throat personal philosophy.[35] In *The Map Reader* (2008) Amelia, despite being a flawed mother and an alcoholic who sometimes lashes out at her son Michael, is still able to gradually instil in him the confidence to leave his room and explore the world by teaching him that he can go anywhere with a map.[36] She also provides him with the practical means to do so by gifting him a passport for his eighth birthday, demonstrating her conviction that he will travel one day. In *Jinx Sister* (2008) it is Hine, a solo mother and minor character in the film, who reverses Laura's self-destructive behaviour and encourages her to begin building relationships with those she loves rather than alienating them.[37] Another version of the mother alone is dramatised on screen in *Home by Christmas* (2010) as Tui lovingly cares for her son during the four years her husband is fighting in World War II, after he signed up without consulting her.[38] In *Fantail* (2013) the solo mother of the film, who is suffering from renal disease, appears only fleetingly on screen, but her daughter Tania is clearly devoted to her and is working nights at the petrol station so she can care for her mother during the day.[39] In a conversation with her brother, both agree categorically that either one will donate a kidney to their mother if she needs it: this highlights their commitment to her and, we can assume, her love and care for them.

Perhaps one of the most heroic mothers alone depicted in recent New Zealand film is the character Sarah from *River Queen* (2005), who risks her life to travel into the dangerous territory of the chief Te Kai Po after her son Boy is kidnapped.[40] This film can be distinguished from other journeys 'into the interior', such as in Joseph Conrad's archetypal 1899 novel *Heart of Darkness* and in the films *Apocalypse Now* (1979), *The Mission* (1986) and *Black Robe* (1991),[41] by the fact that, in *River Queen*, the protagonist making the journey into 'darkness' is a woman and a mother whose motivation is to find her child. Maternal drive replaces the military orders or religious vocation of those other narratives as the catalyst for the journey. The Pākehā character Sarah can be interpreted as one version of the antipodean new woman in a new world who is independent, confident and unconstrained by social convention with regard to her sexuality or to her cultural identity. She is not married to Boy's Māori father before he dies, and she consummates her relationship with her lover Wiremu outside of marriage. At the end of the film Sarah is living with Wiremu and her son in a Māori community: a moko tattoed on her chin confirms that she has adoped Māori culture as her own. Poet and film scholar Olivia Macassey argues that Sarah is a 'proto-New Zealander' whose mixed-race son is 'the true inheritor of the nation'.[42] Sarah transgresses European attitudes of this historical era, in particular the expectations of female passivity, the colonial construction of Māori as exotic 'others', and the patriarchal laws relating to marriage that differed from Māori custom.[43] Significantly for this discussion of the mother alone, Sarah's choices are not individualistic acts of rebellion; rather, she is motivated by the sociality and the care of her maternal role, and by her desire to build a family with her son at the centre.

Unwed mothers in New Zealand history.
Piece of My Heart, Fiona Samuel, 2009, MF Films. Stills photographer: Kirsty Griffin

Reflecting on the past, speaking to the present:
Piece of My Heart (2009) and
Bread and Roses (1993)

Another tactic by filmmakers who intend to engage with cultural attitudes about solo mothers is to make films that critique their historical treatment within wider Aotearoa New Zealand society. The television film *Piece of My Heart* (2009) looks back at New Zealand in the 1960s. It depicts the lives of two women who were thwarted in their attempts to be solo mothers. Kat and Flora meet in a home for unwed teenage mothers.[44] Desperate to keep their children, they make a bargain with the matron to stay silent about a young girl's suicide at the home, and the abuse she suffered from her father that led to her pregnancy and death. After giving birth, Kat and Flora discover too late that they have been tricked and their babies have been legally signed over for adoption, as was the usual policy in maternity homes of the period. The imagery of the institution, in which the young women are underfed and used for hard labour, and the cruel deception of the matron, are an indictment of the maternity homes of the 1960s where young unmarried women were sent to have their illegitimate babies. Years later, in the present day, Kat and Flora are still friends. The profound connection and mutual understanding they share decades after their children were adopted out highlights the devastating psychological consequences for women who are denied the chance to care for their children.

An earlier film that provides another historical perspective is Gaylene Preston's 1993 television biopic *Bread and Roses*.[45] It depicts the challenges for a young Sonja Davies on discovering she is pregnant to an American serviceman in the mid-1940s. They are engaged, but not married, and he has been sent to the Pacific. Sonja's mother calls her a 'stupid girl' when she hears of the pregnancy and suggests termination, despite the fact that she had Sonja in similar circumstances after she became pregnant to an American officer during World War I. Sonja refuses outright, and goes on to give birth to her daughter Penny alone in hospital with very little medical support or care. She stays with friends when her daughter is an infant because her mother and stepfather refuse to let her live with them; she is compelled to return to work to earn money to support herself and her child. Like *Piece of My Heart*, the film highlights the difficulties of mothering alone through the reaction of Sonja's immediate family and the wider public. It represents the social stigma faced by women who had romantic relationships with US servicemen and the challenges of negotiating the military bureaucracy for financial support – as Angela Wanhalla explores in her chapter. In a scene at the post office, for example, a woman overhears Sonja enquiring about the money she should be receiving from the American military. Eyeing Sonja's pram she comments knowingly to another woman in the queue, 'She's not the first to be left high and dry.'

Bread and Roses and the more recent *Piece of My Heart* are part of an international trend in cinema that interrogates the historical attitude towards, and treatment of, unmarried mothers in the postwar era until the late 1960s. In *Mother and Child* (US, 2009), Karen suffers after unwillingly adopting out her illegitimate child at the age of 14 because of pressure from her mother.[46] *Philomena*, a 2013 BBC production based on true events, features the elderly Philomena Lee searching for her son who was forcibly adopted from a maternity home in Ireland in 1952.[47] Both women continue to care deeply about their children in spite of the fact that they knew them only as an infant (in Karen's case) and a toddler (in Philomena's).

As well as contributing to a wider cultural conversation about the fate of unwed mothers historically, *Piece of My Heart* develops the critique first suggested by *Gone Up North for a While*: the film functions as a 'harsh criticism of the conservatism that barred Flora and Kat from keeping their children'.[48] At the same time, it represents the humanity of women who choose – or, in this case, wanted to choose – to mother alone. It foregrounds their utter commitment to their children by showing the severe and ongoing effect of being separated from them. *Piece of My Heart* is typical of the historical film genre in that it draws on history as a 'device to speak of the present time'.[49] It challenges a residual cultural trend in public discourse surrounding solo mothers in New Zealand to moralistically judge the 'choices' made by women who mother alone, especially young women who have children outside of marriage.[50]

New motherhood alone:
The Great Maiden's Blush (2015)

A recent example of the representation of solo mothers in New Zealand feature film is *The Great Maiden's Blush*, directed by Andrea Bosshard and Shane Loader.[51] The film focuses on two women who become mothers in the opening scenes. Bunny is working-class, Māori, a girl racer and taxi driver who is currently in prison and plans to adopt out her son.[52] Aila is middle-class, Pākehā, a failed classical pianist and a passionate gardener, whose infant daughter needs a life-saving heart operation. The two meet in the postnatal ward where they share a room but are otherwise alone (apart from Bunny's security detail). The two women are drawn together through sharing the stresses of first-time motherhood, and with no other support, they form a friendship that becomes instrumental in their lives as they encourage each other to face up to the truth of the unconventional paternity of their children.

The Great Maiden's Blush presents its two mother characters as complicated, nuanced figures. Aila is still mourning the daughter she adopted out as a teenager after an affair with her piano teacher, and has withdrawn from the world since the death of her mother. Bunny is hardened, apparently unemotional, a convicted criminal, who lashes out at those around her and tries to avoid bonding with her son. Both women have kept their pregnancies secret and are determined to have their children alone.

The character Bunny appears to fall outside of the cultural construction of the mother as responsive, sensitive and patient. In one scene she tells the intended adoptive parents of her baby that she 'never wanted him' and shouts at them to take him away and 'piss off'. As the film progresses, however, her character is slowly unpacked and the complexities of her circumstances are revealed. Bunny's growing love for her son, her friendship with Aila and her intense relationships with Aleksander, the father of her child, and his son Andrej highlight her capacity to care – a trait that is combined with her fierce independence. At the film's resolution, Bunny's choice to give her son to his father Aleksander because she knows she will only be allowed to keep him in prison until he is nine months old suggests the tragic consequences of government policies that restrict the access of women prisoners to their children.[53]

Another innovative aspect of this film is its focus on the visceral intensity of the experience of new motherhood for women. Andrea Bosshard explained in an interview that this aspect of the story was inspired in part by her reading of *The Women's Decameron*, a 1987 novel about women in a maternity ward in the Soviet Union who share their stories.[54] It was also prompted by her own experiences of new motherhood in a New Zealand context, particularly the time she spent in a Karitane unit, which she describes as 'a place filled with women who were all dealing with the challenges of new motherhood ... where issues of race, class and religion ... became completely irrelevant.'[55] The film communicates the intensity of new motherhood – which is rarely depicted in cinema in New Zealand or internationally – with scenes of giving birth, the neonatal unit, breastfeeding and breast pumping, and the process of learning the daily routines of maternal care. As Bosshard states, 'I don't know of any other film that treats this incredibly rich time of people's lives with the respect it deserves.'[56] *The Great Maiden's Blush* foregrounds the work involved in learning to mother, and the skill required to care for an infant. It presents two female characters who forge a deep friendship through sharing the process of mastering their new role, despite differences in background, class and ethnicity.

Conclusion

The popularity of the solo mother character on New Zealand screens, and her sympathetic portrayal, suggests something about the perspective of New Zealand filmmakers who are often speaking from the periphery to push forward a cultural conversation. For example, the progressive role of the National Film Unit in the 1970s, which challenged social convention by showing the complex social reality of illegitimate births in New Zealand, was important to the production and themes of *Gone Up North for a While*. Bosshard and Loader's exploration of the complexities of single motherhood, including the consequences for women who are imprisoned and unable to keep their children, is, they argue, 'increasingly relevant' in a context where solo mothers are strongly encouraged to return to work once their youngest child turns two, and women prisoners are limited in being able to care for their children.[57]

Through the varied cinematic work explored in this chapter,[58] filmmakers make visible the growing number of families headed by a solo mother in New Zealand, and emphasise the dedication of solo mothers to their children. In doing so the films circumvent wider public rhetoric about solo motherhood, derived from the historical attitude in colonial New Zealand that single mothers were morally undeserving of financial and social support, and currently manifest in government initiatives that require solo mothers to take on paid work.[59] These filmmakers show the traditional patriarchal family to be detrimental to women; instead they focus on families headed by solo mothers. They represent the high value solo mothers place on their caring maternal role and the centrality of children to their lives, as revealed in sociological research.[60]

The character of the mother alone seems to resonate in distinctive local ways within a New Zealand culture where motherhood has been regarded as important. From a colonial legacy in which women were valued as wives and mothers, through phases of governmental pronatalist rhetoric, to post-World War II suburban domesticity, images of the mother and of family have informed our national identity. Among these historical iterations of women's maternal role, the appeal of the mother alone figure suggests a strongly felt resistance to and critique of the mythologies of man (or woman) alone. Indeed, the mother alone is a strange title for this chapter because, of course, these women are not alone – they are always connected to another or others through what gender scholar Evelyn Fox Keller calls 'dynamic autonomy', an 'interdependent sense of self'.[61] This sociability, this connectedness, is significant because it raises questions about family, care, dependence and responsibility in a culture influenced by a powerful cultural myth of the itinerant, self-sufficient man alone, and intensified by an individualist ideology of self-reliance and self-interest. The figure of the mother alone whose care signals 'an ability to let go of egocentric preoccupations' complicates this archetypal male loner's impulse to reject civilisation.[62] The depiction of the mother alone on screen highlights the ongoing necessity of being in the world, rather than rejecting it, and of remaining responsive and caring towards others, instead of focusing primarily on egocentric needs. The mother alone figure suggests the presence within New Zealand culture of an alternative model of female-centric care outside of conventional ideologies of the family, and of a feminine sensibility that resists the isolationism that continues to be highly visible within New Zealand fiction and is perpetuated by the prevailing neoliberal ideology in Aotearoa New Zealand.

In a recent analysis, filmmaker and scholar Roger Horrocks cites 'Kiwi male culture' as one of four key themes in New Zealand cinema since the 1970s, alongside landscape, horror or unease, and adolescence.[63] However, by taking another perspective on New Zealand cinema – even on films understood to have a 'masculine' vision, such as *Smash Palace* – we can discover a variety of female characters who reflect an alternative experience of life and culture in Aotearoa New Zealand, and of mothering in particular. One such prominent figure is the mother alone. From the early films at the beginning of this chapter to more recent depictions of women mothering alone, this group of films reveal another theme of New Zealand cinema: the celebration of maternal autonomy outside of conventional nuclear families and traditional ideologies of motherhood. These films, in different ways, subvert cultural expectations of women's caring role as necessarily occurring within specific social and familial arrangements, and make visible the skill and commitment of mothers who are caring for their children alone.

Notes

1   The original film no longer exists. These plot details are taken from Bruce Babington, *A History of New Zealand Fiction Feature Film* (Manchester & New York: Manchester University Press, 2007), 49–50.

2   See Heather Devere's chapter in this volume for a discussion of Susan Moller Okin's work.

3   Julia T. Wood, *Who Cares? Women, care and culture* (Carbondale: Southern Illinois University Press, 1994), 98.

4   *Heart of the Stag.* Film. New Zealand. Michael Firth, 1984; *Rain.* Film. New Zealand. Christine Jeffs, 2001.

5   *The Ugly.* Film. New Zealand. Scott Reynolds, 1997; *What Becomes of the Broken Hearted?* Film. New Zealand. Ian Mune, 1999.

6   Margaret Tennant, *Paupers and Providers: Charitable aid in New Zealand* (Wellington: Bridget Williams Books, 1989), 105–08.

7   Gabrielle Hine, 'Shaping motherhood: Representations of pregnancy in popular media', PhD dissertation, University of Otago, 2011, 165.

8   Ibid., 159.

9   Paul Maunder quoted in 'No. 8 wire movie making', *Our National Film Unit.* Short film. New Zealand. NZ On Screen, 2010: www.nzonscreen.com/collection/national-film-unit-collection/background. The Domestic Purposes Benefit – Sole Parent was renamed Sole Parent Support in July 2013.

10   Ian Conrich, *Studies in New Zealand Cinema No. 16*, 1.

11   For a full list of directors in this group see Conrich, 1–2. See also Alistair Fox, Barry Keith Grant, & Hilary Radner, 'Introduction: The history film in New Zealand cinema', in *New Zealand Cinema: Interpreting the past*, eds Alistair Fox, Barry Keith Grant & Hilary Radner (Bristol: Intellect, 2011), 26–27.

12   Russell Campbell 'The Kiwi bloke: The representation of Pakeha masculinity in New Zealand film', in Ian Conrich & Stuart Murray (eds), *Contemporary New Zealand Cinema: From new wave to blockbuster* (London & New York: I.B. Tauris, 2008), 215.

13   Nicholas Reid captions an image of Jacqui from the film with 'The obverse side of Kiwi machismo – alienated woman', *A Decade of New Zealand Film: Sleeping Dogs to Came a Hot Friday* (Dunedin: John McIndoe Publishing, 1986).

14   See Devere's chapter in this volume for a discussion of Annette Baier's work.

15   *Solo.* Film. New Zealand. Tony Williams, 1977; Robin Hyde, *The Godwits Fly* (London: Persephone Books, 1938); Marilyn Duckworth, *A Gap in the Spectrum* (Oxford: Oxford University Press, 1986 [1959]); Keri Hulme, *The Bone People* (Auckland: Spiral/Hodder & Stoughton, 1983).

16   Hilary Radner, 'Screening women's histories: Jane Campion and the New Zealand heritage film, from the biopic to the female gothic', in *New Zealand Cinema*, 260.

17   *The Piano.* Film. New Zealand/Australia/France. Jane Campion, 1993. Ada's status as a mother alone might be debated. Indeed, much scholarship on the film explores the imagery of the 'family' of Stewart, Ada and Flora. In the opening scenes of the film Ada and Flora identify as an independent family unit: Flora says of Stewart, 'I'm not going

to call him Papa.' However, as the film progresses, she begins to follow his instructions and refers to him as 'Papa', at which point it could be argued he is helping to father her. My basis for calling Ada a mother alone is that she does not accept Stewart as the patriarchal head of the family, as her husband or Flora's father, and although Flora identifies him as 'Papa' for a short time, his actions towards Ada in cutting off her finger alienate Flora from him by the conclusion of the film.

18 Bennett E. Roth, '*The Piano*: A modern film melodrama about passion and punishment', *Psychoanalytic Psychology* 17, no. 2 (2000), 410.

19 Alistair Fox, *Jane Campion: Authorship and personal cinema* (Bloomington & Indianapolis: Indiana University Press, 2011), 112.

20 Jane Campion quoted in Thomas Bourguignon and Michel Ciment, 'Interview with Jane Campion: More barbarian than aesthete (1993)', in *Jane Campion Interviews*, ed. Virginia Wright Wexman (Jackson: Virginia University Press of Mississippi, 1999), 111.

21 This trend can be related to two related shifts in New Zealand filmmaking from the 1990s identified by writer and biographer Deborah Shepherd: the increased visibility of women's culture and a strongly oppositional strain within women's cinema. See *Reframing Women: A history of New Zealand film* (Auckland: Harper Collins, 2000), 134.

22 Helen Martin, '*Ruby and Rata*', in Helen Martin & Sam Edwards, *New Zealand Film: 1912–1996* (Oxford: Oxford University Press, 1997), 149.

23 *Maid in Manhattan*. Film. United States. Wayne Wang, 2002; *Good Deeds*. Film. United States. Tyler Perry, 2012.

24 *Topless Women Talk About Their Lives*. Film. New Zealand. Harry Sinclair, 1997.

25 *Magik and Rose*. Film. New Zealand. Vanessa Alexander, 1999.

26 *Apron Strings*. Film. New Zealand. Sima Urale, 2008.

27 Statistics New Zealand figures show that between 1986 and 1996 there was a 57 per cent increase in the number of children living in sole-parent families (the majority of which are headed by women). See New Zealand Statistics, Key Statistics 1999, 7: www.stats.govt.nz/browse_for_stats/people_and_communities/children/nzs-children.aspx

28 Lauri Umansky, *Motherhood Reconceived: Feminism and the legacies of the sixties* (New York: New York University Press, 1996), 3. See also Jane Alpert, 'Mother right', *Off Our Backs* 3, no. 8 (1973), 22–28; and Elizabeth Gould Davis, *The First Sex* (New York: G.P. Putname's Sons, 1971).

29 Niall Richardson & Sadie Wearing, *Gender in the Media* (Houndmills: Palgrave Macmillan, 2014), 66.

30 *Jerry Maguire*. Film. United States, Cameron Crowe, 1996; *One Fine Day*. Film. United States. Michael Hoffman, 1996; *As Good as it Gets*. Film. United States. James L. Brooks, 1997; *Labor Day*. Film. United States. Jason Retiman, 2013; *The Single Moms Club*. Film. United States. Tyler Perry, 2014.

31 *Once Were Warriors*. Film. New Zealand. Lee Tamahori, 1994.

32 Alistair Fox, 'Inwardness, insularity, and the man alone: Postcolonial anxiety in the New Zealand novel', *Journal of Postcolonial Writing* 45, no. 3 (2009), 269.

33 Barbara Brookes, *A History of New Zealand Women* (Wellington: Bridget Williams Books, 2016), 434.

34 *Fracture*. Film. New Zealand. Larry Parr, 2004. The film is based on Maurice Gee's *Crime Story* (Auckland: Penguin, 1994).

35 *Show of Hands*. Film. New Zealand. Anthony McCarten, 2008.

36 *The Map Reader*. Film. New Zealand. Harold Brodie, 2008.

37 *Jinx Sister*. Film. New Zealand. Athina Tsoulis, 2008.

38 *Home by Christmas*. Film. New Zealand. Gaylene Preston, 2010.

39 *Fantail*. Film. New Zealand. Curtis Vowell, 2013.

40 *River Queen*. Film. New Zealand/United Kingdom. Vincent Ward, 2005.

41 Joseph Conrad, *Heart of Darkness* (London: Penguin, 1997 [1899]); *Apocalypse Now*. Film. United States. Francis Ford Coppola, 1979; *The Mission*. Film. United Kingdom/France. Roland Joffé, 1986; *Black Robe*. Film. Canada/Australia/United States. Bruce Beresford, 1991. The book and films cited here and the phrase 'into the interior' are from Annabel Cooper's discussion in 'Tracking Tītokowaru over text and screen: Pākehā narrate the warrior 1906–2005,' in Fox, Grant & Radner, *New Zealand Cinema*, 145–46.

42 Olivia Macassey 'Cross-currents: *River Queen*'s national and trans-national heritages,' in Fox, Grant & Radner, *New Zealand Cinema*, 131.

43 Brookes, *A History of New Zealand Women*, 78.

44 *Piece of My Heart*. Television film. New Zealand. Fiona Samuel, 2009. The film is based on Renée Taylor's novel *Does This Make Sense to You?* (Auckland: Penguin Books, 1995). The home is modelled on the Salvation Army's Bethany maternity homes and the Alexandra Home for Unmarried Mothers in Wellington.

45 *Bread and Roses*. Television film. New Zealand. Gaylene Preston, 1993. The film was based on Sonja Davies's autobiography *Bread and Roses: Sonja Davies, her story* (Masterton: Fraser Books, 1984).

46 *Mother and Child*. Film. United States. Rodrigo García, 2009.

47 *Philomena*. Film. United Kingdom. Stephen Frears, 2013.

48 Hine, 'Shaping motherhood', 177.

49 Pierre Sorlin quoted in Leger Grindon, *Shadows of the Past: Studies in the historical fiction film* (Philadelphia: Temple University Press, 1994), 1.

50 One example of public discourse surrounding young mothers was the debate about, and media treatment of, Keisha Castle-Hughes (the actress who plays the young Kat in the film) when she became pregnant at 16. See Hine, 'Shaping motherhood', 85–86, for a discussion of this debate.

51 *Great Maiden's Blush*. Film. New Zealand. Andrea Bosshard and Shane Loader, 2015.

52 The term 'boy racer' is used in Aotearoa New Zealand to refer to young men who drive their cars (which are often modified) aggressively and loudly. Bunny is a female racer within this subculture.

53 The Department of Corrections in New Zealand (2016) states that 'Some prisoners with babies and children up to the age of 24 months may be eligible to live in self-care units where they can bond in a safe and supportive environment' and that 'mothers

with babies aged less than nine months old who are cared for in the community ...
are permitted daily visits ... where they can feed and bond with their child': 'Women
in Prison': www.corrections.govt.nz/working_with_offenders/prison_sentences/be-
ing_in_prison/women_in_prison.html

54 Julia Vosnesenskaya, *The Women's Decameron* (New York: Henry Holt & Co., 1987).

55 Andrea Bosshard and Shane Loader, interviewed by Bronwyn Polaschek, Wellington,
New Zealand, 4 August 2016.

56 Bosshard, interviewed by Bronwyn Polaschek.

57 Ibid.

58 While this chapter has discussed a variety of feature films, there are other cinematic
texts that could be explored in terms of the representation of the solo mother, such as
short films. For example, in 2017, the excellent *Waru* was released in New Zealand,
a sequence of eight interrelated short films directed by Briar Grace-Smith, Casey
Kaa, Ainsley Gardiner, Katie Wolfe, Chelsea Cohen, Renae Maihi, Paula Jones and
Awanui Simich-Pene. The 10-minute stories include a number of characters who
appear to be solo mothers.

59 Brookes, *A History of New Zealand Women,* 80, 464.

60 For example see Kathryn Edin & Maria Kefalas, *Promises I Can Keep: Why poor wom-
en put motherhood before marriage* (Los Angeles: University of California Press, 2005).

61 Evelyn Fox Keller cited in Wood, *Who Cares?*, 108.

62 Wood, *Who Cares?*, 87.

63 Roger Horrocks, 'Introduction', in Diane Pivac, Frank Start & Lawrence McDonald
(eds), *New Zealand Film: An illustrated history* (Wellington: Te Papa Press, 2011), 20.

10

'THEY THINK I CARE NOT':
Taking account of Takau Rio Love

Rosemary Anderson

At a service at the Terrace Congregational Church in Wellington in August 1940, Takau Rio Love, High Chief Elect of Rarotonga, dedicated her life to her future role. As Makea Nui Ariki, she would soon leave to take up the chiefly duties of her late father.[1] At 34, Takau had spent over half her life in New Zealand. During that time she had become a respected local figure as a visible and active force in Wellington's Māori cultural and welfare organisations, while remaining a loyal ambassador for the Cook Islands.

The Cook Islands were annexed in 1901 and formed part of New Zealand's Pacific empire. The Indigenous people of both sites are known as Māori; they are distinct populations but share a common ancestry. According to oral tradition, Rarotonga served as a starting point for Māori migration to New Zealand.[2] Indigenous trade in the 1860s reopened this ocean passage, and cultural links were further cemented in the first half of the twentieth century. Prominent Māori political leaders were influential in this process. From the 1920s, Cook Island scholars and cultural groups experienced something of life in New Zealand, and occasionally, migrants were absorbed by marrying into New Zealand communities.[3] By 1936, 103 Cook Islanders were resident in New Zealand, but numbers were set to rise dramatically during the war and in the following decades.[4]

Takau Rio Love was one of these migrants. This chapter follows the life trajectory of one woman caught up in divided loyalties between these two distinct sites. Takau's family held a privileged position in the Cook Islands, shared a special relationship with representatives of the New Zealand government and had frequent contact with New Zealand Māori. Takau's marriage to Eruera (Tiwi) Love, the first Māori commander of the 28th Maori Battalion, resulted from these connections. She lived a very public life and was subject to scrutiny in public and private spheres; this fact was reflected in the wording she chose for an 'In Memoriam' notice on the anniversary of Tiwi's death at El Alamein in 1942.

> 'Keep smiling darling', was your last message. Through the long weary year I did.
>
> They think I care not.
>
> Yet, each day and night with tears in my heart, I whisper to the winds, 'Mizpah',
>
> For I know, God will watch over you and me,
>
> When we are apart.
>
> Some day, somewhere, dearest we will meet,
>
> I will still be smiling.[5]

The words 'They think I care not' reflect private grief, the tears in her heart, but they also allude to an inner conflict of balancing private and public duty with the expectations of others. Her story is one of double duty – to her family and to her people, operating across two countries. Through an examination of a successful woman operating in the public sphere, this chapter considers political and cultural leadership as a form of public care – for caring is not limited to the realm of the intimate and personal. Caring and care work are political, but this is also shaped by cultural considerations, as Takau's public life demonstrates. Taking an expansive definition of justice and care, and examining these ideas in a cultural and colonial context through the life of one woman, highlights how to be just to one – the nation – might place constraints on the other – duty to family.

Interpreting the dynamics of Takau's life in any personal sense is problematic because of the limited sources. Aspects of Takau's early years can be gleaned from the memoirs of her younger sister Makea Nui Teremoana Ariki CBE, although Takau is seldom mentioned directly there. There are no private memoirs, letters or reflections to call on, and so we must often rely on articles in newspapers and magazines, published for their newsworthy value. In the press, the leadership qualities of the Makea Nui Ariki are subject to a pronounced Eurocentric bias, openly sanctioning and encouraging a cooperative relationship between the Indigenous peoples of the Cook Islands and representatives of the New Zealand government. During World War II, mainstream newspapers played a key role in fostering patriotic fervour. Glowing accounts of fundraising activities, along with the dignitaries and personalities involved, take on a distinctly laudatory tone. While these articles project a vivid and colourful picture of Takau's role as a public figure, the dearth of personal sources means this image cannot be balanced by accounts of private and family life. Using these sources highlights the dilemma between her care for the nation and care for her family, which is also the historians' dilemma in seeking a balanced portrayal of her life.

Early years

In many respects, because of her love for Tiwi, Takau's life took a very different path to that envisaged by her parents. She was born Takau Upoko Ngariki Tinirau in 1904 on Taputapuatea marae at Rarotonga. She belonged to a senior family of Ngāti Makea, one of three chiefly families on the island. The London Missionary Society and New Zealand government officials regarded the Makea Nui as the premier title of Rarotonga and, by extension, of the whole of the Cook Island group, although not all Indigenous leaders shared this interpretation.[6] Takau grew up in the grounds of the Para O Tane Palace, and was an inheritor of a long tradition of female leadership – notably her grandmother, Makea Takau Ariki I (1839–1911), who was popularly known as the 'Queen of Rarotonga.'[7]

For more than 40 years, Takau's grandmother was the prominent 'face' of the Cook Islands, welcoming all important visitors to Rarotonga, including New Zealand governors and prime ministers. More than a figurehead, by 1870 she dominated local trade with Europeans.[8] She proved a strong and dignified leader, guiding her people through a period of rapid political and social change. The outcome of the Cook Islands annexation to New Zealand in 1901 was not as expected: indigenous leaders retained prestige and influence among their own people, but their decision-making powers were significantly diminished. More than 50 years elapsed before the Cook Islands people regained any significant political voice.[9]

Takau grew up at the centre of island life at Para O Tane Palace, in the watchful care of her grandmother. There she was exposed to the key political figures of the age. Her father, Makea Nui Tinirau, had a cordial relationship with New Zealand officials, including with Hugh Ayson, the long-serving resident commissioner of the Islands. He was also a close friend of Māui Pōmare, a prominent Māori health reformer and minister of the Cook Islands from 1916 to 1928.[10] In 1921 Tinirau's succession to the Makea title was celebrated in the New Zealand media: he was extolled as a progressive and popular leader and his loyalty to the New Zealand administration was emphasised. Tinirau's cooperation with government earned him a privileged position and he was rewarded with official visits to New Zealand and royal honours.[11]

These New Zealand influences, along with closer connections with New Zealand Māori, shaped the future course of Takau's life. Julia T. Wood, in discussing how young girls develop a gendered identity, suggests this is rooted in 'encouragement to "form" themselves into the person who will be of benefit to others'.[12] This was especially pressing for Takau who, as the eldest child, would inherit the Makea title that involved a role determined not by gender alone. Her father's role engaged with broader political aspects of island life, seeking strategies to meet his people's material needs. In working towards a society with a 'fair distribution of work and benefits', his was a traditional, masculine 'ethic of justice' approach to caring (as described by Heather Devere in her chapter).

Takau's mother Teariki Tutini was devoted to church and community. Hers was a female-centred, 'ethic of care' approach to duty, one that emphasised interpersonal relationships and emotional empathy. Teremoana remembered the women gathering on the marae, singing and talking as they worked at their various crafts. They discussed their lives, families and community, and collectively sought solutions to problems; and Tutini offered advice or practical help wherever possible.[13] In this setting, the women's togetherness might function as a form of 'therapeutic communication' by creating an empathetic space where, ideally, those who expressed themselves were not judged or their opinions invalidated. The apparent effectiveness of this approach to care demonstrates 'the importance of active responsiveness to others as essential to caring'.[14] Women raised in such an environment would have 'a marked tendency ... to feel more connected to others and to be more inclined to care for them'.[15] Within the ethic of care debate, some theorists would consider these supportive activities as a basic, but tangible level of civic participation, regardless of whether it was recognised as such.[16]

Marriage and mobility

In 1920 Tinirau set in train a journey that complicated Takau's life by creating a dual allegiance between the Cook Islands and New Zealand. Tinirau felt disadvantaged by his limited knowledge of English, particularly in dealings with officials and traders. He wished his children to be more proficient and better equipped for future leadership roles, so he chose to send them to New Zealand to complete their education. Takau was one of the first Cook Island girls to attend Hukarere Maori Girls' College in Napier.[17] While in New Zealand she was the ward of Sir Māui and Lady Mīria Pōmare and spent most school holidays with the family. On one occasion she was billeted with Rīpeka and Wi Hapi Love, one of Wellington's leading Māori families, and it was at their home in Lower Hutt that she first met their son Tiwi.[18]

In 1926, aged 22, Takau completed her education and returned to Rarotonga where she was expected to remain. But Takau and Tiwi were destined to meet again soon. Tiwi joined the Maori All Blacks on an overseas tour, and when the ship stopped over at Rarotonga on the return voyage they rekindled their friendship.[19] Shortly after, Takau told her father she wished to return to New Zealand to train as a nurse: she would be living in Wellington, and it was a convenient excuse to be closer to Tiwi.[20] The couple wished to marry, and eventually their families agreed. The wedding took place at Para O Tane in September 1928.[21] Three daughters, including twins, were born during their three years in the Cook Islands before the family returned to Wellington in 1931, where a fourth daughter was born in 1934.

Life in New Zealand

Takau settled in to life in Lower Hutt, raising her children and engaging in community activities. She was a popular guest speaker at local clubs and events, where she often talked about Rarotongan life and customs. She told her audiences it was unheard of for women to speak in public in the Cook Islands but that, nevertheless, they 'had many and important duties to carry out in the life of the community; "in fact ... we have more to do than the men have".[22] Takau was referring to the *au vaine*, women's committees, that were active throughout the Cook Islands group from the mid-1920s. Under the direction of Dr Edward Pohau Ellison, the New Zealand Māori medical officer, high-ranking women promoted and enforced public hygiene measures to counter tuberculosis and other endemic diseases and to help reduce infant mortality. Although their methods were regarded as authoritarian, the au vaine relationship with the community was generally accepted as a partnership of care.[23]

Living in New Zealand, Takau was not part of these initiatives, but she was kept informed on island happenings through regular visitors and through letters from friends and family.[24] She became involved in caring for her adopted Māori family, working in similar ways to the au vaine. As women of high rank, Rīpeka Love and Lady Mīria Pōmare shared a long history of working for the benefit of their people, and were fine examples and mentors. During the economic depression of the 1930s they gave practical assistance to those affected by poverty, and supported young Māori who were facing the social challenges of urbanisation.

In the early 1930s the Love family donated land for Te Tatau o te Po, a meeting house and marae on the Hutt Road. Takau and Tiwi took an active role in raising funds for the facility and were involved in many of its functions. Socials, concerts, church services and sporting events were organised and hosted through Te Tatau o te Po, and the marae accommodated Māori and Cook Island groups visiting the area.[25] In 1935 Takau was instrumental in establishing the Te Ropu Maori Girls' Club, which aimed to foster pride in Māori heritage by reviving and promoting Māori culture, arts and crafts. As patroness, Lady Pōmare and other important guests were welcomed at club events – including Janet Fraser, wife of the prime minister, Peter Fraser.[26] Mīria and Rīpeka were also founders and loyal supporters of the Ngati Poneke Young Maori Club, established in 1937;[27] the club evolved as a meeting place for the growing urban Māori population of Wellington and functioned in a similar way to Te Tatau o te Po, only on a larger scale. Janet Fraser became an acknowledged leader in the association, as did Takau, and the two women became well acquainted through their shared connections and active involvement in Māori welfare.

Takau Rio Love, Lady Mīria Pōmare and Miriama Hekata (shown in detail) are in the foreground of this image of the Monte Carlo Russian Ballet Company visiting 'eminent Maori women' at Hiwiroa, Lower Hutt, 1937.

W. Hall Raine, National Library of Australia, nla.obj-224084913

New responsibilities

When Tinirau passed away in Rarotonga in January 1939 after several years of failing health, Takau prepared to return to take up her father's title. Her new responsibilities raised conflicting notions of duty and care. After the declaration of war in September 1939, Tiwi was seconded to help establish the 28th Maori Battalion, and in May 1940 he sailed for war. At that time, preparations were underway in Rarotonga for a traditional coronation ceremony and feast – a strange juxtaposition of sorrow and joy for Takau.[28] Her many friends in the Hutt Valley said their goodbyes, and her contribution to the welfare of the community was publicly recognised.[29] The *Auckland Star* wrote that she was a devoted leader who would 'do much to still further cement the good relations between the New Zealand Government and the native people'.[30] As if to quash any doubts over her long absence from the islands, the article mentioned how Takau had prepared for the role while in New Zealand. She had studied the social problems that resulted from changes to traditional island life, and researched ways of improving island exports. According to the article, the administration's choice was 'a happy one'.[31] This was certainly the case for the administrators, and for Auckland traders, who would benefit from the islanders' ongoing acquiescence. The cooperative approach of Indigenous Cook Island leaders was important in sustaining this relationship.

But while everyone was projecting a straightforward and positive future, the reality was somewhat different. Takau's plans were disrupted when an appeal against her leadership claim was lodged with the Supreme Court of New Zealand. Questions were being asked about the degree of responsibility she felt towards the Cook Islands – there was a perception that because she had married 'out of the family' and had lived away from the islands for too long, her succession rights were fragile.[32] On that basis Willie Browne, husband of Tuvaine Browne, a cousin of Takau's, claimed hereditary rights of accession on his wife's behalf. Browne also claimed, among other things, that customary succession favoured a male – an odd assertion given that Takau's grandmother had previously held the title.[33] In February 1940 Judge Ayson of the High Court of Rarotonga dismissed Browne's appeal and Takau was officially declared successor to the Makea Nui Ariki title, on condition that she reside permanently in Rarotonga.[34] Takau prepared to leave New Zealand once again, but at a time of great personal strain and distress.[35] Tiwi had been wounded in Crete, but not seriously enough to be evacuated. She also faced separation from her daughters, who were aged between eight and 11. She had agreed to leave them with their grandparents in Lower Hutt, to continue their education in New Zealand.[36]

Bereavement and questions of care

After nine months' residence in Rarotonga, Takau received news of Tiwi's death. Wartime shipping restrictions delayed her return to New Zealand so she was unable to attend memorial services held in his honour. After three months of grieving in relative privacy she returned to Wellington where another three months elapsed before she spoke to the press. Six months was considered an acceptable mourning period in Cook Island culture at that time, although New Zealand society may have expected a longer observance.[37] Takau told a *Star* reporter she was delighted to be reunited with her daughters but that she was also 'anxious' to further serve the war effort, and was seeking 'a wartime post'.[38] These contradictory emotions suggest this was a very unsettling time for Takau, a period of conflicting allegiances and great uncertainty as to where her immediate duty lay.

The terms of her accession to the Ariki title specified her continued and permanent residence in Rarotonga. Instead, Takau chose to stay in New Zealand and actively reengaged in patriotic activities. She visited convalescent servicemen of the Maori Battalion and maintained a watchful oversight over island women working throughout the North Island.[39] More than 100 young migrants had arrived since 1941 through a quasi-government scheme that allowed Cook Island administrators to recruit domestic workers for service in some privileged private homes.[40] In Wellington, Takau organised troupes of Cook Island singers, musicians and dancers to perform in public concerts and to entertain soldiers at camps and hospitals. She composed music and songs for these events, and often joined in the performance. These entertainments were enthusiastically received, and were especially popular with the American servicemen who began arriving from June 1942 and who, as Angela Wanhalla discusses in her chapter, created families but left the main burden of care to women in the host communities.[41]

Concerned for Cook Island workers in more isolated rural areas, Takau visited to check on the women's situations. She removed those who were

Cook Island entertainers and American troops, Wellington, c. 1943. Takau Rio Love is seated in the front row, fourth from the right. Private collection of Grace Hutton

unhappy or potentially at risk from their place of employment. Where possible, she took them to family or friends elsewhere; others she placed in the care of a friend who ran a reputable boarding house in central Wellington. This served as a refuge for those in difficulty, where the young women were supported, given advice and helped into other employment.[42] Most left domestic service at the earliest opportunity and moved to higher paid and less restrictive employment in factories and hospitals.

As thousands of American troops flooded into the country, however, the Cook Islands Department became increasingly concerned for the welfare of the young migrants: it believed they were unprepared for the moral dangers of cities in wartime. Their fears appeared to be justified when several women fell pregnant. Some were afraid to go home and face the disappointment of their family; in one case Takau offered to accompany the young woman to

Rarotonga and negotiate that meeting.[43] Evidence suggests that her concerns for these young women, along with her desire to be with her daughters, were factors that delayed her permanent return to Rarotonga.[44] And by staying in New Zealand, she was fulfilling the obligation she clearly felt to make an active contribution to the war effort.

Rituals and expectations

During World War II grieving New Zealand families were expected to present an impassive public face, in light of similar losses borne throughout the empire.[45] According to historian Joy Damousi, society governed public displays of emotion: grief was seldom articulated in the community, and responses were restrained by obligation and duty.[46] Being so far removed from the battlefields, families were deprived of a body, and Māori and Pākehā mourners alike had to forgo the familiar and comforting processes of lament and burial. Under normal circumstances, these rites were an essential element in expressing grief and coming to terms with loss.[47]

'In memoriam' or 'roll of honour' notices published in newspapers were one of the few places to publicly express personal grief. According to Ffion Murphy, families who were trying to make some sense of war clung to 'a traditional set of values and languages – high diction, euphemisms about battle, notions of duty, glory, heroism and the hallowed dead'.[48] This can be seen in the notices placed by Tiwi's family, in phrases such as 'died while doing his duty' and 'for God, for King and for Country'.[49] At the same time, these notices exhibited women's emotion and agency: composing and sharing a more personalised message that reflected on individual trauma might be the first step taken in coming to terms with loss. Bereavement was made more bearable through belief in an afterlife, and families took comfort in using this forum to refer to their loved ones as part of the eternal family story.[50] Takau's plaintive appeal, cited at the start of this chapter, confirms the faith she shared with her husband: she is proclaiming her unwavering belief that she will be reunited with Tiwi.

Takau's high public profile may ultimately have been to her detriment, both socially and emotionally. Women in wartime Europe faced danger in a literal sense, but those on the home front came under fire in other ways. Men, before they left for war, often advised their wives on how to proceed if they did not return.[51] Takau spoke openly of her agreement with Tiwi, of a promise made and a promise kept, to continue on and keep smiling. This seems at odds with society's expectations of mourning, but it is in keeping with their shared ethos of care and duty. Others might have expected Takau to take a quieter, less public role in the wake of her husband's death. In referring to 'the long weary year', she alludes to the emotional toll of keeping her promise, the endurance required. By publicly disclosing their understanding, she made a clear statement: she did not carry on regardless of her loss, but because of it. The fact that Takau candidly and publicly expressed what she believed others thought of her suggests she felt misunderstood and unfairly criticised; while at the same time, the public nature of this statement reflects the public way she chose to live her life. Yet, in spite of these emotive overtures she did not court sympathy, nor offer an apology. Instead, by explaining the reasons for her ongoing determination and drive, she sought some 'inclusion in an empathic moral community'.[52]

Political awakenings

Socially and economically, World War II brought mixed fortunes to the Cook Islands. The establishment of US military bases on Aitutaki and Penrhyn brought unprecedented prosperity to those islands, while conditions elsewhere in the group grew increasingly impoverished. In 1943 several hurricanes left some communities gravely short of food, and many islanders believed the government was unaware of their problems.

Takau formed an unlikely alliance with Willie Browne, her former adversary in the courts. Browne kept her well informed on wartime conditions, and Takau, still resident in Wellington, relayed island concerns directly to PM Peter Fraser. They suggested means of reducing pressure on island resources, but these were declined in favour of a government scheme to supply labourers to mine phosphate at Makatea in French Polynesia.[53]

In June 1944 Takau was quietly advised by friends in the Cook Island Department that some in the islands were unhappy at her protracted stay in New Zealand. She returned immediately rather than face another challenge to her title.[54] In August Takau visited some of the outer islands where, according to the *Pacific Islands Monthly*, she received a 'royal welcome'.[55] However, in a letter to Cyril McKay, secretary of the Island Territories Department in Wellington, Takau acknowledged leadership could not be legitimised so easily. Hinting at underlying dissent, she wrote, 'the trip has gained for me the confidence and trust of the people ... I am trying my best for all, so far so good.'[56]

In 1945 Takau returned permanently to Rarotonga. The issues she addressed on her return give some indication of her intended course. She joined island leaders on a visit to the outer islands to foster solidarity among fruitgrowers and encourage higher production. She successfully fought to improve pay rates for workers in Rarotonga, and helped investigate complaints over dangerous and unsanitary conditions for workers at Makatea. Island leaders condemned the scheme and initiated some improvements, but failed to bring about its closure. Life on isolated islands was especially hard for the elderly and infirm, and many World War I soldiers suffered ongoing health problems resulting from their overseas service. These men received no support from the New Zealand government, and island leaders intended to address this issue. Another of Takau's aims was to establish a museum at Rarotonga, to promote interest in Cook Island history and to ensure historic sites were preserved.[57]

Underlying these activities was a groundswell of anti-colonialist sentiment and a growing resentment over the domination of New Zealand officials who failed to listen to the islanders' concerns. In 1932, Eastern Māori MP Āpirana Ngata described an ariki system that was 'stereotyped by mission influence and confirmed by the courts, that is the government'. He viewed this as a deep-rooted problem, a symptom of a highly stratified society.[58] Takau, and her father before her, were regarded as 'pro-establishment' figures who collaborated with government officials in return for 'added prestige'.[59] Many islanders were no longer willing to accept this hegemonic style of leadership.

By 1945 the political situation was moving beyond Takau's conciliatory influence. While she was outwardly supportive of moves towards greater autonomy, she appeared unwilling to 'shut the door' on New Zealand. Having experienced its advantages, she likely viewed migration as an extension of island life, a future direction for the young. This was certainly the view of Ngata, who noted the favourable reactions of young islanders visiting New Zealand, 'the country with which the destiny of the Cook Islands is linked'. This 'revelation of possibilities' often proved an unsettling experience, however, and many wished to stay in New Zealand to take advantage of education and employment opportunities.[60] Takau, who had personally experienced this magnetism, had no wish to jeopardise future relations with New Zealand if this meant young islanders might be deprived of the benefits of future access.

Who cared for Takau?

Takau was 'quietly married' in Rarotonga in January 1946 to Tutupu Ariki Ara-ite, a mata`iapo almost 20 years her junior. Soon after, she was afflicted by multiple sclerosis – she was paralysed in the lower body, and unable to swallow and speak. Her husband cared for her for a time, but in June 1947 he left her. William Tailby, former secretary of the Cook Islands Department in Wellington and now the islands' resident commissioner, arranged for family to be at her bedside and ensured she received the best possible care in the local hospital. Takau passed away on 16 September 1947 at the age of 43. Tailby considered this a 'merciful release ... for none of us who have known Takau when she was full of vitality and the joy of living could have wished her any prolongation of her last months of agony and misery'.[61] Messages received from official and private circles in New Zealand reflected the respect she had earned. Local businesses and government offices closed on the day of her funeral, and relays of young men carried her coffin to the church. A few weeks later, a memorial service was held.

Takau was a wife and mother. She was also a woman who cared for others in a very public and political sense. She was raised and surrounded by strong, proactive, highly motivated women who worked tirelessly to safeguard the welfare of their people. Their duty of care extended well beyond the domestic sphere, and into their communities at large. Takau invested energy in caring for New Zealand Māori, while preparing for her future leadership role in the Cook Islands. During wartime she sustained a high public profile, even in the wake of personal loss. Her goals and motivations were complicated by changing perceptions of 'home', of where she belonged, and where her duty lay. When 'home' is understood as a place of intimate relationships and memories, a gathering of things, stories and practices, we can better comprehend how the essence of home is not necessarily fixed in any one place but can shift and change over time.[62]

Within island society during this period, traditional forms of leadership were being usurped by new ideals. Some opposed what they perceived as

Takau's dual allegiances; they believed an island leader could not have 'a foot in both camps', especially at a time of rising independence movements throughout the Pacific. Given her many friends and influential contacts in New Zealand, and her willingness to seek redress for island problems at the highest level of government, Takau might be regarded as having bridged, rather than divided her worlds – her Rarotongan home and her adopted home in New Zealand, as well as family and cultural and political responsibilities. In fact, Takau served as a link between many peoples – connecting, uniting, supporting and mobilising, and epitomising the value and strength of Indigenous women in a leadership role.

Notes

1 'Religious services', *Evening Post*, 3 August 1940.
2 Debbie Futter-Puati, 'Maki maro: Tuberculosis in the Cook Islands: A social history, 1896–1975', MA thesis, University of Auckland, 2010, 2.
3 Rosemary Anderson, 'The origins of Cook Island migration to New Zealand, 1920–1950', MA thesis, University of Otago, 2015, 20–24.
4 Anthony Hooper, 'The migration of Cook Islanders to New Zealand', *Journal of the Polynesian Society* 70, no. 1 (1961), 13.
5 'New Zealand Roll of Honour', *Evening Post*, 12 July 1943.
6 'Not a queen', *Press*, 1 February 1943.
7 Eva Saar, *Memoirs of Makea Nui Teremoana Ariki CBE* (Rarotonga: Paula Lineen, 2014), 18.
8 Jeffrey Sissons, *Nation and Destination: Creating Cook Islands identity* (Rarotonga: Institute of Pacific Studies & University of the South Pacific Centre in the Cook Islands, 1999), 13, 18.
9 Richard Gilson, *The Cook Islands, 1820–1950*, edited by R.G. Crocombe (Wellington: Victoria University Press in association with the Institute of Pacific Studies, University of the South Pacific, 1980), 48–51; 'Changes to succession to Makea Nui tribal title?', *Cook Islands Herald* online edition, 22 April 2009.
10 Saar, *Memoirs*, 30.
11 'Biographical notes', *Evening Post*, 3 June 1933. 'Island loyalty', *Evening Post*, 24 February 1927.
12 Julia T. Wood, *Who Cares? Women, care and culture* (Carbondale: Southern Illinois University Press, 1994), 91.
13 Saar, *Memoirs*, 21.
14 Wood, *Who Cares?*, 106.
15 Ibid.
16 See Heather Devere's chapter in this volume.
17 Saar, *Memoirs*, 34, 39, 40. There was no secondary schooling in the Cook Islands at that time.

18 Susan Love de Miguel, 'Love, Eruera Te Whiti o Rongomai', from the Dictionary of New Zealand Biography: www.teara.govt.nz/en/biographies/5l17/love-eruera-te-whiti-o-rongomai

19 'Nearing home', *Auckland Star*, 9 February 1927; Love de Miguel, 'Love, Eruera'.

20 Saar, *Memoirs*, 47.

21 Love de Miguel, 'Love, Eruera'.

22 'Hutt Valley News', *Evening Post*, 18 August 1938.

23 D. Futter-Puati, L. Bryder, J.K. Park, J. Littleton & P. Herda, 'Partnerships for health: Decimating tuberculosis in the Cook Islands, 1920–1975', *Health & Place* 25 (2014), 11.

24 Saar, *Memoirs*, 49; 'Cook Islands', *Auckland Star*, 16 March 1940.

25 Love de Miguel, 'Love, Eruera'; Angela Ballara, 'Love, Ripeka Wharawhara', from the Dictionary of New Zealand Biography: www.TeAra.govt.nz/en/biographies/3l14/love-ripeka-wharawhara

26 'Hutt Valley News', *Evening Post*, 12 December 1938; 'Cook Islands', *Auckland Star*, 16 March 1940; 'A Rarotongan air', *Evening Post*, 13 March 1941.

27 'Maori mourning', *Evening Post*, 8 March 1945.

28 'News summary', *Nambour Chronicle and North Coast Advertiser* (Queensland), 19 July 1940.

29 'Rarotonga's Queen', *Evening Post*, 10 July 1940; 'Farewell parties', *Evening Post*, 19 September 1941.

30 'Cook Islands', *Auckland Star*, 16 March 1940.

31 Ibid.

32 'Native title', *Auckland Star*, 10 June 1941; 'These names make news', *World's News* (Sydney, NSW), 9 May 1942.

33 'Paramount chief', *New Zealand Herald*, 10 June 1941.

34 'Title stands', *New Zealand Herald*, 19 June 1941.

35 'Here and there', *Evening Post*, 16 September 1941; 'Farewell parties'.

36 'Rarotonga's new Makea', *Pacific Islands Monthly*, October 1941, 6.

37 Aka`iti Ama, '"Maeva" – Rites of passage: The highlights of family life', in R.G. Crocombe & Marjorie Tuainekore Crocombe (eds), *Akono`anga Maori – Cook Islands Culture* (Suva, Fiji; & Rarotonga: Institute of Pacific Studies in association with the Cook Islands Extension Centre, University of the South Pacific, the Cook Islands Cultural and Historic Places Trust & the Ministry of Cultural Development, 2003), 122.

38 'For women: Mrs Rio Love', *Auckland Star*, 26 January 1943.

39 'Personal notes', *Evening Post*, 20 January 1944.

40 This scheme is discussed in detail in Charlotte Macdonald, 'Taking colonialism home: Cook Island "housegirls" in New Zealand, 1939–1948', in Victoria Haskins & Claire Lowrie (eds), *Colonization and Domestic Service: Historical and contemporary perspectives* (Routledge: New York, 2014), 272–88; and Rosemary Anderson, 'Distant daughters: Cook Islands domestics in wartime New Zealand, 1941–1946', *Journal of Pacific History* 48, no. 3 (2013), 267–85.

41 'Rarotongan girls', *Evening Post*, 23 January 1943.

42 Lady Superintendent, Napier Hospital to Cook Islands Dept, 8 June 1945 and McKay to National Service (Manpower Division). n.d., 1944, IT121/1/6, Part 5: Natives – Cook Island Girls for Domestic Service in New Zealand, Island Territories Department, Wellington, ANZ.

43 Resident Commissioner to Cook Islands Dept, 13 August 1942 and Cook Islands Dept to Resident Commissioner, 5 October 42, IT121/1/6, Part 2, and McKay to Minister of Island Territories, 9 July 45, Resident Commissioner to Dept Island Territories, 16 August 44, and Resident Commissioner to Dept Island Territories, 11 July 1945, IT121/1/6, Part 5.

44 Makea Nui Ariki to Bishop of Aotearoa, 14 April 1943, IT102/3/1, Part 1.

45 'The war effort', *Evening Post*, 28 June 1941.

46 Joy Damousi, *Living with the Aftermath: Trauma, nostalgia and grief in post-war Australia* (Cambridge: Cambridge University Press, 2001), 3.

47 Rachel Patrick, 'Bereavement and mourning (New Zealand)', in 1914–1918 Online, International Encyclopaedia of the First World War, edited by Ute Daniel, Peter Gatrell, Oliver Janz, Heather Jones, Jennifer Keene, Alan Kramer & Bill Nasson, Freie Universität Berlin, Berlin, 2015-02-19. doi: http://dx.doi.org/10.15463/ie1418.10557

48 Ffion Murphy, 'In Memoriam: Women, war and communal lament', *Hecate* 40, no. 2 (2014), 104.

49 'New Zealand Roll of Honour', *Evening Post*, 12 July 1943.

50 Murphy, 'In Memoriam', 110, 116.

51 Ibid., 110.

52 Ibid., 115.

53 McKay to Minister of Island Territories, 9 July 1945, IT121/1/6, Part 5: Takau Love to PM Fraser, 27 May 1943, and Willie Browne to Makea Nui Takau Ariki, 28 April 1943, IT102/2/1, Part 1: Department of Island Territories to Acting Minister of Island Territories, 7 July 1944, IT102/4/16, Part 2.

54 Resident Commissioner, Rarotonga, to Department of Island Territories, Wellington, 19 June 1944, IT102/3/1, Part 1.

55 'Ariki Nui Returns', *Pacific Islands Monthly*, November 1944, 22.

56 Makea Takau Ariki to Cyril McKay, Dept of Island Territories, IT102/3/1, Part 1.

57 'Island orange bloc urged', *Pacific Islands Monthly*, August 1945, 23; 'General News', *Press*, 2 November 1942.

58 Ngata to Buck, 17 September 1932, in *Na to Hoa Aroha – From Your Dear Friend: The correspondence between Sir Apirana Ngata and Sir Peter Buck, 1932–50*, vol. 3, edited by M.P.K. Sorrenson (Auckland: Auckland University Press, 1986), 116.

59 Dick Scott, *Years of the Pooh-Bah: A Cook Islands history* (Rarotonga/Auckland: CITC/ Hodder & Stoughton, 1991), 236, 294.

60 Ngata to Buck, 17 March 1934, in *Na to Hoa Aroha*, 142.

61 Cook Islands Administration to Dept of Island Territories, 29 January 1946, 26 August and 24 September 1947, IT102/3/1, Part 1.

62 Tim Cresswell, *Place: An introduction* (Oxford, England: Wiley Blackwell, 2015), 53.

11

HELPERS, REFORMERS AND MUDDLERS:
Social work and the professionalisation of caring

Margaret Tennant

As the oldest daughter in a Longburn farming family, Bertha Zurcher was almost inevitably destined for domestic caring.[1] Oversight of younger siblings was followed by an early exit from school when Bertha was only 12. With an authoritarian father and a mother increasingly incapacitated by arthritis, Bertha ran the Zurcher household and tended to her mother from the mid-1920s. One respite from hard work in the home and on the farm was her involvement in the Methodist Church and the uplifting fellowship of its youth activities. Another was the local Workers' Education Association (WEA), which helped to widen her horizons and extend her learning opportunities.

A life shift came in 1943 when Bertha was aged 30: with the support of friends she left home and went to train as a nurse at Wellington Hospital. She completed her training in 1946, and later gained maternity and midwifery qualifications. Although she returned to the family home and resumed her responsibilities there, it was with a parallel professional life as a different kind of carer, first in the maternity unit at Palmerston North Hospital and later as a district nurse. While she was tending to the household – to her bedridden and emotionally dependent mother, and to a brother who had had a stroke – she took on increasing responsibilities in her nursing role. In 1955 Bertha was selected to attend the Postgraduate School of Nursing course in Wellington, and when she returned to the Manawatū, 'Sister Zurcher' was appointed assistant medical social worker or 'almoner' at Palmerston North Hospital. She was not the first almoner in the Manawatū, but she took the role in new directions, associating it with a broader social work identity. In 1964 she became a foundation member of the New Zealand Association of Social Workers and, as a member of its education and training standing committee, she helped promote the move toward professional qualifications for social workers.[2]

When Bertha retired as senior medical social worker, she entered another phase in her life of care. At the age of 60 she was inducted into the Order of St Stephen, a Methodist fellowship for volunteers, and began an association with the Manawatū Methodist Social Services as a family support worker.[3] The support she gave was utterly practical, in situations where a mother was in hospital, a couple had separated, or where parents desperately needed a break together, and children required care and a stable household routine. Bertha would move in to the household (or turn up with her caravan) and take on the role of surrogate mother for a period, thus avoiding the need for children to be placed in foster care or to face other disruptions. She would pack lunches and see children off to school, do housework and prepare meals, and be in the home for the children's return from school.[4] Over 13 years she assisted hundreds of families under stress. After her retirement from this role in the late 1980s she became a visitor to those in need, travelling from one end of town to the other on her mobility scooter.[5]

Bertha never considered herself a person of significance, and her reputation is largely local, Manawatū-based – though deeply embedded in her community. Her life experience encompasses many of the practical registers of 'caring' explored in this volume, as well as the more philosophical understandings discussed in Heather Devere's chapter. She cared for others her entire life. She cared for family members and for complete strangers; she did so as a matter of family obligation, but also on a voluntary basis beyond her own immediate kin. She worked in a caring capacity as an employee of a public hospital, and as an unpaid associate of a voluntary agency. She worked within hierarchical institutional structures, in looser community contexts and in private homes. As a nurse she was a member of an increasingly regulated group that had claimed its own professional identity since the 1900s in New Zealand; and she supported and participated in the emergence of professional social work. Her association with the Methodist Church underlines the view some still have of social work as an outward expression of faith; while her work as a nurse and then as a medical social worker shows

Bertha Zurcher on her retirement as the Manawatu Methodist Social Services live-in home support worker in 1988, with one of her former charges. Over 14 years in the role she had cared for hundreds of children in more than 240 families. Reproduced with permission Fairfax Media/ Manawatu Standard

how nursing (and teaching) often provided the skills base for social work before it refined its own corpus of knowledge. The two areas are often labelled 'the caring professions', and both are heavily dominated by women – nursing was 94 per cent female in 2013, and social work 80 per cent.[6] Nonetheless, their professional trajectories, though intersecting, were different.

This chapter focuses on caring beyond the familial context and the antecedents of twenty-first century social work – just one of the many threads in Bertha Zurcher's life of caring. As with the history of nursing, the history of social work is heavily focused on its 'professionalisation project' and the move towards formal education and credentials.[7] The lens here is directed first at the public deployment of 'caring' activities by an earlier generation, mostly women, who were also labelled social workers, or social service workers; their legacy fed into the multiple strands of modern social work with its ambivalent attitude towards notions of 'caring'. There are three stages to the transition: the extension of social caring beyond the home, generally on an unpaid basis; the emergence of the financially supported or waged social service worker – usually but not exclusively female and undertaking casework; and attempts to professionalise social work as an occupation with a distinct knowledge base and formal training.

'Proto' social workers

The naming of activities and occupations is significant, and meanings crystallise over time. In his analysis of the development of social work in the United States, Daniel Walkowitz noted that the term 'social work' entered the national vocabulary around the end of the nineteenth and start of the twentieth century. Terms such as charity work, social service work, welfare work and philanthropy competed in the first two decades of the twentieth century, until 'social work' was overwhelmingly embraced by a cadre of full-time paid workers wanting to distinguish their activities from personal and religious charity work.[8] This transition was not without conflict between the new generation of social workers who were championing training, credentials, objectivity and systematic casework, and the supposed emotionalism and inconsistency of their largely evangelical predecessors.

In New Zealand the transition was less clear, and slower to embrace the professional enterprise. When the term first appeared in New Zealand the 'social' (which supposes knowledge of communal needs) was emphasised over the 'worker', at least in any sense of work as employment. As New Zealand moved beyond its early colonial period and cities expanded, new (or newly apparent) social needs began to impinge on the public consciousness. From the 1890s there were numerous references in newspapers to 'social workers' who were well known in their New Zealand communities, as well as to prominent individuals overseas, including church personnel, philanthropists and social reformers. These women and men generally aimed to extend their influence beyond the home and immediate church congregation into a wider public sphere. And yet the 'work' part of the equation was not insignificant: on their death, eulogies acknowledged their hard graft, often over decades and in contexts where battles, personal and political, were hard fought. Such work was not necessarily paid, however.

There has been a good deal written about the social mobilisation of women's caring in New Zealand during and after the campaign for women's suffrage.[9] Faced with the casualties of a rapidly urbanising late-colonial society, middle-class women, often those of an age to be free of childcare, felt empowered to operate beyond the home. Initially this occurred through the churches and established benevolent societies, but soon they formed other, women-centred organisations such as the Women's Christian Temperance Union (established in New Zealand in 1885) and the National Council of Women (1896). Such bodies combined a political agenda for change with opportunities to intervene more directly in others' lives. The language they used did not pose a challenge to the nineteenth-century notion of separate spheres, for their activities were often justified as a form of extended housekeeping. Women's claims to a public role were promoted as a necessary counterbalance to the male role.

Eveline Willett Cunnington is a good example of this first generation of social workers. A foundation member of the Canterbury Women's Institute, the National Council of Women, the Canterbury Fabian Society and the WEA, she was also a prominent committee member of the Canterbury Female Refuge and an elected member of the North Canterbury Charitable Aid Board. In 1895 she became one of the first two women in New Zealand to be appointed official prison visitors.[10] Cunnington was said to possess 'a witty and sometimes caustic pen', and was described in the *Auckland Star* after her death as having 'the brain of an unusually able man ... combined [with] the sweet sympathy of the tenderest woman'[11] – a rare combination of qualities, it was implied, but clearly one that made her both acceptable and effective in the context of her time. Suffragist Kate Sheppard's more radical claims were similarly softened by reassuring comments on her 'womanliness' and unthreatening appearance, and Cunnington had previously deflected criticism by noting that although she was sometimes called 'a new woman', she 'was an old woman in the sense that she had great faith and confidence in her husband, who had shared and consented to her work'.[12] As one involved in rescue work with 'fallen women' and with prison visitation, Cunnington worked to help those who had fallen foul of the law and of social mores. But she also agitated for a mixed package of wider legislative reforms, including infant life protection, raising the age of sexual consent to 21, and the appointment of women police (in what was arguably a 'social work' role). Increasingly she promoted a socialist agenda for a complete change in the economic order and, as an Anglican, she attempted to bring the church and the socialist movement closer together.[13]

Cunnington's 1916 obituary in the *Maoriland Worker* claimed that 'no social worker has been more respected nor better known than Mrs. Cunnington'.[14] As a prolific writer she had already applied her acute eye to the notion of social work in 1897: it was, she wrote, a generic term, 'covering all those people who engage in work outside of their immediate and natural obligations'; those who voluntarily 'assume[d] labours and responsibilities which [did] not fall to their lot in the course of ordinary private life'.[15] She classified social workers into three categories: social helpers, social reformers and 'social muddlers'. The latter she dismissed as ill informed, erratic and inconsistent in their responses to social issues: 'the social muddler is kind to-day and severe tomorrow; full of extravagant generosity at one hour and insanely mean at another'. Seemingly well intentioned, such persons were also able to exert political influence, and Cunnington considered that 'the oscillation and bewildering see-saw of our social life is due to the influence of these people'. Caring was not enough in itself and, indeed, it could be socially regressive if it was based on a superficial and emotionally driven understanding of facts.

In contrast, the social helper was represented by the rich combination of workers in Cunnington's own Christchurch community: Salvationists, Anglican and Catholic orders of nuns and ladies of the St Saviours Guild, all undertaking their work 'quietly, steadfastly and unweariedly'. Their different modes and methods of caring she saw as a positive, for 'the coat of charity, like Joseph's garment, should be of many bright hues. Poor humanity needs so much cheering ... He wants every particle of help that can be given him by the different social workers of the world.'[16] Uniformity and standardisation of attributes were not part of the remit.

But it was the social reformers that Cunnington saw as the 'true martyrs', the 'noble army that goes down into the arena and fights ... generally against terrible odds, established custom, crystallised, law-hardened prejudice', despite the sneers of others. Such reformers gathered facts and data, used them to inform theory, then tried to turn theories into actualities. Here Cunnington foreshadowed the notion of evidence-based social research as underpinning social action: she might have been welcome in many a sociology department of a later era. Her critiques of poverty and social class and her espousal of Fabianism would have made her sympathetic to the ethic of justice discussed in chapter 2. But in her own terms, she was both reformer and helper; and speaking, it seems, from experience, she noted how altruistic work invariably crushed its workers 'till tired brain and weary foot give way, broken down by the sheer bigness of the work'. Social caring could come with a high personal price.

Cunnington's article on social work was a product of the late nineteenth century, but it anticipated tensions that still exercise social workers: whether the core task of social work is to work with individuals to effect personal change, or whether wider social action and a commitment to social justice and equity should be prioritised – perspectives that are aligned with the 'ethic of care' and the 'ethic of justice', but are also more simplistically represented, since the 1970s, as social control and social change, or as individualist and collectivist responses to social problems.[17] Cunnington's analysis was not explicitly gendered: she used a universalised 'he' and 'him' in relation to each of her categories, even though the examples given of 'social helpers' were largely women's organisations or religious orders. The 'social reformer' was represented in the article by the fact-gathering university professor, but there is a strong sense that 'social muddlers' could be of either sex. The key thrust of Cunnington's argument was the need for analysis and thought; for the exercise of the brain as well as the heart, despite the personal calumnies and opposition this invited. Social caring was to be *informed* caring.

Paid to care: Early strands in social work as an occupation

Cunnington's social workers took caring outside the home, but they were not necessarily remunerated for their work: indeed, her definition, while not excluding a paid occupation, emphasises the voluntary impulse. While the term 'social worker' was widely used in the early twentieth-century for those with collective concerns and social programmes, it was not until 1926 that it appeared in the New Zealand census, along with 'welfare worker', as the occupational descriptor.[18] Before 1926 the relevant occupational categories drew in those 'ministering to charity', 'officers of benevolent institutions', 'officers of charitable or benevolent institutions' and 'others involved in social welfare work'. At this time the United States census placed religious, charity and welfare workers as 'sub-professionals' in the midst of a heterogeneous list of other occupations, including notaries, sportsmen, fortune tellers and keepers of pleasure resorts and race tracks.[19] The New Zealand census included social workers within a larger professional grouping, alongside doctors, barristers and accountants, though external perceptions of their status were not quite so clear. The term was later submerged as the New Zealand census focused on location of work rather than occupations, but it re-emerged in 1966 to capture those not otherwise recorded as undertaking welfare activities on a paid basis.[20]

The 1926 census showed that there were 70 women and 47 men classified as social workers in New Zealand, alongside 34 deaconesses, 81 organisers (69 of them male, and probably associated with unions and bodies such as the Young Men's Christian Association), and 1309 Sisters of Mercy and Compassion under the same subcategory. Members of the deaconess and other religious orders undertook caring work beyond the confines of their churches (though some of the Sisters of Mercy would also have been teachers). Of the 70 women specifically described as social or welfare workers, nearly 80 per cent had never married and a further 17 per cent were widowed or separated, compared with a minority (38 per cent) of the men living outside of a marital situation.[21] 'Helping' work was still considered the domain of dedicated women workers, even when it was performed outside of religious orders: they were the devoted, unattached daughters, the Bertha Zurchers, now caring for the wider social family. Social work was, and continued to be, 'womanly' work.

While nineteenth-century evangelicalism had at first seen Christians move into missionary work with the heathen overseas, by the end of the century the focus was also on the unchurched and the needy closer to home. A large number of welfare workers identified by the census were individuals who were maintained by religious denominations to run an expanding number of welfare institutions, especially church homes for children. Others worked under the umbrella of city missions and newer denominational agencies that were more directly concerned with welfare: the Presbyterian Social Service Association (PSSA), started in Dunedin in 1906, is a prime example of this. The Salvation Army had an especially strong social welfare arm: its credo of 'soup, soap and salvation' captured evangelical aspirations to bring individuals to God while ministering to their bodily needs. For evangelicals, care and conversion were closely intertwined; souls as well as bodies were the the focus of concern. Although the secularisation of social work was to proceed over the twentieth century, Auckland city missioner Jasper Calder was exaggerating only slightly when he claimed in 1928 that 'there are no social workers anywhere except those who are inspired by some religious conviction'.[22]

Christian belief provided a durable thread within social work. When the New Zealand Association of Social Workers was formed in 1964, a number of its leaders were either associated with church agencies, or came to their role with strong religious conviction: Merv Hancock, the first president, was a Methodist lay preacher who acknowledged the social gospel as a major influence in his life; the vice-president and first chair of its education and training committee, Major Thelma Smith, was matron of the Salvation Army's Auckland Bethany Hospital; and the secretary, Arch Elliffe, was a Presbyterian minister and former superintendent of the Otago PSSA.[23] If conversion was no longer an explicit outcome of Christian caring, there was still the belief that faith should be expressed through social action and a modelling of Christ's work in the modern world.[24] As Bertha Zurcher, another foundation member of the association, wrote, 'to tell people they matter is one thing; to actually show them in the name of the Church they do is quite another'.[25]

A more secular strand of modern social work was in place by the early twentieth century. The Society for the Protection of Women and Children (SPWC), first formed in Auckland in 1893, was an especially significant organisation in the voluntary sector. By the late 1900s there was an SPWC in all of the main centres, and each employed a woman visitor or, more inquisitorially, 'inspector' in what was essentially a caseworker role. Keeping case records was a feature of organisations in Britain and the United States that promoted the idea of a 'scientific charity' based on systematic investigation of needs and targeting of responses rather than an uncoordinated and emotionally driven distribution of alms (the kind of response Cunnington attributed to her 'social muddlers'). In New Zealand, case records were used by agencies such as the hospital and charitable aid boards to discourage welfare abuse – to identify clients who did the rounds, imposing on multiple sources of charitable aid. The SPWC took casework beyond a basic record-keeping function to integrate it with counselling, domestic support, legal assistance, and advocacy for legislative changes. Its women caseworkers, situated in ones and twos in offices, undertook work that was physically and emotionally hard: it involved long hours, travel (often by bicycle), and interaction with families in crisis, with a good deal of domestic violence in the client mix. Their employment typically involved decades in the job, and signals occupational issues that were to remain important for social workers throughout the twentieth century: high caseloads, low salaries, occasional difficulties with the voluntary committees they reported to, and the stress of a position on the boundaries of the public and the private, and of volunteer and worker identities.[26] And given that they were paid workers answerable to voluntary committees of 'ladies and gentlemen', they were also working on the boundaries of class.

Many of these early SPWC workers brought other forms of experience to their role. Winefride Dive described her transition into a case worker:

> When the war began at the end of 1939 my sons enlisted and my daughters were also away. I decided to do something and didn't feel like going back to teaching so I decided to go into social work. I answered the advertisement of the Protection Society; but I approached it with considerable trepidation – a raw recruit, you might say....
>
> I found myself dealing with domestic upheavals, unmarried mothers, old people, neighbours' quarrels ... Social Security benefits had hardly been established then and the unfortunate wives who sought Court Orders for maintenance had a pretty raw time.... I approached Mr Parry, the Minister for Social Security, and told him about the plight of these women. We urged the deserted wives pension and eventually it was granted, but it took a long time.[27]

Dive's account shows the almost serendipitous nature of entry into social work at the time, and how age, background 'life experience' and alternative professional training – in her case as a teacher – were substitutes for a social work education.

The SPWC's paid workers were women, backed up where necessary by police and other authority figures. While most histories of social work have focused on the feminisation of the helping professions and on social work as a locus of female employment, social work was always less exclusively female than nursing, and there were contexts where men were predominant. The Prisoners' Aid and Rehabilitation Society was one such setting. Local prisoners' aid societies emerged in the late nineteenth-century, bringing into sharp juxtaposition two extremes of colonial and post-colonial manhood. The prisoners' aid worker was typically a family man with strong church connections, often a cleric who could combine prison chaplaincy with an assisting role beyond the prison gates. His pastoral and welfare role led him to interact with other men whose excessive expression of rough frontier masculinity – in inappropriate contexts – brought them into conflict with the law.

George Moreton combined the role of Discharged Prisoners' Aid Society secretary and Anglican chaplain to Mount Eden Prison from the late 1920s. He, like a number of city missioners of his time, epitomised the 'muscular Christian' – the male church worker who represented the masculine face of the churches against concerns that Christianity was becoming overly feminised. Many had previously been involved in bodies such as the YMCA and the Brotherhood of St Andrew. They were charged with leading an inspirational social work among young men, while providing strong and principled role models to their weaker brethren. In these organisations' publicity the sporting prowess and physicality of such men were often emphasised, and their written reports sometimes picked up on the vernacular of their clientele. These particular male social workers worked on the boundaries between an authoritarian role and an *over*-caring one, and it was easy for prison visitors to endanger relationships on either side. George Moreton, for example, was evicted from his rented prisoners' aid office because of neighbourhood complaints about the 'parson and his scaly friends', but his next office was burgled by what he termed 'the alumni of Rock College' (Mount Eden Prison). When, in the mid-1940s, Moreton moved from assistance to advocacy, publicly criticising conditions in Mount Eden, his chaplaincy and access to the prison were terminated.[28] The tension between individual support and social critique was most apparent for those needing to interact with state agencies.

The employment of social workers within statutory agencies increased from the mid-twentieth century. Whereas in the United States the most important developments in the emergence of a social work identity had taken place within the voluntary sector, in New Zealand public agencies led the way. Nursing provided one important strand. There were forms of nursing that took its practitioners beyond a hospital setting into the homes of the sick poor. Initially provided by private philanthropic bodies, district nursing became a legislative responsibility of hospital boards in 1926. The boards wanted to relieve their wards of chronically ill patients who were a drain on resources, and found the nurses were an effective way of easing the transition from hospital to home, or averting admission in the first place.[29] As trained personnel who went into private homes, the district nurses often reported on matters that were not strictly medical. In this sense their concerns overlapped with those of social workers, who were also interested in the connections between health, hygiene and moral and financial wellbeing. The Department of Health encouraged the development of hospital-based social work as a means of linking district nurses and in-patient care. As an article in the nurses' journal *Kai Tiaki* said in 1929, 'A physical restoration unaccompanied by a restoration of self-respect, suitable occupation, and satisfaction with life, is but at best a part service.' It added that 'successful social service is only possible for a woman with a missionary spirit – it is more, perhaps than any other social service, vocational'.[30] Nursing had long referenced the religious language of vocation and sisterhood, so it was not surprising that medical social work, staffed initially by nurses, invoked missionary endeavours as its practitioners ventured beyond the hospital.

In the 1930s the director of nursing, Mary Lambie, rejected the American and British precedent of using laypersons as almoners and this established the role as one for nurses, many of whom acquired an elite status via the postgraduate diploma in nursing administered by Victoria University and the Department of Health.[31] The Palmerston North Hospital Board appears to have been the first to appoint a nurse 'almoner' in 1939, and other hospital boards followed, more often using the label 'medical social worker'.[32] In 1972 only 23 per cent of the 188 social workers employed in the health services had a qualification specific to social work.[33] After this time the hospital boards actually led the way in requiring their social service appointees to have a social work qualification or prior social work experience, or both.[34] Medical social workers became an important subset of the profession in the late twentieth century.

In the meantime, nursing provided a professional underpinning to women's social work in the state social service sector. After the Child Welfare Act was passed in 1925 a cadre of state social workers developed within the Child Welfare Branch of the Department of Education, and they soon provided a vitally important cluster of experience and knowledge. From an initial 20 officers gazetted after the Act came into force, numbers increased to nearly 100 in the mid-1940s and 291 field officers by 1971 (in addition to residential and clerical staff).[35] In March 1945, 43 of the 53 female child welfare officers had nursing qualifications – and often more than one; the men, on the other hand, came mostly from a teaching background.[36] The branch perpetuated existing gender divisions within social work by employing women as 'child welfare officers' to deal with small boys, girls and young women, and the male employees as 'boys' welfare officers' to work mostly with boys aged over 12. Before the late 1940s, female officers, like the majority of women within the public service, did not have permanent status. Differential promotion and pay scales were reinforced by separate supervision and in-service training of the officers within head office. A 1945 report noted that the pay scales of the female officers, in particular, were far below what they could earn in their former professions, especially at senior levels, and that the conditions of work were often more challenging and strenuous:

> Child Welfare work is an essential service which tends to attract socially conscious women. It is felt that they should not receive less recognition financially than they would receive by remaining in their previous positions … The responsibility involved in this work is unusually heavy and demands an outstanding type of woman, with a broad outlook, initiative and human sympathy.[37]

If self-sacrifice was a feature of women's domestic caring, it was extended into 'caring' forms of employment and, indeed, was institutionalised within state structures.

A minimum age of 25 (over 30 in practice) ensured that, as well as any former professional training, the appointees had at least some experience of life, but they otherwise learned on the job.[38] Charlie Peek, superintendent of child welfare from 1946 to 1964, was an advocate for professional social work training, but quoted with approval a statement by John A. Lee that 'when dealing with children, big hearts are better than big heads'. There was, in Peek's view, no real substitute for experience: 'no person, however well prepared otherwise, begins as a "good officer".'[39] In the mid-twentieth century, recruitment prioritised life experience in the absence of more formal avenues of training; and this recognition of experience, life skills and cultural capital is still an important factor in the credentialling of social workers. In the early twenty-first century formal social work education has promised a foreshortening of experience and the production of a more effective, flexible, culturally attuned and socially aware practitioner.[40] Big hearts have given way to assessed 'competencies'.

The Child Welfare Branch (later 'Division') soon became the largest single employer of social workers within state agencies.[41] Its employees worked within a hierarchical public service structure with the usual requirements to shift around as part of the promotion process: they were exposed to 'efficiency tests' after 1937, and had access to increasingly formalised forms of in-service training. Initially these were mostly to do with administrative processes, appointees' responsibilities as public servants and the statutory basis of their work – a reminder that these particular social workers were agents of a government department, were invested with considerable state powers and were dealing with a largely involuntary clientele.[42] They were part of what has been termed 'the policing of families', whereby 'experts' in health, hygiene, child rearing and discipline gained an authority to make pronouncements on, or, in the case of child welfare workers, to actively intervene in families that were deemed dysfunctional – where caring was absent, insufficient or misdirected.[43]

Officers inspected the private children's homes that supplemented the state's own institutions, supervised foster-home placements, followed up on the welfare of ex-nuptial children, spent considerable time in the children's courts, and engaged in what was optimistically termed 'preventive work'. As Bronwyn Dalley's history of child welfare in New Zealand points out, this kind of investigation could delve into all aspects of a family's life, and sometimes involved supervision of household expenditure, judgement of the quality of housework and of marital relations; and, despite the goal of keeping families together, it could end with children being placed in state care or in supervision.[44] However caring and pragmatic they may have been as individuals, child welfare officers as a group came to be seen as a threat even beyond the families they worked with, largely because of their association with court work and the removal of children from unsatisfactory homes. (How many children of the mid-twentieth century were threatened with 'the welfare' if they misbehaved?) The balance between care and control was, and is, most finely tested in the area of child welfare work.

A range of social work functions were carried out within public agencies by 1970, when plans for a merged Department of Social Welfare were afoot: it was estimated in 1969 that approximately 70 per cent of New Zealand's social workers were employed within statutory and local body agencies such as hospital and education boards.[45] There were probation officers, Māori welfare officers working within the Department of Maori Affairs and social workers within the Department of Social Security, as well as the child welfare officers. In localities the work of the officers overlapped with that of visiting teachers who were appointed within schools to liaise with the home on issues of truancy and learning, the Health Department's public health nurses, and the hospital boards' medical social workers. Social work had become bureaucratised under the umbrella of the caring (and controlling) state. The effects of this process were partially mitigated by the strong and pragmatic personalities of many of the women and men employed within its structures. This expansion occurred during the heyday of New Zealand's welfare state. It prompted the last superintendent of Child Welfare, Lewis Anderson, to reflect on rises in child offending despite increased assistance to needy families and a period of relative prosperity over the 1950s and 1960s: 'Working towards improved living standards is still desirable, and even essential, but he or she is a foolish person who thinks it constitutes the universal panacea for social problems.' The caring state still needed its social workers, 'the people on the spot in a face-to-face-relationship with . . . clients'.[46] But these social workers had increasingly become part of the state apparatus, and even those who acted beyond it were enmeshed in its demands. This is a situation that still exercises the profession's analysts and practitioners, for 'social work can be conceptualised as a profession hovering in uncomfortable places, caught between aspirations to contribute to social justice and bureaucratic constraints'.[47]

The professionalisation of caring

Histories of New Zealand social work invariably record the response of education minister Peter Fraser in 1949 to requests for funding to set up a School of Social Work at Victoria University College. Fraser apparently replied: 'Nonsense, we've done all the social work needed in New Zealand'! (When the principal of Victoria, Sir Thomas Hunter, went back to Fraser with a proposal for a 'School of Social Science', Fraser replied, 'Fine, how much money do you want?')[48] The story encapsulates the tension between government investment in benefits given as of right, and the development of social services extended to individuals and families. The New Zealand focus on the former is sometimes seen as a reason for the relatively late professionalisation of social work there compared to other countries. Other possible reasons include the small scale of New Zealand society, the dispersal of many social workers and their embeddedness, often long-term, in specific local communities where trust and interpersonal relations probably counted for more than professional credentials.

Social workers (like nurses) have long agonised over definitions of 'professionalism' and the characteristics of a professional, which involve far more than getting paid for doing a job. Sonya Hunt refers to 'a politically charged project, achieved through a series of strategic alliances with those in power ... while at the same time evidencing technical knowledge and competence, promoting ethical standards and public interest while separating the discipline from competing groups with alternative cultural capital'. She and others underline the power relations in this process, especially where alliances need to be formed with government in order to advance professional interests. An associated theme is the tendency towards occupational closure, exclusiveness and control of standards, encapsulated in debates over social worker registration.[49] Other defining characteristics of a profession are the emergence of a specialised education imparting a recognised and distinctive body of knowledge, skills and values; the formation of a professional association; and agreement on a code of ethics. The recent history of social work in New Zealand has been well canvassed by social work educators including Hunt, Nash and Beddoe, who have highlighted key dates such as the establishment of the School of Social Science and its first intake of students in 1950, the beginning of a generation of highly influential graduates from the course; the formation of the New Zealand Association of Social Workers (NZASW) in 1964; the first undergraduate Bachelor of Social Work degree established at Massey University in 1976; and the Social Workers Registration Act of 2003, which provided for voluntary registration.[50]

Social work moved towards professionalisation very late compared with New Zealand's other main 'caring' profession, nursing. Social work and nursing were both female-dominated occupations with strong religious undertones to their foundations, but New Zealand nurses gained registration via a state examination from 1901. They had a sufficiently strong collective voice to stave off competition from voluntary auxiliary nursing aides during World War I, and to ensure that volunteer aides remained firmly under their control during the next world war. They formed their own national organisation in 1909 and eventually gained control over their own body of knowledge and accreditation processes from the 1970s, when training moved from an apprenticeship model into the tertiary education sector. They were initially assisted towards professional status by elements that nursing leaders later challenged: a high level of advocacy (and control) from the director of nursing within the Department of Health, and close association with the prestigious domains of medical knowledge. Nurses were readily distinguishable because they wore uniforms and, since most were located in hospitals, they formed a critical mass and their activities were visible to the public. Those they assisted came from all walks of life; and there was an assumption that nurses' efforts would result in patient improvement if not cure – an assumption not quite so readily extended to social workers and their more marginalised client base. Like social workers, nurses have often chafed against their association with 'caring', especially the domestic and devotional associations of the term, though in the case of nursing it did gain them a high level of public approval. Social workers, or at least those in statutory agencies, have had to contend with the historically more authoritarian elements of their role: as a speaker at the AGM of the Mental Health Association said in 1972, 'A social worker is still a curious creature in New Zealand of unknown origin, unknown parentage to many people[,] doing an obviously worthy task to be sure but with slightly grisly and, or suspicious overtones or undertones.'[51]

Mary Nash suggests that social work's pathway to professional status was hindered by internal as well as external factors. High on the list of external factors in the mid century were beliefs about the efficacy of New Zealand's benefit-based welfare state: Fraser's view on this has already been noted. John McCreary, lecturer (and later professor) in the School of Social Science, stated at the inaugural conference of the NZASW in 1964:

> We have believed, both as Public Service administrators and in
> Government that by passing social legislation we can solve social problems.
> What is very clear to me is that social legislation without social service
> is uneconomic and ineffectual, and it is only with the development of
> adequate social services that social legislation becomes effective.[52]

His emphasis was on the need for better linkages between social legislation and the experience gained from social casework practice.

By the end of the century the situation was very different and the redistributive welfare state was on the wane. As the welfare state contracted from the mid-1980s and market principles prevailed, even social workers found themselves subject to business models, their tasks sometimes broken down into units of performance and contracted on an hourly basis. In social work, as in other employment areas, public policy goals were expressed in terms of economic rather than social benefits.[53]

The impetus to professionalise was also disrupted by some profound divisions within social work itself. The wider activism of the 1960s and 1970s fuelled social workers' own analyses of their remit, and rifts developed between those who were making a pragmatic effort to consolidate as a profession within a range of employment contexts, and those who prioritised social justice, social action and community work as the core tasks of social work. Even if they did not necessarily use the same terminology, the 'ethic of care' and the 'ethic of justice' discussed elsewhere in this volume were concepts that implicitly framed the theoretical and practical debates that exercised social workers of the time. Advocates of social justice were more likely to be hostile to the professional project, which they saw as elitist, exclusionary, and distancing social workers from their clientele. Anti-racist critiques pointed out the inconsistency of Pākehā social workers working with a primarily Māori clientele in many contexts, and asserted the primacy of cultural competencies as part of indigenous social work. Such internal ambivalence was compounded by the tendency of some social workers to identify with their agencies rather than with any wider professional agenda; and by debates over the nature of training – where it should take place (in universities, technical institutes or teachers colleges), the length of courses (from short certificates to two-year diplomas to four-year degrees, for example), and who should control it (social work educators or employers). There was anxiety that competency-based training might undermine the wider, more critical, social justice components of social work programmes.[54]

There has been ongoing disagreement over mandatory registration, too: some agencies and individuals have expressed disquiet about the degree of state control over the registration process and its potential to exclude competent practitioners, especially those from Māori and Pasifika backgrounds. The cost for non-profit agencies, 86 per cent of whose social workers were estimated to be unregistered in 2013, has also been a concern.[55] In 2016 there were 5000 social workers on the register, compared with some 18,000 self-identified social workers in the 2013 census.[56] This gap, and government agencies' increasing risk aversion in fields such as child protection and mental health, has brought mandatory registration ever closer.[57] The title 'social worker' is likely to be restricted by law, in line with similar professions such as nurses, pharmacists, medical practitioners and dieticians.

Conclusion

Would Bertha Zurcher be registered or even recognised as a 'social worker' today? In her own professional field of medical social work – one of the first to tighten requirements – she would probably be required to have a qualification specifically in social work; her postgraduate nursing qualification unlikely to suffice. The 2003 Social Workers Registration Act does provide for recognition of prior experience, but Bertha would be obliged to provide comprehensive written evidence to prove that she was 'fit and proper' to practise, and she might be required to undertake a face-to-face competency interview. In particular, she would need to demonstrate that she has 'specific competencies to work with Māori and other cultural and ethnic groups'.[58] She might also have to undertake ongoing professional development. Even as a volunteer going into private homes for an agency, Bertha would be subject to police checks and would probably be obliged to undertake a degree of training.

In the public sphere, 'caring' is not enough: a risk-averse society requires oversight of carers and assessment of skills to ensure that helping is indeed helping in specific contexts. Misdirected caring has been linked with a potentially dangerous emotionalism and a lack of self-reflexivity. For social workers, as for nurses, the notion of caring has been complicated by the elaboration of 'competencies' – a process that is possibly less challenging for nurses, with their specific clinical requirements, than for social workers. The national 'core competencies' of social workers do include personal qualities commensurate with 'caring' as it appears elsewhere in this volume: the social worker is to be 'compassionate, empathetic and respectful ... to understand others to adequately assess their needs', for example. And wider social caring has not altogether disappeared from the social work curriculum; indeed, it is given its own tick boxes under headings such as 'Competence to promote the principles of human rights and social and economic justice', 'Competence to engage in practice which promotes social change', and 'Competence to promote empowerment of people and communities to enable positive change'. This is some distance from the thrust of Eveline Cunnington's 'social reformers', for it supposes a closer affinity with clientele than nineteenth-century reformers would have envisaged: a less paternalistic – or maternalistic – interaction with them (in theory at least). Those who take on the mantle of 'social helpers' are expected to 'partner' with clients and, in working with Māori, to demonstrate practice that is 'culturally sustaining, strengthens relationships, is mutually contributing and connecting and encourages warmth' (though the nature of that 'warmth' is not specified). In this they have a more demanding brief than Cunnington's religiously inspired Christchurch colleagues of the 1890s and 1900s.[59] The approach of those early workers was unambiguously top-down, monocultural and more confidently informed by the certitudes of religion than of academic curricula. Bertha would nonetheless have found Christian fellow travellers among the ranks of current social workers – those who still see social work as 'more than just a job, it is a vocation and a spiritual calling of service', inspired by the example of Christ[60] – terminology that earlier generations of deaconesses, nuns and devout laypersons would have been equally comfortable with. Recognition of Māori spirituality and respect for spiritual as well as cultural markers are now part of the package of formal social work competencies.

In her role of domestic carer Bertha Zurcher would have been free from public accountabilities and largely invisible. She was part of the 'shadow' labour force – mostly women – identified by Ivan Illich.[61] If the demands of the workplace became too much for her, as they did for many employed women, she might today draw on the services of paid external caregivers, or her parents might end up in institutional care – as, indeed, did Bertha herself: she died a resident of Palmerston North's Brightwater Home in 2014, aged 100. Her life exemplified the many dimensions of care and changing understandings of social work over the span of a century.

Notes

1   Many thanks to Charlotte Macdonald and Annabel Cooper for detailed comments on this chapter, and to others partaking in the 'Caring Histories' workshop for helpful suggestions.

2   Biographical information is based on June MacMillan, *And All Shall Be Well: The life of Bertha Zurcher* (Palmerston North: Keeling & Mundy Print, 2010).

3   On Zurcher's relationship with Manawatu Methodist Social Services, see Helen Dollery, 'Social service, social justice or a matter of faith? The Palmerston North Methodist Social Service Centre 1963–2000', Masters thesis, Massey University, 2005, 60–70.

4   Florence M. Baber, *Towards Wholeness: A history of the Manawatu Methodist Social Service Centre 1963–1983* [n.p., 1983].

5   'And all shall be well', http://anzasw.nz/wp-content/uploads/Bertha-Zurcher.pdf

6   Statistics New Zealand, *Women at Work: 1991–2013*, 15, www.stats.govt.nz, 2015.

7   The key work here is Mary Nash, 'People, policies and practice: Social work education in Aotearoa/New Zealand from 1949 to 1995', PhD thesis, Massey University, 1998. For a shorter summary see Mary Nash, '"That terrible title, social worker": A time of transition in social work history 1949–53,' *Social Work Review* 10, no. 1 (March 1998), 12–18; and Mary Nash, 'Educating social workers in Aotearoa New Zealand', in Marie Connolly (ed.), *New Zealand Social Work: Contexts and practice* (Melbourne: Oxford University Press, 2001), 265–78. A much-cited review of the early years of the school under its first professor, D.C. Marsh, is J.R. McCreary, 'The School of Social Science – Part One: The Martians', *New Zealand Social Worker* 7, no. 1 (1971), 9–49.

8   Daniel Walkowitz, *Working with Class: Social workers and the politics of middle-class identity* (Chapel Hill: University of North Carolina Press, 1999), 27.

9   Chapters in Anne Else (ed.), *Women Together: A history of women's organisations in New Zealand Ngā rōpū wāhine o te motu* (Wellington: Daphne Brassell Associates/Historical Branch, Department of Internal Affairs, 1993) draw on a range of existing literature to make this point: see, especially, Raewyn Dalziel on 'Political organisations', 55–69; Margaret Tennant, 'Welfare organisations', 109–19; Sandra Coney, 'Health organisations', 241–53; Dorothy Page, 'Service organisations', 289–99. See also Barbara Brookes, *A History of New Zealand Women* (Wellington: Bridget Williams Books, 2016), chs 5 & 6.

10 Roberta Nicholls, 'Cunnington, Eveline Willett'.

11 *Auckland Star*, 5 August 1916, 17.

12 *Press*, 21 February 1904, 7.

13 Nicholls, 'Cunnington, Eveline Willett', from the Dictionary of New Zealand Biography: www.TeAra.govt.nz/en/biographies/3c44/cunnington-eveline-willett

14 *Maoriland Worker*, 9 November 1916, 3.

15 This, and the following summary is based upon an article by Eveline Cunnington in the Christchurch *Star*, 27 November 1897, 6.

16 Ibid. I have written previously on the social work of women church personnel in 'Sisterly ministrations: The social work of Protestant deaconesses in New Zealand 1890–1940', *New Zealand Journal of History* 32, no.1 (1998), 3–22. Other histories

that touch on churchwomen's social work in New Zealand include Ruth Fry, *Community of the Sacred Name: A centennial history* (Christchurch: Community of the Sacred Name, 1993); Jessie Munro, *The Story of Suzanne Aubert* (Auckland: Auckland University Press/Bridget Williams Books, 1996); and Margaret McClure, *Saving the City. A history of the Order of the Good Shepherd and the Community of the Holy Name in Auckland, 1894–2000* (Auckland: David Ling Publishing, 2002).

17 For an excellent article on different approaches to social work professionalisation in New Zealand see Sonya Hunt, 'The social work professionalization project before the 1990s in Aotearoa New Zealand: The dream', *Aotearoa New Zealand Social Work* 28, no. 3 (2016), 15–25.

18 *Census of New Zealand*, 1926, vol. IX, 49.

19 Walkowitz, *Working with Class*, 29.

20 *Census of New Zealand*, 1926, vol. IX, 23 and 49; *Census of New Zealand*, 1966, vol. IV, 73.

21 'Occupations,' *Census of New Zealand*, vol. X, 1926, 49.

22 Report on Auckland City Mission, [Auckland] *Diocesan Yearbook*, 1927–28, Auckland Anglican Diocesan Archive.

23 Merv Hancock, interviewed by Margaret Tennant, 29 July 1998, Hancock tape 11, Massey University Archives. On Elliffe's role in the Presbyterian Social Service Association's Dunedin office for more than 25 years, see Ian Dougherty & Jane Thomson, *Making a Difference: A centennial history of Presbyterian Support Otago* (Dunedin: Presbyterian Support Otago, 2006), 64–65.

24 For one explanation of faith-based social work from the director of a Presbyterian-based pastoral counselling centre, see E.M. [Rev. Evan] Sherrard, 'A philosophy behind a church social work agency', *New Zealand Social Worker* 5, no. 1 (1969), 35–41.

25 Quoted in Dollery, 'Social service, social justice', 66.

26 For more detail on this body nationally, see Margaret Tennant, 'New Zealand Federation of Home and Family Societies 1893–', in Else, *Women Together*, 132–34; and, for Auckland, Raewyn Dalziel, *Focus on the Family: The Auckland Home and Family Society 1893–1993* (Auckland: Home and Family Society/David Ling Publishing, 1993).

27 *New Zealand Social Worker*, January 1970, 11.

28 Melville Harcourt, *A Parson in Prison: A biography of the Rev. George Edgar Moreton* (Auckland: Whitcombe & Tombs, 1942). For an overview of Prisoners' Aid work see Margaret Tennant, *Through the Prison Gate: 125 Years of prisoners' aid and rehabilitation* (Wellington: New Zealand Prisoners' Aid and Rehabilitation Society, 2002).

29 Pamela Wood & Kerri Arcus, 'Poverty, philanthropy and professionalism: The establishment of District Nursing Service in Wellington, New Zealand, 1903', *Health and History* 13, no. 1 (2011), 44, 60.

30 *Kai Tiaki*, 1 November 1929, 60; an article by director of nursing, Mary Lambie, on 'Hospital social service work done in Toronto' appears in *Kai Tiaki*, October 1925, 192. See also a report on the advantages of appointing an 'almoner' to Wellington Hospital, *Evening Post*, 1 March 1935, 10.

31 See correspondence in H1 21/93 23033, Archives New Zealand, Wellington.

32 Jo Kellaway & Mike Maryan, *A Century of Care: Palmerston North Hospital 1893–1993* (Double Bay, Australia: Focal Books, 1993), 70; Patricia E. Johnstone, 'How medical social work developed in New Zealand', *New Zealand Social Worker* 5, no. 1 (1969), 35–37.

33 T.H.J. Austin, 'The Department of Health's policy regarding social work services', in Papers relating to Medical Social Workers' Seminar March 1973, in author's possession.

34 Lambie, 'On hospital social service work', 192; Nash, 'People, policies and practice', 160. On Lambie's preference for nurses as almoners see correspondence in ADZB 16163 (H1 21/93), Archives New Zealand.

35 Bronwyn Dalley, *Family Matters: Child welfare in twentieth-century New Zealand* (Auckland: Auckland University Press/Historical Branch, Department of Internal Affairs, 1998), 96, 173.

36 See Child Welfare Officers' Salaries, 'Report on Female Child Welfare Officers for the Consultative Committee', E1 19/28/38a, Archives New Zealand.

37 Ibid.

38 Dalley, *Family Matters*, 97. For a child welfare officer's views on this see Annie Tocker, 'Recollections from 1926', *New Zealand Social Worker* 5, no. 4 (1969), 21–3; Lorna Hodder, 'Recollections from 1940', *New Zealand Social Worker* 5, no. 4 (1969), 27. Such in-service training as occurred seems to have been largely procedural, covering relevant laws and responsibilities as public servants.

39 C.E. Peek, 'A superintendent looks back', *New Zealand Social Worker* 5, no. 4 (1969), 15–19.

40 Liz Beddoe, 'A matter of degrees: The role of education in the professionalization journey of social work in New Zealand', *Aotearoa New Zealand Social Work* 26, nos 2 & 3 (2014), 23.

41 Nash, '"That terrible title, social worker"', 14.

42 Tocker, 'Recollections from 1926'), 21–23; Kathleen M. Stewart, 'Recollections from 1930', *New Zealand Social Worker* 5, no. 4 (1969), 25; Hodder, 'Recollections from 1940', 27–29.

43 See Jacques Donzelot, *The Policing of Families* (Pantheon: London, 1979); Barbara Ehrenreich & Deirdre English, *For Her Own Good: 150 years of experts' advice to women* (London: Pluto Press, 1979). I discuss resistance to such interventions, at least in the case of health professionals, in Margaret Tennant, '"Missionaries of health": the School Medical Service during the inter-war period', in Linda Bryder (ed.), *A Healthy Country: Essays on the social history of medicine in New Zealand* (Wellington: Bridget Williams Books, 1991), 128–48.

44 Dalley, *Family Matters*, 148–49, 161; see also 'Reminiscences', *New Zealand Social Worker* 5, no. 4 (1969).

45 T.H.J. Austin & W.S. Buxton, 'Training for the future of social work in New Zealand', *New Zealand Social Worker* 5, no. 1 (1969), 5.

46 Lewis Anderson, 'Child Welfare Division', in author's possession. Anderson was superintendent from 1964 to 1972. Youth court appearances rose from 2000 in

1948/49 to more than 12,000 in 1971/72 (Dalley, *Family Matters*, 172). The number of children and young people in regular contact with the division was more than 16,000 by the end of 1971.

47 Liz Beddoe, 'A "profession of faith" or a profession: Social work, knowledge and professional capital', *New Zealand Sociology* 28, no. 2 (2013), 44–63.

48 J.R. McCreary, 'The School of Social Science Part One – The Martians', *New Zealand Social Worker* 7, no. 1 (1971), 11; also cited, for example, by Nash in '"That terrible title, social worker"', 12.

49 Sonya Hunt, 'The social work professionalization project' contains an excellent short summary of approaches to professionalism and 'the professionalisation project' in New Zealand. Beddoe, 'A "profession of faith" or a profession', provides a more theoretically informed discussion of the attributes of professional capital associated with modern social work.

50 See Hunt, 'The social work professionalization project'; Beddoe, 'A "profession of faith" or a profession'; Nash, 'People, policies and practice'; Angeline Barretta-Herman, 'The development of social work in New Zealand: 1969–1988: The social welfare policy context', *Social Work Review* 5, no. 4 (1993), 4–8.

51 Rosemary Treadgold, 'Professionalism for social work in New Zealand', *New Zealand Social Worker* 10, no. 2 (1974), 3.

52 J.R. McCreary, 'Keynote address', in New Zealand Association of Social Workers Inc., *Report of Inaugural Conference Auckland 4 to 7 February 1964* (Auckland: Pelorus Press, 1964).

53 Nash, 'People, policies and practice', 417.

54 Ibid., ch. 13.

55 Barbara Gilray, 'Social worker registration: A decade of development, debate and delivery', *Aotearoa New Zealand Social Work* 25, no. 3 (2013), 30. See also Gavin Rennie, 'Registration ten years on: A perspective from a social work educator', *Aotearoa New Zealand Social Work* 25, no. 3 (2013), 3–10 for another debate: about proposals to raise the bar for registration from a diploma as the benchmark for registration, to a four-year degree.

56 Stacey Kirk, 'New Zealand heading towards compulsory registration of social workers, MPs unclear of path', 6 April 2016: www.stuff.co.nz/national/politics/78614486/NZ-heading-towards-compulsory-registration-of-social-workers-MPs-unclear-of-path

57 See Beddoe, 'A "profession of faith" or a profession', 50–52 on risk aversion and the late twentieth-century 'crisis of trust' in social work, some of it attributable to highly publicised failures of practice in New Zealand and elsewhere.

58 Gilray, 'Social worker registration', 29, 30.

59 On social work competencies see Social Workers Registration Board: www.swrb.govt.nz/competence-assessment/core-competence-standards

60 Enriqueta Hernandez, 'Spirituality in social work practice', MSW (Applied) research report, Massey University, 2014, 10.

61 Quoted by Barbara Brookes in her chapter in this volume.

SELECT BIBLIOGRAPHY:
Women, work and care

Violeta Gilabert

This select bibliography assembles notable publications that address the multiple intersections between women, work and care from a historical perspective. It is arranged into two sections: New Zealand and International. In the New Zealand section, we have aimed to provide a wide selection of writings on aspects of caring, even if 'care' is not the key focus of analysis. In the listing of international scholarship, since there is more work that directly addresses care as an analytical concept, we have collated a selection of works that provide good entry points into what is a growing area of scholarly enquiry.

These works include books, edited collections, journal articles, book chapters, and a selection of postgraduate research essays and dissertations. While academic rigour was a primary concern in our selection process, so too was breadth of work that would render visible the diverse histories of women and care in New Zealand and beyond. It is intended to help the new researcher locate texts that represent good entry points into particular fields of inquiry, while providing a useful overview of contemporary thought, research, and analysis for general and scholarly readers alike.

NEW ZEALAND
General histories

Brookes, Barbara, *A History of New Zealand Women* (Wellington: Bridget Williams Books, 2016)

_____, Annabel Cooper & Robin Law (eds), *Sites of Gender: Women, men, and modernity in Southern Dunedin, 1890–1939* (Auckland: Auckland University Press, 2003)

_____, Charlotte Macdonald & Margaret Tennant (eds), *Women in History: Essays on European women in New Zealand* (Wellington: Allen & Unwin/Port Nicholson Press, 1986)

_____, *Women in History 2: Essays on Women in New Zealand* (Wellington: Bridget Williams Books, 1992)

Bunkle, Phillida & Beryl Hughes (eds), *Women in New Zealand Society* (Auckland: Allen & Unwin, 1980)

Coney, Sandra, *Standing in the Sunshine: A history of New Zealand women since they won the vote* (Auckland: Viking, 1993)

Cox, Shelagh (ed.), *Public and Private Worlds: Women in contemporary New Zealand* (Wellington: Allen & Unwin/Port Nicholson Press, 1987)

Du Plessis, Rosemary & Lynne Alice (eds), *Feminist Thought in Aotearoa New Zealand: Connections and difference* (Auckland: Oxford University Press, 1998)

Park, Julie (ed.), *Ladies a Plate: Change and continuity in the lives of New Zealand Women* (Auckland: Auckland University Press, 1991)

Porter, Frances, Charlotte Macdonald & Tui Macdonald, *'My Hand Will Write What my Heart Dictates': The unsettled lives of women in nineteenth-century New Zealand as revealed to sisters, family and friends* (Auckland: Auckland University Press & Bridget Williams Books, 1996)

Care professions: Education and health

Aitken, Jo, 'Wives and mothers first: The New Zealand teachers' marriage bar and the ideology of domesticity, 1920–1940', *Women's Studies Journal* 12, no. 2 (1996), 83–99

Belgrave, Michael, 'A subtle containment: Women in New Zealand medicine, 1893–1941', *New Zealand Journal of History* 22, no. 1 (1988), 44–55

Bishop, Joanna, '"The first line of defence": Domestic health care in colonial New Zealand, 1850s–1920s', *Health and History* 16, no. 2 (2014), 1–23

Bryder, Linda, '"An area peculiarly our own": Women and childbirth in early to mid-twentieth century New Zealand', *New Zealand Journal of History* 51, no. 1 (2017), 92–112

_____, '"What women want": Childbirth services and women's activism in New Zealand, 1900–1960', in Janet Greenlees & Linda Bryder (eds), *Western Maternity and Medicine, 1880–1990* (London: Pickering & Chatto, 2013), 81–98

Clarke, Alison, *Born to a Changing World: Childbirth in nineteenth-century New Zealand* (Wellington: Bridget Williams Books, 2012)

Cody, Paula, 'Women psychiatrists in New Zealand, 1900–1990: An oral history', in Barbara Brookes & Jane Thomson (eds), *'Unfortunate Folk': Essays on mental health treatment, 1863–1992* (Dunedin: Otago University Press, 2001), 215–35

Coleborne, Catharine & Ondine Godtschalk, 'Colonial families and cultures of health: Glimpses of illness and domestic medicine in private records in New Zealand and Australia, 1850–1919', *Journal of Family History* 38 (2013), 403–21

Fry, Ruth, *It's Different for Daughters: A history of the curriculum for girls in New Zealand schools, 1900–1975* (Wellington: New Zealand Council for Educational Research, 1985)

Jenkins, Kuni, 'Mana wahine: Māori women and leadership of Māori schools in Aotearoa/New Zealand', *New Zealand Journal of Educational Studies* 40, no. 1/2 (2005), 45–59

Matthews, Kay Morris & Kuni Jenkins, 'Knowing their place: The political socialisation of Maori women in New Zealand through schooling policy and practice', *Women's History Review* 7, no. 1 (1998), 86–107

McKegg, Alexandra, 'The Maori Health Nursing Scheme: An experiment in autonomous health care', *New Zealand Journal of History* 26, no. 2 (1992), 145–60

Mein Smith, Philippa, *Maternity in Dispute: New Zealand, 1920–1939* (Wellington: Government Printer/Historical Publications Branch, 1986)

Middleton, Sue (ed.), *Women and Education in Aotearoa* (Wellington: Allen & Unwin/ Port Nicholson Press, 1988)

Morris Matthews, Kay, *In Their Own Right: Women and higher education in New Zealand before 1945* (Wellington: NZCER Press, 2008)

Parkes, C.M., 'The impact of the medicalisation of New Zealand's maternity services on women's experience of childbirth, 1904–1937', in Linda Bryder (ed.), *A Healthy Country: Essays on the social history of medicine in New Zealand* (Wellington: Bridget Williams Books, 1991), 165–80

Rogers, Anna, *While You're Away: New Zealand nurses at war 1899–1948* (Auckland: Auckland University Press, 2003)

Shaw, Louise, 'More than the ordinary domestic drudge: Women and technical education in Auckland 1895–1922', *History of Education Review* 38, no. 1 (2009), 3–15

———, 'From family helpmeet to lady dispenser: Women pharmacists 1881–1939', *New Zealand Journal of History* 32, no. 1 (1998), 23–42

Tennant, Margaret & Lesley Courtney, '"The Karitane": The rise and fall of a semi-profession for women', *New Zealand Journal of History* 51, no. 1 (2017), 113–34

Family formation and parenting

Adams, Jane, 'Fertility factors: infertility, medicine and the law in New Zealand, 1950–2014', PhD, University of Otago, 2017

Brookes, Barbara, '"Cherishing hopes of the impossible": Mothers, fathers, and disability at birth in mid-twentieth-century New Zealand', in Tracy Penny Light, Barbara Brookes & Wendy Mitchinson (eds), *Bodily Subjects: Essays on gender and health, 1800–2000* (Montreal: McGill–Queen's University Press, 2014), 178–99

Else, Anne, 'A question of adoption: Closed stranger adoption in New Zealand, 1944–1974', in Barbara Brookes, Charlotte Macdonald & Margaret Tennant (eds), *Women in History 2: Essays on women in New Zealand* (Wellington: Bridget Williams Books, 1992), 225–53

———, '"The need is ever present": The Motherhood of Man movement and stranger adoption in New Zealand', *New Zealand Journal of History* 23, no. 1 (1989), 47–67.

Frank, Tim, 'About our father's business: Fatherhood in New Zealand, 1900–1940', PhD, University of Auckland, 2004

Jenkins, Kuni & Helen Mountain Harte, *Traditional Maori Parenting: An historical review of literature of traditional Maori child rearing practices in pre-European times* (Auckland: Te Kahui Mana Ririki, 2011)

Koopman-Boyden, Peggy G. (ed.), *Families in New Zealand Society* (Wellington: Methuen Publications, 1978)

Macdonald, Charlotte, 'Too many men and too few women: Gender's "fatal impact" in nineteenth-century colonies', in Caroline Daley & Deborah Montgomerie (eds), *The Gendered Kiwi* (Auckland: Auckland University Press, 1999), 17–37

May, Helen, *Minding Children, Managing Men: Conflict and compromise in the lives of postwar Pakeha women* (Wellington: Bridget Williams Books, 1992)

Metge, Joan, *New Growth From Old: The whānau in the modern world* (Wellington: Victoria University Press, 1995)

Mikaere, Ani, 'Maori women: Caught in the contradictions of a colonised reality', *Waikato Law Review* 2 (1994), 125–49

Olssen, Erik, 'Families and the gendering of European New Zealand in the colonial period, 1840–80', in Caroline Daley & Deborah Montgomerie (eds), *The Gendered Kiwi* (Auckland: Auckland University Press, 1999), 37–63

Palmer, G.R., 'Birth mothers: Adoption in New Zealand and the social control of women, 1881–1985', MA, University of Canterbury, 1991

Pool, Ian, Arunachalam Dharmalingam & Janet Sceats, *The New Zealand Family: A demographic history* (Auckland: Auckland University Press, 2007)

Thomson, David, 'Marriage and family on the colonial frontier', in Tony Ballantyne & Brian Moloughney (eds), *Disputed Histories: Imagining New Zealand's pasts* (Dunedin: Otago University Press, 2006), 119–43

Toynbee, Claire, *Her Work and His: Family, kin and community in New Zealand, 1900–1930* (Wellington: Victoria University Press, 1995)

Gender and the state

Armstrong, Nicola, 'Handling the Hydra: Feminist analyses of the state', in Rosemary Du Plessis with Phillida Bunkle, Kathie Irwin, Alison Laurie & Sue Middleton (eds), *Feminist Voices: Women's studies texts for Aotearoa/New Zealand*, (Oxford: Oxford University Press, 1992), 224–38

Briar, Celia, Robyn Munford & Mary Nash (eds), *Superwoman Where Are You? Social policy and women's experience* (Palmerston North: Dunmore Press, 1992)

Dalley, Bronwyn & Margaret Tennant (eds), *Past Judgement: Social policy in New Zealand history* (Dunedin: Otago University Press, 2004)

Else, Anne, 'To market and home again: Gender and the New Right', in Rosemary Du Plessis with Phillida Bunkle, Kathie Irwin, Alison Laurie & Sue Middleton (eds), *Feminist Voices: Women's studies texts for Aotearoa/New Zealand* (Oxford: Oxford University Press, 1992), 239–51

Hyman, Prue, *Hopes Dashed?: The economics of gender inequality* (Wellington: Bridget Williams Books, 2017)

_____, *Women and Economics: A New Zealand feminist perspective* (Wellington: Bridget Williams Books, 1996)

_____, 'The use of economic orthodoxy to justify inequality: A feminist critique', in Rosemary Du Plessis with Phillida Bunkle, Kathie Irwin, Alison Laurie & Sue Middleton (eds), *Feminist Voices: Women's studies texts for Aotearoa/New Zealand* (Oxford: Oxford University Press, 1992), 252–65

Labrum, Bronwyn, 'Persistent needs and expanding desires: Pakeha families and state welfare in the years of prosperity', in Bronwyn Dalley & Bronwyn Labrum (eds),

Fragments: New Zealand social & cultural history (Auckland: Auckland University Press, 2000), 188–211

Millar, Grace, 'Families and the 1951 Waterfront Dispute', PhD, Victoria University of Wellington, 2013

Molloy, Maureen, 'Citizenship, property, and bodies: Discourses on Gender and the inter-war Labour government in New Zealand', *Gender & History* 4, no. 3 (1992), 293–304

Nolan, Melanie, *Breadwinning: New Zealand Women and the State* (Christchurch: Canterbury University Press, 2000)

_____, '"Politics swept under a domestic carpet"? Fracturing domesticity and the male breadwinner wage: Women's economic citizenship, 1920s–1940s', *New Zealand Journal of History* 27, no. 2 (1993), 199–217

Sutch, W.B., *Women with a Cause* (Wellington: Price Milburn & Co., 1973)

Waring, Marilyn, *Counting for Nothing: What men value and what women are worth* (Wellington: Allen & Unwin/Port Nicholson Press, 1988)

Employment and labour relations

Anderson, Rosemary, 'Distant daughters: Cook Islands domestics in wartime New Zealand, 1941–1946', *Journal of Pacific History* 48, no. 3 (2013), 267–85

Bardsley, Dianne, *The Land Girls: In a man's world, 1939–1946* (Dunedin: Otago University Press, 2000)

Brookes, Barbara & Catherine Smith, 'Styling gender: From barber shops and ladies' hairdressers to the unisex salon, 1920–1970', *New Zealand Journal of History* 51, no. 1 (2017), 184–207

Collins, Jenny, 'Glorified housekeepers or pioneering professionals? The professional lives of home science graduates from the University of New Zealand', *History of Education Review* 37, no. 2 (2008), 40–51

Corner, Margaret, *No Easy Victory: Towards equal pay for women in the government service, 1890–1960* (Wellington: New Zealand Public Service Association, 1988)

Dalziel, Raewyn, Focus on the Family: *The Auckland Home & Family Society, 1893–1993* (Auckland: The Society, 1993)

Du Plessis, Rosemary, 'Stating the contradictions: The case of women's employment', in Rosemary Du Plessis with Phillida Bunkle, Kathie Irwin, Alison Laurie & Sue Middleton (eds), *Feminist Voices: Women's studies texts for Aotearoa/New Zealand* (Oxford: Oxford University Press, 1992), 209–23

Emery, Michelle, Jill Hooks & Ross Stewart, 'Born at the wrong time? An oral history of women professional accountants in New Zealand', *Accounting History* 7, no. 2 (2002), 7–34

Fitzgerald, Tanya, 'An absent presence: Women professors at the University of New Zealand, 1911–1961', *Journal of Educational Administration and History* 39, no. 3 (2007), 239–53

_____, & Jenny Collins, *Historical Portraits of Women Home Scientists at the University of New Zealand, 1911–1947* (Amherst: Cambria Press, 2011)

Harrison, Barbara & Melanie Nolan, 'Reflections in colonial glass? Women factory inspectors in Britain and New Zealand 1893–1921', *Women's History Review* 13, no. 2 (2004), 263–89

Locke, Cybèle, 'Building solidarity at the flax-roots: Standing committees for women, Māori, and Pacific Island members inside the Wellington Hotel and Hospital Workers' Union, 1979–1989', *Labour and Industry* 25, no. 3 (2015), 170–84

———, 'Maori sovereignty, Black feminism, and the New Zealand Trade Union Movement', in Carol Williams (ed.), *Indigenous Women and Work* (Chicago: University of Illinois, 2012), 254–68

Macdonald, Charlotte, 'Strangers at the hearth: The eclipse of domestic service in New Zealand homes c.1830–1940s', in Barbara Brookes (ed.), *At Home in New Zealand: History, houses, people* (Wellington: Bridget Williams Books, 2000), 41–56

———, 'Taking colonialism home: Cook Island "housegirls" in New Zealand, 1939–1948', in Victoria K. Haskins & Claire Lowrie (eds), *Colonisation and Domestic Service: Historical and contemporary perspectives* (London & New York: Routledge, 2014), 273–88

McCabe, Jane, 'Settling in, from within: Anglo-Indian lady-helps in 1920s New Zealand', in Victoria K. Haskins & Claire Lowrie (eds), *Colonisation and Domestic Service: Historical and Contemporary Perspectives* (New York: Routledge, 2014), 63–79

Montgomerie, Deborah, 'Men's jobs and women's work: The New Zealand Women's Land Service in World War II', *Agricultural History* 63, no. 3 (1989), 1–13

———, 'The limitations of wartime change: Women war workers in New Zealand', *New Zealand Journal of History* 23, no. 1 (1989): 68–86

———, *The Women's War: New Zealand women 1939–1945* (Auckland: Auckland University Press, 2001)

Nolan, Melanie, 'Gender and the politics of keeping left: Wellington Labour women and their community', in Barbara Brookes & Dorothy Page (eds), *Communities of Women: Historical perspectives* (Dunedin: Otago University Press, 2002), 147–63

Pickles, Katie, 'Empire settlement and single British women as New Zealand domestic servants during the 1920s', *New Zealand Journal of History* 35, no. 1 (2001), 22–44

Feminism and politics

Alberti, Johanna, 'The turn of the tide: Sexuality and politics, 1923–31', *Women's Studies Journal* 1, no. 2 (1992), 169–91

Brookes, Barbara, 'A weakness for strong subjects: The women's movement and sexuality', *New Zealand Journal of History* 27, no. 2 (1993), 140–56

Brown, Hayley M., '"A woman's right to choose": Second wave feminist advocacy of abortion law reform in New Zealand and New South Wales from the 1970s', MA thesis, University of Canterbury, 2004

Cahill, Maud & Christine Dann (eds), *Changing Our Lives: Women working in the women's liberation movement, 1970–1990* (Wellington: Bridget Williams Books, 1991)

Coleman, Jenny, *Polly Plum: A firm and earnest woman's advocate* (Dunedin: Otago University Press, 2017)

Coney, Sandra, *Out of the Frying Pan: Inflammatory writings 1972–89* (Auckland: Penguin Books, 1990)

Dalziel, Raewyn, 'The colonial helpmeet: Women's role and the vote in nineteenth-century New Zealand', *New Zealand Journal of History* 11, no. 2 (1977), 112–23

Dann, Christine, *Up From Under: Women and liberation in New Zealand, 1970–1985* (Wellington: Bridget Williams Books, 1985)

Elphick, Judith, 'What's wrong with Emma? The feminist debate in colonial Auckland', *New Zealand Journal of History* 9, no. 2 (1975), 126–41

Grigg, A.R., 'Prohibition and women: The preservation of an ideal and a myth', *New Zealand Journal of History* 17, no. 2 (1983), 144–65

Grimshaw, Patricia, 'Politicians and suffragettes: Women's suffrage in New Zealand 1891–1893', *New Zealand Journal of History* 4, no. 2 (1970), 160–77

_____, 'Settler anxieties, Indigenous peoples, and women's suffrage in the colonies of Australia, New Zealand, and Hawai`i, 1888 to 1902', *Pacific Historical Review* 69, no. 4 (2000), 553–72

_____, *Women's Suffrage in New Zealand* (Auckland: Auckland University Press, 1972)

_____, '*Women's Suffrage in New Zealand* revisited: Writing from the margins', in *Suffrage and Beyond: International feminist perspectives* (Auckland: Auckland University Press, 1994), 25–42

Hutching, Megan, *Leading the Way: How New Zealand women won the vote* (Auckland: Harper Collins, 2010)

Kedgley, Susan Jane & Mary Varnham (eds), *Heading Nowhere in a Navy Blue Suit: And other tales from the feminist revolution* (Wellington: Daphne Brasell Associates Press, 1993)

Labrum, Bronwyn, '"For the better discharge of our duties": Women's rights in Wanganui, 1893–1903', *Women's Studies Journal* 6, no. 1 (1990), 136–51

Lovell-Smith, Margaret, *How Women Won the Vote: A Canterbury perspective* (Christchurch: Canterbury Museum, 1993)

_____, *The Woman Question: Writings by the women who won the vote* (Auckland: New Women's Press, 1992)

Macdonald, Charlotte, *The Vote, the Pill and the Demon Drink: A history of feminist writing in New Zealand, 1869–1993* (Wellington: Bridget Williams Books, 1993)

Malthus, Jane, '"Bifurcated and not ashamed": Late nineteenth-century dress reformers in New Zealand', *New Zealand Journal of History* 23, no. 1 (1989), 32–46

McCallum, Janet, *Women in the House: Members of Parliament in New Zealand* (Picton: Cape Catley, 1993)

McCulloch, Alison, *Fighting to Choose: The abortion rights struggle in New Zealand* (Wellington: Victoria University Press, 2013)

Rei, Tania, *Maori Women and the Vote* (Wellington: Huia, 1993)

Wallace, Sandra, 'Members for everywoman? The campaign promises of women parliamentary candidates', *New Zealand Journal of History* 27, no. 2 (1993), 187–98

Institutional care

Beagle, Margaret, 'Children of the state: A study of the New Zealand industrial school system, 1880–1925', MA thesis, University of Auckland, 1974

Cooke, Allan, 'State responsibility for children in care', PhD, University of Otago, 2014.

Dalley, Bronwyn, *Family Matters: Child welfare in twentieth-century New Zealand* (Auckland: Auckland University Press, 1998)

Stanley, Elizabeth, *The Road to Hell: State violence against children in postwar New Zealand* (Auckland: Auckland University Press, 2016)

Tennant, Margaret, 'Disability in New Zealand: A historical survey', *New Zealand Journal of Disability Studies* 2 (1996), 3–34

_____, 'Elderly indigents and old men's homes, 1880–1920', *New Zealand Journal of History* 17, no.1 (1983), 3–20

_____, 'Magdalens and moral imbeciles: Women's homes in nineteenth century New Zealand', *Women's Studies Journal* 9, no. 5 (1986): 491–502

_____, '"Maternity and morality": Homes for single mothers, 1890–1930', *Women's Studies Journal* 2, no. 1 (1985), 28–49

Material culture

Hamon, Jan, 'The New Zealand dressmaker: Experiences, practices and contributions to fashionability, 1940–1980', PhD, RMIT, 2007

Labrum, Bronwyn, Fiona McKergow & Stephanie Gibson (eds), *Looking Flash: Clothing in Aotearoa New Zealand* (Auckland: Auckland University Press, 2007)

Nicholson, Heather, *The Loving Stitch: A history of knitting and spinning in New Zealand* (Auckland: Auckland University Press, 1998)

Sprecher, Danielle, 'Good clothes are good business: Gender, consumption, and appearance in the office, 1918–39', in Caroline Daley & Deborah Montgomerie (eds), *The Gendered Kiwi* (Auckland: Auckland University Press, 1999), 141–63

Organisational histories

Bryder, Linda, *A Voice for Mothers: The Plunket Society and infant welfare, 1907–2000* (Auckland: Auckland University Press, 2003)

_____, *Not Just Weighing Babies: Plunket in Auckland, 1908–1998* (Auckland: Pyramid Press, 1998)

Byron, Isolde, *Nga Perehitini: The Presidents of the Māori Women's Welfare League, 1951–2001* (Auckland: Māori Women's Development Inc., 2002)

Dougherty, Ian, *Without Compromise: A brief history of the New Zealand Women's Christian Temperance Union* (Auckland: New Zealand Women's Christian Temperance Union, 2013)

Else, Anne, *Women Together: A history of women's organisations in New Zealand: Nga ropu wahine o te motu* (Wellington: Historical Branch, Department of Internal Affairs, 1993)

Shaw, Louise, *Latching On: 50 years of breastfeeding support. La Leche League in New Zealand, 1964–2014* (Porirua: La Leche League New Zealand, 2014)

Szaszy, M., A. Rogers & M. Simpson, *Early Stories from Founding Members of the Maori Women's Welfare League – Te Tīmatanga Tātau Tātau, Te Ropu Wahine Maori Toko i te Ora* (Wellington: The League/Bridget Williams Books, 1993)

Tennant, Margaret, 'Matrons with a mission: Women's organisations in New Zealand, 1893–1915', MA thesis, Massey University, 1976

Religion

Fitzgerald, Caroline (ed.), *Letters from the Bay of Islands: The story of Marianne Williams* (Auckland: Penguin, 2004)

Fitzgerald, Tanya, '"To unite their strength with ours": Women and missionary work in Aotearoa/New Zealand', *Journal of Pacific History* 39, no. 2 (2004), 147–61

Grant, Susannah, *Windows on a Women's World: The Dominican Sisters of Aotearoa* (Dunedin: Otago University Press, 2017)

Matthews, Angela, 'An easy passage? An Anglican female priesthood in New Zealand', in John Stenhouse and Jane Thomson (eds), *Building God's Own Country: Historical essays on religions in New Zealand* (Dunedin: Otago University Press, 2004), 209–23

Paterson, Lachy, 'The rise and fall of women field workers within the Presbyterian Māori Mission, 1907–1970', in Hugh Morrison, Lachy Paterson, Murray Rae & Brett Knowles (eds), *Mana Māori and Christianity* (Wellington: Huia, 2012), 179–205

Piercy, Karen-Maree, 'Patient and enduring love: The deaconess movement, 1900–1920', in John Stenhouse & Jane Thomson (eds), *Building God's Own Country: Historical Essays on Religions in New Zealand* (Dunedin: Otago University Press, 2004), 196–209

Porter, Frances, 'All that the heart does bear: A reflection on the domestic life of missionary wives', in Robert Glen (ed.), *Mission and Moko: The Church Missionary Society in New Zealand* (Christchurch: Latimer Fellowship, 1992), 110–33

Ross, Cathy, *Women with a Mission: Rediscovering missionary wives in early New Zealand* (Auckland: Penguin Books, 2006)

Rountree, Kathryn, 'Re-making the Maori female body: Marianne Williams's mission in the Bay of Islands', *Journal of Pacific History* 35, no. 1 (2000), 49–66

Stenhouse, John, 'Christianity, women and the working class: A Dunedin case study, 1885–1935', in John Stenhouse & G.A. Wood (ed.), *Christianity, Modernity, and Culture: New perspectives on New Zealand history* (Adelaide: ATF Press, 2005), 157–80

Tennant, Margaret, 'Sisterly ministrations: The social work of Protestant deaconesses in New Zealand 1890–1940', *New Zealand Journal of History* 32, no. 1 (1998): 3–22

_____, '"Woman's peculiar mission": Ladies' benevolence in the New Zealand setting', in Barbara Brookes & Dorothy Page (eds), *Communities of Women: Historical perspectives* (Dunedin: Otago University Press, 2002), 69–81

Whitelaw, Brooke, 'A message from the missahibs: New Zealand Presbyterian women missionaries in the Punjab, 1910–1940', MA thesis, University of Otago, 2001

Reports

Ministry of Social Development, *Caring for the Carers – He Atawhai i te Hunga Ngākau Oha o Aotearoa: The New Zealand Carers' Strategy Action Plan for 2014 to 2018* (Wellington: Ministry of Social Development, 2014)

New Zealand Human Rights Commission, *Caring Counts* (Wellington: New Zealand Human Rights Commission, 2012)

Society for Research on Women in New Zealand Inc., Wellington Branch, *Those Who Care* (Wellington: Society for Research on Women, 1976)

Society for Research on Women in New Zealand Inc., Auckland Branch, *Those Who Care in Auckland* (Auckland: Society for Research on Women, 1979)

INTERNATIONAL

Abel, Emily K., *Hearts of Wisdom: American women caring for kin, 1850–1940* (Cambridge, MA: Harvard University Press, 2000)

_____, *The Inevitable Hour: A history of caring for dying patients in America* (Baltimore: John Hopkins University Press, 2013)

Abel, Emily K. & Margaret K. Nelson (eds), *Circles of Care: Work and identity in women's lives* (New York: State University of New York Press, 1990)

Boris, Eileen (ed.), *Intimate Labors: Cultures, technologies, and the politics of care* (Stanford, CA: Stanford University Press, 2010)

Clement, Grace, *Care, Autonomy and Justice: Feminism and the ethic of care* (Boulder, CO & Oxford, UK: Westview Press, 1996)

DeVault, Marjorie L., *Feeding the Family: The social organization of caring as gendered work* (Chicago & London: University of Chicago Press, 1991)

Duffy, Mignon, *Making Care Count: A century of gender, race, and paid care work* (New Brunswick, NJ: Rutgers University Press, 2011)

Fraser, Nancy, 'Contradictions of capital and care', *New Left Review* 100 (2016): 99–117

_____, *Fortunes of Feminism: From state-managed capitalism to neo-liberal crisis* (New York: Verso Books, 2013)

Garey, Anita I. & Karen V. Hansen (eds), *At the Heart of Work and Family: Engaging the ideas of Arlie Hochschild* (Brunswick, NJ: Rutgers University Press, 2011).

Held, Virginia, *The Ethics of Care: Personal, political and global* (Oxford: Oxford University Press, 2006)

Hochschild, Arlie R., *The Managed Heart: Commercialization of human feeling* (Berkeley: University of California Press, 1983)

Meyer, Madonna H. (ed.), *Care Work: Gender, labor and the welfare state* (London/New York: Routledge, 2000; New Brunswick, NJ: Rutgers University Press, 2011)

Noddings, Nel, *Caring: A feminine approach to ethics and moral education* (Berkeley, CA: University of California Press, 1984)

Powell, Lindsay, William Southwell-Wright & Rebecca Gowland (eds), *Care in the Past: Archaeological and interdisciplinary perspectives* (Philadelphia: Oxbow Books, 2017)

Robinson, Fiona, *Globalizing Care: Ethics, Feminist Theory, and International Relations* (Boulder, CO: Westview Press, 1999)

Sevenhuijsen, Selma, *Citizenship and the Ethics of Care* (London: Routledge, 1998)

Sweet, Helen & Sue Hawkins (eds), *Colonial Caring: A history of colonial and post-colonial nursing* (Manchester: Manchester University Press, 2015)

Wood, Julia T., *Who Cares? Women, care and culture* (Carbondale: Southern Illinois University Press, 1994)

CONTRIBUTORS

Rosemary Anderson is a PhD candidate with the Department of History and Art History at the University of Otago. Her MA thesis explored the social realities of New Zealand's colonial relationship with the Cook Islands, and highlighted political, familial and cultural associations between New Zealand and Cook Island Māori. An article, 'Distant daughters: Cook Island domestics in wartime New Zealand', published in the *Journal of Pacific History* in 2013, examined the experiences of early Cook Island migrants to New Zealand.

Barbara Brookes is professor of history at the University of Otago. She has published extensively on gender relations in New Zealand, as well as on the history of health and disease in New Zealand and Britain. Her most recent book is *A History of New Zealand Women* (Bridget Williams Books, 2016), which won the Illustrated Non-Fiction category of the 2017 Ockham New Zealand Book Awards.

Katie Cooper is curator of colonial histories at the Museum of New Zealand Te Papa Tongarewa. Her doctorate, completed in 2017 at the University of Otago, examined rural communities in New Zealand from 1840 to 1940, focusing in particular on foodways, domestic technology and gender.

Heather Devere is director of practice in the National Centre for Peace and Conflict Studies at the University of Otago. Her teaching focuses on peace traditions of Aotearoa and conflict resolution practice. She has published widely on issues including peace journalism, women and politics, women in the media, refugee resettlement, children's rights, Indigenous peace traditions and the politics of friendship.

Violeta Gilabert is a researcher and PhD candidate in the Department of History and Art History at the University of Otago. Her doctoral thesis examines the causes and consequences of 'caring' in Māori and Pākehā relationships, and how marriage and its affective demands changed over the twentieth century.

Antje Lübcke is research services librarian at the University of Otago Library. She has worked with historical photographs from the Pacific and New Zealand in her time as a postgraduate student and as an archives assistant in archives in Canberra, Australia and in Dunedin. She successfully completed her PhD on the early photographers of New Guinea, W.G. Lawes and J.W. Lindt, through the Australian National University in January 2017. Her contribution to this volume is based on her MA research on the photograph albums of the New Zealand Presbyterian mission to the New Hebrides that she completed in the Department of History and Art History at Otago in 2009.

Jane McCabe is a lecturer in history at the University of Otago, where she teaches papers on modern India, colonial India, migration to New Zealand, and global history. Her monograph *Race, Tea and Colonial Resettlement: Imperial families, interrupted* (Bloomsbury, 2017) examined a Presbyterian scheme that resettled 130 mixed-race children from Indian tea plantations to New Zealand in the early twentieth century. Jane's current research project, funded by a Royal Society of New Zealand Marsden Grant, is a cross-cultural history of land and inheritance.

Bronwyn Polaschek is an independent scholar and teacher based in Wellington. Her research focuses on popular culture and gender theory. She has published work on the cinema genres of the biopic and documentary, historical narratives of femininity, and contemporary celebrity, and is author of *The Postfeminist Biopic* (Palgrave Macmillan, 2013).

Margaret Tennant has honorary research and professor emeritus status at Massey University. She is a social historian whose work has also focused on the history of social policy, and of the non-profit sector in particular. Her most recent book was *Across the Street, Across the World: A history of the Red Cross in New Zealand* (New Zealand Red Cross, 2015), and she currently leads the Palmerston North History Project.

Angela Wanhalla teaches in the Department of History and Art History at the University of Otago. She is a historian of race, gender and colonialism. Her most recent books include *He Reo Wāhine: Māori Women's Voices from* *the Nineteenth Century* (Auckland University Press, 2017), co-written with Lachy Paterson, and *Mothers' Darlings of the South Pacific: The children of indigenous women and US servicemen, World War II* (University of Hawai`i Press/Otago University Press, 2016), co-edited with Judith A. Bennett.

Melissa Matutina Williams is of Te Rarawa and Ngāti Maru descent. She completed a PhD in history, and lectured in Māori and New Zealand history at the University of Auckland. Melissa's publications include her award-winning book, *Panguru and the City: Kāinga Tahi, Kāinga Rua: An urban migration history* (Bridget Williams Books, 2015), which is based on the oral histories of her whanaunga who migrated from North Hokianga to Auckland, 1930–1970. Melissa continues to research and write in the fields of Māori and New Zealand history and enjoys spending time with her mokopuna.

INDEX

Page numbers in **bold** refer to images.

child abuse, neglect and maltreatment 14, 32, 66

child care and child rearing: balance between care and control in welfare work 250, 251; child bearing conflated with capacity to care 137–38; children with physical or intellectual disabilities 10, 18, 19, 26–27; commercial context 20, 30, 174, 175; early childhood education 21; equal responsibilities of men and women 48; European settler society 22–23; family home as place for children's emotional and physical development 153–54; by family support workers 238; foster homes 250; institutional care 14, 250 (*see also* St Andrew's Colonial Homes, Kalimpong); by Kalimpong emigrants 96; by Māori 12, 17, 21–22, 59, 65–66; Māori children placed with Pākehā families 66; obligation to properly care for the young 44–45; in rural areas 153–55; tamariki atawhai 65–66; *see also* ayah care

child offending 251

child poverty 14, 32

Child Welfare Act 1925 248

Child Welfare Branch (later Division), Department of Education 182, 184–85, 248–49, 250, 251

childbirth, colonial women 22

children: care of younger siblings 20; duty of care returned to parents in later life 18, 24, 26, 30, 237, 238; economic contribution to rural families 154; separation from mothers to erase mother's culture 82; training in caring 20; *see also* American war children, New Zealand

church groups 20

churches: validation of women's caring work 20–21, 23, 30; welfare agencies 244–45, 247; women's role 29, 30, 31

citizenship and the ethic of care 42, 49

city missions 244, 245, 247

civic friendship model 42, 49

civic participation, care as 49

Clarke, Alison 22

Clarke, John 200

class 41, 84, 85, 86, 87, 212, 242, 246

Clegg, Ellen 179

Clement, Grace 42

clothing, crafts and care: home sewing and knitting 164–65, 166–67, 168–69, 172–73, 174–75; knitted teddies 170–71; ready-made clothing 174–75; sun bonnet 162–63

Cobbes' department store, fabric section 164, 165

Cochrane, Donald 106

Cockburn, George 23

coercion 44

collectivism 59, 222, 243

colonialism 12, 59, 208, 213, 231

communitarianism 39

community, care role 11, 12, 20, 59, 138, 139, 155–56, 222–23, 224, 232; *see also* social work

community/social groups 20

Conrad, Joseph, *Heart of Darkness* 208

contract theory 38–39, 45

Cook Islands: changing political ideals 231, 232–33; labourers for phosphate mining, Makatea 230, 231; migrants to New Zealand 12, 219, 227–29, 231–32; relationship with New Zealand 219–21, 231–32; women 12, 223–24, 227–29, 232; World War I veterans 231; World War II 221, 230; *see also* Love, Takau Rio

Cook Islands Department 230, 232

Cooper, Katie 13–14, **174**

Cooper, Whina 57, 206

cost of caring 10

critical race theory 38–39

Crook, Gerald 189

Cruise, Richard 17

Cunnington, Eveline Willett 241–43, 256